The Urban R's:

race relations as the problem
in urban education

The Center for Urban Education, a nonprofit corporation
chartered by the New York State Board of Regents, conducts
research and development studies into the problems of contemporary urban education. The CENTER seeks both to clarify
these problems and to find effective and workable solutions
to them, and its publications program (which includes the
preparation of individual papers and also a journal) is part of
this effort. Publications are chosen on the basis of merit and
should not be read as expression of official policy. The CENTER
is located at 33 West 42 Street, New York, N.Y. 10036.

The Urban R's:
race relations as the problem in urban education

Edited by:
**ROBERT A. DENTLER
BERNARD MACKLER
MARY ELLEN WARSHAUER**

Published for
THE CENTER FOR URBAN EDUCATION
by FREDERICK A. PRAEGER, *Publishers*
New York · Washington · London

FREDERICK A. PRAEGER, PUBLISHERS
111 Fourth Avenue, New York, N.Y. 10003, U.S.A.
77-79 Charlotte Street, London W.1, England

Published in the United States of America in 1967
by Frederick A. Praeger, Inc., Publishers

This publication results from work performed
under a contract with the United States
Department of Health, Education, and Welfare,
Office of Education.

Library of Congress Catalog Card Number: 67-24987

Printed in the United States of America

To the late Theresa M. Barmack,
colleague and friend

Acknowledgments

Although these empirical studies and social scientific interpretations of selected problems in urban education were edited and published within the Center for Urban Education, many of them grew out of work generated or guided in some degree by the staff of the Institute of Urban Studies at Teachers College, Columbia University. The Institute was active from 1962 through 1965, when its staff was merged into the new, much larger Center for Urban Education where the editors of this volume now work.

We have dedicated this volume to the memory of our colleague and friend, the late Theresa M. Barmack, who, as Administrative Assistant of the Institute for Urban Studies, sustained the egos and made the arrangements so vital to the work of many of our authors, including the editors themselves. She looked forward to the publication of this volume and contributed directly to its preparation.

We also acknowledge with special thanks the help of Harris Dienstfrey, senior editor on the staff of the Center, who led us patiently toward clear exposition, provided ideas about organization and emphasis, and most importantly, weeded out several entries among the manuscripts.

The interpretations and conclusions expressed in the introductions and studies contained in this book are not necessarily those of the Center for Urban Education. All responsibility rests with the editors.

Contents

Introduction

The achievement differences between white, Negro, and Puerto Rican students are very great. At grade six, the average Negro student in the metropolitan Northeast is more than one and three-fourths years behind the average white in reading comprehension. At grade nine, he is more than two and one-half years behind; at grade twelve, he is nearly three years behind. The record for the Puerto Rican is even poorer. At grade six, the average Puerto Rican pupil is more than three years behind the average white and a year to a year and a quarter behind the average Negro; and the gap does not narrow over the next six grades.

This educational fact has been widely if not well understood among urban educators in the North since the 1954 *Brown* decision of the Supreme Court. For nearly the entire decade from 1955 to 1965, the causes of this cumulative failure were for the most part attributed to two sources: family conditioning, and deficiencies in the facilities and programs of the metropolitan area public school. Those inside the educational establishment emphasized family deficiencies. Those pressing for reform from the outside emphasized the failure to teach effectively.

Neither the fact of cumulative failure nor the debate about its causes would have attracted great public interest save for the civil rights revolution. Again and again, the struggles for equal employment, fair housing, and political equality came together on the common ground of a call for educational opportunity. Not only had the first legal successes of the revolution pointed up the strategic importance of education, but the tasks of achieving improved employment, better housing, and political equality seemed to depend for their ultimate realization upon preparing a generation of youth for the utilization of equal rights.

Of course, there were other reasons as well for the intensification of public interest in urban education during this decade. An absolute doubling of the youth population together with an automating economy combined to stimulate public demands for effective educational performance on all fronts. Some of these demands—for example, the hopes of city youths to get into college or to qualify for elite technical and vocational high schools—might have been met quickly to the satisfaction of all. But the civil rights revolution had induced a crisis in confidence. As competition for the best of scarce educational resources quickened, suspicions swelled. Was it true that each city contained but a few effective schools as islands in a sea of administrative confusion and inept construction? Was the entire scheme of urban public education dangerously out of date?

Three monumental, federally sponsored studies of these and related educational issues—the Coleman-Campbell Report (*Equality of Educational Opportunity*), the Civil Rights Commission Report (*Racial Isolation in the Public Schools*), and *Project Talent*—reinforce each other profoundly in identifying the prime sources of school success and failure. Each demonstrates that student achievement is influenced mainly by family conditioning, personal motivation, and the social climate of the school.

These major sources of academic success or failure are inextricably connected with race or ethnicity. In the metropolitan North, social and economic differences in family conditioning amount, at the extremes, to differences between Negroes and whites. In the twelve largest central cities of the North, more than half of the families subsisting at or below the poverty line are Negro.

Similarly, the social climate of an urban public school is also heavily affected by race. Coleman and Campbell have shown: "Of all the characteristics of schools which distinguished the education being provided the average white and Negro students, it is the environment provided by the fellow students where the differences are most dramatic." Social climate thus depends upon who goes to school with whom. Admittedly, it also develops out of the relations between staff members and between teachers and pupils. But in racially changing communities even these social relations are symbolized most dramatically in the instance of race relations.

As for personal motivation, this factor blends aspects of individual personality with family conditioning and the social influence of the school, as these are perceived by the child. But it is particularly the racially isolated Negro in the Northern city or suburban school who finds himself at a disadvantage on at least two of these three counts.

For these reasons, the most urgent urban educational challenge of the day is not curriculum or instruction. It is the challenge of changing race relations. As the studies in *The Urban R's* reveal, the challenge of changing race relations presents itself with equal significance in the desegregating community, in the all-Negro school in the inner city, and in the all-white school in the adjacent suburb where children are deprived of significant contacts with the groups that will comprise their worlds as adults.

The studies in *The Urban R's* were conducted between 1964 and 1966, before the results of the three great reports just mentioned had been published in full. Some of what we found confirms the Coleman-Campbell Report. But other parts of our work go deeper and offer greater focus and more precise illumination.

For instance, we offer a very concrete approach to the definition of school segregation and desegregation which is not available elsewhere. We show what school desegregation looks like when it occurs as a result of community conflict and litigation. We improve upon the literature about the effects of school integration upon young children. And we begin to make the critical distinction between race relations within naturally unsegregated schools—those located in zones of residential transition—and race relations in schools where integration has been planned.

We also set some limits upon the dangerous assumption that ethnic condition and individual development are uniformly correlative. For example, we report on Harlem adolescents who are sensitively alive to and well informed about social issues, regardless of their measured level of literacy. And we report on low-income urban mothers who rear their children in strikingly similar ways, whether they are themselves Negro, Puerto Rican, or white.

A careful reading of *The Urban R's*, then, should persuade the reader that race relations represent the most urgent challenge to urban education—but in ways that are expressive and symptomatic of, rather than intrinsic to, the urban condition. Race relations thus carry one into the heart of the contemporary educational challenge, but the full scope of the task before us is to rectify deficiencies in the urban social organization as these can be identified in the larger process of human relations.

If urban educators are failing, they are failing at the points where the newly emergent culture of the urban society itself has failed to specify adequately either ends or means for the educator and his clientele. For example, we find in *The Urban R's* that impoverished urban Negro parents do not participate in local school affairs, power struggles to the contrary notwithstanding. This finding raises the questions: Involvement and participation to what ends? What in the life of the city school (or its suburban counterpart) is relevant to contemporary family life? Similarly, if New York City's special schools for the maladjusted and the disturbed are racially segregated and educationally ineffective, as *The Urban R's* shows, the issue thrown into relief is only superficially one of a cultural predisposition toward many minority groups. At a deeper level, it is the fact that we are in a period when the place of all children in this culture is in transition.

Urban race relations in public education offer an excellent index of this transition. When the culture of the urban school has changed so that it fosters the growth of low-income Negro children, we will know that American urban culture as a whole has been significantly redesigned. *The Urban R's* offers standards for assessing some of these occasions.

The Urban R's:

race relations as the problem in urban education

PART I

The Urban Context of Education

The years since the Brown Decision of 1954 may be divided into three stages of social scientific and educational research, at least on matters of concern to the urban North. Most of the decade of the 1950's was given over to finding out whether unequal educational services were associated with segregated school staffs and student bodies. The evidence in the case of dozens of Northern cities and suburbs was dramatic enough to stimulate political action and reaction.

From about 1959 through 1963, research and commentary about Northern school segregation were given over chiefly to prescription. The earlier documentation of less qualified teachers, poorer facilities, and cumulative failures in learning in minority segregated schools all reinforced the belief that immediate remedies were required. Limited attention was given, in outlining plans for change, to the ways in which racial school segregation was entwined with economic segregation, subcultural discontinuities between school and community, and dislocations in teaching and learning. This stage of prescription was also a stage of hardening ideologies. From proponents of instant, total desegregation, to advocates of experimental pairing and balancing to program compensators and black separatists, all parties tended to promote dogmas of solution or accommodation.

In this period, some natural experiments in desegregation began in the urban North. Yet, not one superintendent funded, designed, or managed to execute careful evaluations of the effects upon students or teachers. The trail of research thinned at just the twist on the path when crucial choices were being made in the revision of policies and practices.

Moreover, where school desegregation was planned by local officials, plans often fell short of including mechanisms for receiving transferred students in an encouraging fashion, reorienting staffs in the transition, or modifying programs of instruction to meet changes in the *status quo*. Desegregation was approached, at least initially, as a matter unto itself, until opponents began to emphasize the neglect of so-called quality considerations as essential adjuncts to change.

We are now in a third phase, that of refinement of interpretation.

3

In their paper "A New Definition of School Segregation," for example, Warshauer and Dentler attempt to limit the concept of school segregation. Their index is crude, but it is less arbitrary than the indicators used in earlier stages of planning and research. It is sensitive to the variability of population composition from city to city, and its formulation is amenable to extension beyond racial (or Negro versus white) categories. Their formulation makes it possible to take into account the permeable boundary between public and parochial systems within the same community. It distinguishes between segregation, desegregation, and integration, and it offers a basis for gauging the extent of *social class* as well as ethnic segregation peculiar to any urban school district. Under the auspices of the Center for Urban Education, the approach has been applied to plans for school desegregation of New York City, Buffalo, and Bridgeport, Connecticut, among other Northeastern localities.

Robert La Frankie's case history of Englewood, New Jersey, refines our knowledge of the conflict a school district is likely to experience if its leaders choose the route of litigation and civil rights tokenism as against early, deliberate, and comprehensive steps toward school desegregation. His study further details the topic by relating the ways in which the issue of school segregation is linked in the metropolitan North to long-standing, indeed century-old, neglect of racial equality on the one hand, and to the partially exclusive character of public school control by class and ethnic groups on the other.

Kurt Lang and Gladys Engel Lang, in their paper "Resistance to School Desegregation: A Case Study of Backlash Among Jews," refine our views of the school segregation question in quite another way. They reveal, through opinion research, that the usual generalizations about who favors or opposes desegregation in a Northern community are not valid. They show how the attitudes of second generation Jewish parents are affected by social status, upward mobility, and feelings about territory. Earlier Jewish attitudes based upon immigrant morality and the sacredness of scholarly learning have been transformed. Racial desegregation of schools has become a question considered in terms of its perceived impact upon the life chances and life space of particular ethnic and social groups.

All three papers suggest ways in which the school desegregation question is unbounded. Affected by old patterns of settlement and intergroup relations, influenced by the vast heterogeneity of ethnic and class interests, and depending for its resolution at all points upon matters that involve more than racial balance, Northern school desegregation represents the complex of relations between the changing metropolis and its public schools. It is *the* symbol of the context; the best criterion for gauging changes in urban public services; and the first wedge to be placed between the cornerstone of education and the foundation of the community.

A New Definition of School Segregation

Mary Ellen Warshauer and Robert A. Dentler

Since the historic decision by the United States Supreme Court in Brown versus Topeka, much attention has been directed to the existence of de facto school segregation in Northern communities. Many studies have been undertaken to determine the nature and extent of school segregation or "racial imbalance" as it is commonly called. One basic concern of these studies has been the identification of segregated schools.

However, once *de jure* segregated conditions are eliminated, there can be no legal definition of what constitutes a segregated school. Definitions, therefore, become sociological and vary according to the situation at hand and the planner's, educator's, or researcher's purpose. As a result, many different standards for identifying segregated schools have been employed in different communities. Some of these have been exact and based on numerical ratios while others have tended to be subjective in nature and not explicitly delineated. The researcher, educator, planner, or interested individual is thus confronted with a difficult task if he is interested in comparative data; what is considered a segregated school in one community may not be so classified in another. In addition, where no numerical or empirical standards have been employed, variation in identifying segregated schools *within* a community might also arise.

Although no one definition of a segregated school can be considered "right" or "wrong," it is possible to evaluate the usefulness of a definition by its applicability to the problem being studied. For meaningful sociological research, any standard employed should be based empirically on the ethnic composition of a given area to permit accurate classification, and be flexible enough to enable adaptation to specific situations and change over time. In addition, the definition must have equal relevance and value in all types of communities.

Sociologically, "segregation" is a condition that tends to exclude or minimize association between groups, restricting the relationships that do occur to subordinate-superordinate roles. It is hard to determine the nature or quality of the relationships between various groups; thus, standards for identifying segregated schools have been primarily concerned with the *opportunity* for association based on the presence of a

6

diverse or ethnically mixed student population. Although everyone agrees that a school whose student population is 100 per cent Negro, Puerto Rican, Chinese, Mexican, etc., is segregated, less unanimity exists for other varying proportions.

One index that has been employed (in Chicago—Advisory Panel on Integration of the Public Schools ["The Hauser Report"], 1964; in Massachusetts—Massachusetts State Advisory Committee, 1965; and in New York—Public Education Association, 1955; Urban League, 1963; State Education Commissioner's Advisory Committee ["The Allen Report"], 1964), referred to as the 90-10 ratio, holds that:

> *Schools whose student body is less than 10 per cent Negro will be classified "white" segregated schools; if less than 10 per cent of the student body is white, the schools will be considered "Negro" segregated schools; the remainder will be referred to as "integrated" schools. (Hauser Report, 1964, p. 17.)*

In New York City the index has been modified to include both Negroes and/or Puerto Ricans, but the proportions have been kept the same (Allen Report, 1964).

Basically the rationale for this index is that in a school where more than 90 per cent of the students is of one ethnic group,[1] the opportunity for association with other groups is minimal. Therefore, meaningful and satisfactory relations between or among groups cannot be easily established.

Given this rationale, the 90-10 ratio seems to be a realistic index of extreme public school segregation in the cities (New York, Chicago, and Boston) where it has been employed. However, it has some major flaws that reduce its value. These flaws not only apply to the 90-10 ratio in particular but can also be seen to apply to the use of this type of static ratio as such. In fact, some data suggest that the specific cutoff point used, whether it is 90, 80, or 70 per cent, makes little difference in the number of segregated schools that are identified. For example, the Allen Report found little difference in classification of Negro and/or Puerto Rican segregated schools with the 90-10, 80-20, and 70-30 intervals. It showed that:

> *Under the criterion of 10% we used, 22% of the elementary schools in the city were minority segregated in 1963. Under a 20% criterion, this increases to 29%; and under a 30% criterion this increases to 31%. Thus our 10% standard contains 131 elementary*

[1] In the Allen Report, Negroes and Puerto Ricans were treated as one minority group in relation to the dominant white or "other" majority.

*schools, while the apparently much wider 30% criterion would in-
clude 183. Our standard includes nearly ¾ of this 183. (Allen
Report, 1964, p. 3.)*

At the other end, the Hauser Report showed little difference between
the 90-10 ratio and a more liberal ratio of 99-1. Using the 10 per cent
criterion, 91 per cent of Chicago's elementary schools were segregated,
while using the 1 per cent criterion, 77 per cent of the schools were
still so classified (Hauser Report, 1964, p. 17).

The discussion below deals specifically with the 90-10 ratio for purposes of clarity, but we believe it applies to all similar standards.

The 90-10 ratio is not based on the ethnic composition of a given
area, but is imposed upon a community from without. Thus, although
it may be a realistic measure for identifying schools in which extreme
segregation has already become an objective reality (in such cities, for
example, as New York, Chicago, and Boston that have a large Negro
population), it has less relevance and value for communities that have
a small number of Negroes. For example, let us assume that a community has a very small percentage of Negroes and all of these
Negroes attend *one* school in the system. However, due to their small
proportion in the community, the number of Negroes in this school
equals only 45 per cent. The 90-10 ratio, or similar measures, would
not classify this school as Negro segregated, although in social fact
the system is extremely segregated. Thus, the ability of static ratios
to lead to accurate classification in all types of communities is questionable.

A second limitation of the 90-10 ratio is the fact that it is a static
index. It lacks the capacity to adjust to demographic shifts in the total
population, shifts that have been of considerable magnitude in Northern communities over the last several decades. The index, therefore, is
insensitive to emerging community patterns and to the dynamics of
change and is not able to identify those schools in which the degree of
segregation is increasing and likely to accelerate to an extreme condition.

The final limitation of the 90-10 ratio derives mainly from its use
in New York City. However, the conditions underlying this flaw are
not specific to this city but may occur in any community where the
segregation of more than one minority group is under study.

One of the basic features of the 90-10 ratio in New York is its combination of Negroes and Puerto Ricans to establish levels and patterns
of ethnic concentration. This procedure can be reliable and valid, however, only to the extent that each major group exhibits similar mo-

bility. In New York, in an effort to test this assumption, we examined whether the intracity movement of Puerto Ricans differed from that of Negroes as both were reflected crudely in public school enrollment data for 1962 and 1963.

Our main test was to see, as summarized in Tables 1 and 2, whether movement among Puerto Rican students involved movement into and out of the same schools as movement among Negro students. We clas-

TABLE 1

NUMBER AND PER CENT OF NEW YORK CITY ELEMENTARY AND JUNIOR HIGH
SCHOOLS CLASSIFIED ACCORDING TO INCREASE OR DECREASE (± 50)
IN NUMBER OF NEGRO OR PUERTO RICAN STUDENTS, 1962-63

	Increase Negro		Decrease Negro		No Change Negro		Total	
	#	%	#	%	#	%	#	%
Manhattan								
Increase Puerto Rican	5	46	0	0	6	55	11	10
Decrease Puerto Rican	1	8	3	23	9	69	13	12
No Change Puerto Rican	10	11	8	9	70	80	88	79
Total	16	14	11	10	85	76	112	101[a]
Queens								
Increase Puerto Rican	3	100	–	–	–	–	3	2
Decrease Puerto Rican	–	–	–	–	–	–	0	0
No Change Puerto Rican	18	12	7	5	120	83	145	98
Total	21	14	7	5	120	82	148	100
Bronx								
Increase Puerto Rican	15	58	0	0	11	42	26	21
Decrease Puerto Rican	4	36	1	9	6	55	11	9
No Change Puerto Rican	20	23	2	2	65	75	87	70
Total	39	31	3	2	82	66	124	100
Brooklyn								
Increase Puerto Rican	11	50	1	5	10	45	22	10
Decrease Puerto Rican	1	8	7	58	4	33	12	5
No Change Puerto Rican	29	15	10	5	153	80	192	85
Total	41	18	18	8	167	74	226	100
Total City								
Increase Puerto Rican	34	55	1	2	27	44	62	10
Decrease Puerto Rican	6	17	11	31	19	53	36	6
No Change Puerto Rican	77	15	27	5	408	80	512	84
Total	117	19	39	6	454	75	610	100

[a]*Figures in this and subsequent tables do not always total 100% because fractions have been eliminated and the percentages rounded to the nearest whole number.*

TABLE 2

PER CENT OF ELEMENTARY AND JUNIOR HIGH SCHOOLS IN NEW YORK CITY
HAVING AN INCREASE OR DECREASE OF FIFTY OR MORE
NEGRO OR PUERTO RICAN STUDENTS, 1962-63

	Increase Negro	Decrease Negro	No Change Negro	Total
Manhattan				
Increase Puerto Rican	4	0	5	9
Decrease Puerto Rican	1	3	8	12
No Change Puerto Rican	9	7	62	78
Total	14	10	75	99
N = 112				
Queens				
Increase Puerto Rican	2	0	0	2
Decrease Puerto Rican	0	0	0	0
No Change Puerto Rican	12	5	81	98
Total	14	5	81	100
N = 148				
Bronx				
Increase Puerto Rican	12	0	9	21
Decrease Puerto Rican	3	1	5	9
No Change Puerto Rican	16	2	52	70
Total	31	3	66	100
N = 124				
Brooklyn				
Increase Puerto Rican	5	0	4	9
Decrease Puerto Rican	0	3	2	5
No Change Puerto Rican	13	4	68	85
Total	18	7	74	99
N = 226				
Total City				
Increase Puerto Rican	6	0	4	10
Decrease Puerto Rican	1	2	3	6
No Change Puerto Rican	13	4	67	84
Total	20	6	74	100
N = 610				

sified a school as "Increase Puerto Rican" if it had 50 more Puerto
Rican students in 1963 than in 1962. School "Decrease" involved a
loss of 50, and "No Change" occurred in schools where less than 50
Puerto Ricans were added or subtracted. The same criteria were used
for Negro students, and the schools were cross tabulated. Table 1 pre-

sents the results with percentages computed horizontally. Table 2 presents the same numbers computed by each cell as a per cent of the total school system.

Through this procedure, we noted that the two groups differ greatly in size and distribution. The Negro population of New York City is about *twice as large* as the Puerto Rican population. At one extreme stands Queens, where Puerto Ricans constitute 1 per cent of the borough population, compared with 9 per cent Negroes. At the other extreme—the Bronx—Puerto Ricans comprise 13 per cent of the population, and Negroes about 12 per cent.

In addition, school stability and change in per cent Puerto Rican versus per cent Negro varied even across two years. Most public schools served the same number of Puerto Rican *or* Negro students in 1962 as in 1963. But the stability of the Puerto Rican student population was greater than that of the Negro for the city as a whole. The Bronx revealed more change than any of the other boroughs. The changes that took place were most often *increases* in level of minority concentration, not decreases. This held true for both Negroes and Puerto Ricans everywhere except in Manhattan. There, a decrease in the concentration of Puerto Rican students took place. We also found that public schools showed greater increases in Negro than in Puerto Rican pupils.

Puerto Rican movement and settlement differ in several ways from that of Negroes in New York City. Therefore, any gross combination of the two minority groups in a mapping of the terrain of segregation in this city leads to an unreliable depiction of the situation. Although further study is needed to determine whether the combination of two minority ethnic groups in other communities would lead to a similar unreliable picture of the degree of segregation, we feel that more can be gained from treating each group separately. In this manner, the opportunity for distortion is eliminated.

The 90-10 ratio (and similar static measures), then, has certain flaws that reduce its value as an index for defining public school segregation. We are therefore led to ask if there is a better yardstick for defining public school segregation in Northern communities.

We believe there is a procedure that classifies accurately, provides sufficient flexibility for specific situations and change over time, is grounded in the reality of the ethnic composition of a given area, and has equal value in all types of communities. We call this procedure the Interval Method because it states segregation levels in terms of a range of percentages. While a number of applications of this procedure can be made, for purposes of illustration we have chosen one rooted in the totals of ethnic population in a given community. We will discuss other possible bases later in the paper.

The Interval Method states that a school is ethnically segregated if it contains more than *two times* the community population proportion of a given minority group. A school may also be defined as segregated if it enrolls *less than half* the proportion of a population group characteristic of its community.

To illustrate how this Interval Method would work in a given community, we have applied it here to the situation in New York City. Table 3 presents the percentage intervals for segregated and unsegregated schools in the city. The intervals are based on the respective percentages of Negroes and Puerto Ricans in each borough. The borough breakdown was employed here because of the large population base of the whole city, and the differing settlement and migration trends of the minority groups in each borough. The size of each borough, however, can be viewed as comparable to that of most medium-sized and large cities in which the interval should be applied on a citywide basis.

TABLE 3

PERCENTAGE INTERVALS FOR SEGREGATED AND UNSEGREGATED SCHOOLS
FOR NEW YORK CITY BY ETHNICITY AND BOROUGH

Borough	Segregated		Unsegregated		Segregated Other	
	% Negro	% Puerto Rican	% Negro	% Puerto Rican	% Negro	% Puerto Rican
Bronx	26-100	26-100	6-25	6-25	0-5	0-5
Brooklyn	31-100	16-100	7-30	3-15	0-6	0-2
Manhattan	51-100	26-100	13-50	6-25	0-12	0-5
Queens	21-100	10-100[a]	5-20	2-10[a]	0-4	0-1[a]

[a]*Classification of the Puerto Rican population in Queens is not based on a true estimate since they constitute only 1 per cent of the borough population and classifying a school containing 2 per cent Puerto Rican as segregated seemed unreasonable. We have therefore adjusted the interval.*

To see how the specific intervals were arrived at, we can use Brooklyn, New York, as an example. In 1963, 15 per cent of the population of Brooklyn was Negro. Therefore, any public school in Brooklyn having more than 30 per cent Negroes (twice 15 per cent) would be classified as "Segregated Negro." At the other end of the scale, any school in Brooklyn containing less than 7 per cent Negroes (less than one-half of 15 per cent) would be classified as "Segregated Other" because it contains "too few" Negroes. A school containing between 7 per cent and 30 per cent Negroes in Brooklyn would thus be considered "Unsegregated" because it does not contain either more than two times or less than half the borough percentage of Negroes. The same logic and procedures, when applied to the population level of Puerto Ricans in Brooklyn (7 per cent) leads to the intervals presented in Table 3.

One rationale for this index can be found in many studies of residential segregation conducted over the last couple of years. In a recent study, Taeuber and Taeuber (1965, p. 29) offered the following rationale in support of their index of residential segregation:

> *Suppose that whether a person was Negro or white made no difference in his choice of residence and that his race was not related to any other factors affecting residential location. . . . Then no neighborhood would be all-Negro or all-white, but rather each would be represented in each neighborhood in approximately the same proportion as in the city as a whole. Thus in a city where Negroes constitute half the population, the residents of any city block would be about equally divided between Negroes and whites. In a city where Negroes constitute 10 per cent of the population, one of every ten households in each block might be expected to be Negro.*

This rationale can be applied to public school enrollment. If *no* segregation existed one would, ideally, expect to find the same proportions of minority group members and whites in a given school as in the community as a whole.

Although this situation may be envisioned ideally, in fact there is always some variation from the pattern. However, it is not feasible to determine mathematically what the variation from this ideal proportion should be. In the past, therefore, when this basic rationale has been used, the definition of segregation which has been employed has not been explicitly delineated. For example, in a study entitled *De Facto Segregation in the Berkeley Public Schools,* the following definition was advanced: "De facto segregation exists in any school whose white-nonwhite ratio varies significantly from the same ratio of the District as a whole" (Berkeley De Facto Segregation Study Committee, 1963, p. 4). "Significantly" was never defined, nor were any numerical percentages established. Instead, the committee "left it for reasonable men to recognize de facto segregation where it exists" (Berkeley, 1963, p. 4). As our earlier discussion noted, the lack of precise standards leads to confusion and uneven classification, and therefore, in our opinion, is unsatisfactory for the study of de facto segregation.

To explicitly delineate the intervals of this new index we have chosen a measure that is *two times* or *less than half* the proportion of a given minority group in the community. Although this measure is exact, in the absence of empirical data, the specific cutoff points remain arbitrary.

At first, we believed that the criterion of two times the *local* proportion of minority group members should be established on the assumption that when a school approximates this ratio it tends to be perceived as undesirable from the point of view of the majority group in the community. Thus, the ratio would function as a "critical point"— a point where the rate of change of white out-migration and subsequent nonwhite in-migration tends to accelerate.

Our use of the "critical point" concept is not new; it is based on work done by Robert J. Havighurst in connection with his discussion of status ratios of the schools. Havighurst (1962, p. 332) introduced the concept of status ratio which he defined as "simply the ratio of the number of pupils of middle-class families to the number of children in working-class families." His formula for determining the status ratio was two times the upper-middle class plus the lower-middle class divided by the upper-lower class plus two times the lower-lower class; the weighting of the upper and lower classes is designed to balance the status ratio according to the proportion of these groups in the larger society. From the status ratio concept, Havighurst went on to suggest that there is probably a "critical point" in the status ratio of a school at which middle-class parents will consider removing their children from the school; in other words, a point at which the status ratio of the school will begin, at an accelerated rate, to show an increase in the proportion of upper-lower and lower-class pupils. Havighurst asserted that the critical point is subjective but arrived at consistently at the same time by a majority of parents whose children attend the given school. He suggested that a number of factors affect the status ratio of a school, one being the racial composition of the school community.

Thus, we postulated at first that when a school reaches the point where the proportion of minority group members is more than *two times* the proportion of this group in the total population, the "critical point" would have been reached, and this school, from the point of view of the majority population, would become defined subjectively as less desirable. This would be the case because ethnicity is still a symbol, a clear indicator of disadvantage.

Although this thesis seems to be a realistic assessment of the situation, the lack of empirical evidence prevents us from adopting it as a rationale for our index. To our knowledge no studies have been conducted dealing with the relationship between white out-migration and the percentage of minority group members attending the schools in a given area.

In addition, Peter Rossi, in his study *Why Families Move* (1955, p. 140), showed:

> . . . *the overwhelming importance of space complaints as a primary factor in decisions to move. Almost half (45 per cent) of the families cited their complaints with the space in their old abodes as the primary reason for moving.*
>
> *Considerably fewer households pointed to the neighborhood or costs as important reasons for leaving their former houses. The impact rating of neighborhood complaints was 14 per cent and the same figure for cost complaints was 12 per cent.*

Furthermore, Dan Dodson, in *A Proposal for Quality Education in Middle Grade Desegregation of Public Schools of Brooklyn, New York* (1965, p. 20), observes that:

> *An objective analysis of the data on Brooklyn would suggest that large numbers of whites do not mind living in interracially mixed neighborhoods and sharing common institutional facilities, provided the encounters their children have with differences does not too seriously threaten their group's own value structure.*

The examples usually used in support of the thesis of white out-movement as a result of school desegregation are Washington, D.C., and Baltimore, Maryland. In these two cities the public schools were desegregated and then quickly became resegregated as massive white out-migration occurred. The example of these two communities among others has increased the discussion of the "tipping point" as that point where the withdrawal would occur.

We believe, however, that the lack of clarity of this concept has led to its misuse in many instances. The "tipping point" is not a function of the level of minority group members in a given school, but is related to the rate of change. In a recent discussion dealing with the clarification of this concept Richard Boardman (unpublished paper) shows that on the basis of the mathematics of the logistic curve:

> *The tipping point may be defined as the point at which the ethnic composition of a given school begins an accelerated change from a relatively stable pattern. If this rate of change in ethnic composi-*

16 *The Urban R's*

tion intensifies over a three to five year period from a prolonged pattern of relative stability, it will continue until a complete cycle has been run and the opposite ethnic composition is obtained. The tipping point is specifically then that point in time at which a relatively stable ethnic composition pattern is replaced by a pattern of heightened change.

Therefore, the "tipping point" can be reached at any level of ethnic composition—10 per cent, two times the proportion of minority group members, 50 per cent, 70 per cent, etc., or, for example, in New York City, "where the percentage of whites drops more than five per cent in any one year, or more than ten per cent in any two to three year period" (Boardman, unpublished paper).

Finally, using the "tipping point" concept in this manner, we are still presented with the question as to what caused the initial change of 5 or 10 per cent. Without empirical evidence all that can be said is that it may be due to a combination of many factors operating simultaneously or any one of a multitude of independent conditions, of which school integration is only one.

In light of the above discussion, the classification of a school as segregated if it contains more than *two times* or *less than half* the local population proportion of a given minority group of the community in which the school is located, cannot be empirically justified. As we noted, the *two times* or *less than half* figures, although exact, are arbitrary.

They represent to us, however, a reasonable variation from the ideal pattern that one would expect by chance if *no* segregation existed. In addition, we feel that when a minority group's population in a given school more than doubles its level in the community as a whole, the presence of this group becomes visible and, therefore, the negative associations assigned to ethnicity would become more evident, regardless of its effect on white out-migration.

The logic of this statement is incorporated into the mechanics of the interval. As the population proportion of a minority group increases, the numerical spread of the unsegregated category increases, resulting in greater leeway in defining a school as unsegregated. This pattern is a result of the mathematical logic of the method, but it also embodies social logic. As the community population of a minority group increases, the group becomes socially more visible. Therefore, the fraction of minority-group pupils in any school would have to reach a higher level before its presence would be sensed and before the negative associations assigned to ethnicity would become evident.

Finally, a measure of *two times* or *less than half* is easily arrived at and employed.

Granting the limitations of the exact cutoff points themselves, we feel that the Interval Method is a more realistic measure for defining public school segregation for many reasons.

In the first place, the Interval Method is based upon the ethnic proportions of a given city; hence, it permits accurate and uniform classification across all types of communities. A school that has more than twice the community proportion of Negroes would be considered segregated whether the total percentage of Negroes in the community was, for example, 1, 5, 10, or 20 per cent. This can be seen in Table 3 for the four boroughs of New York City. In each borough the intervals for segregated and unsegregated schools vary considerably, reflecting their differing proportions of Negroes and Puerto Ricans. Thus, this classificatory scheme has equal value and relevance in all communities whether they have a small or a large minority group population.

Secondly, the Interval Method is not a static measure; it has the ability to adjust to demographic shifts in the total population. As the proportion of nonwhites in the community shifts, the limits of each category will change, reflecting the new community pattern and the dynamics of the change. For example, the intervals for segregated and unsegregated schools for the Negro population of Manhattan, New York, presented in Table 3, are based on a Negro population of 25 per cent. If the proportion of Negroes increased to 30 per cent, then the intervals would be as follows: Segregated Negro, 61 per cent to 100 per cent; Unsegregated, 15 per cent to 60 per cent; and Segregated Other, 0 per cent to 14 per cent. Likewise, if the percentage of Negroes decreased in Manhattan to 20 per cent, the new intervals would be: Segregated Negro, 41 per cent to 100 per cent; Unsegregated, 10 per cent to 40 per cent; and Segregated Other, 0 per cent to 9 per cent. Therefore, since the Interval Method is not static, the criterion of ethnic segregation becomes sensitive to the local conditions of the community rather than being imposed from without.

Another advantage of this classificatory scheme is that it provides the researcher with more information than the static methods discussed previously. The researcher is not only able to identify those schools in which *extreme* segregation has already become an objective reality, but he can also identify those schools that are more or less likely to become segregated.

For example, suppose 20 per cent of a community's population is Negro, then all schools with a 10 to 40 per cent Negro population would be considered unsegregated. Those schools that are in the lower or middle range of this interval are less likely to become segregated than those that have a Negro population very close to 40 per cent. In this manner, the Interval Method can provide some indication of probable future trends.

The final advantage of this scheme is its separate treatment of *each* minority group in relation to the dominant group in a community. As a result of this procedure it is possible to achieve greater conceptual precision in the classification of every school. For example, in New York City separate intervals were established for the Negro and Puerto Rican groups, as Table 3 shows. By applying these intervals each school can be precisely classified. It may be: (1) Segregated Negro and Segregated Puerto Rican; (2) Segregated Negro and Unsegregated Puerto Rican; (3) Unsegregated Negro and Segregated Puerto Rican; or (4) Unsegregated Negro and Unsegregated Puerto Rican. Each school may also be segregated or unsegregated for one group and Segregated Other (containing less than half the borough percentage) for the remaining group. The Interval Method can similarly be applied to any group—such as Mexicans, Chinese, Japanese, etc.—in any community. It can be applied as well to economic groupings. This classificatory scheme, therefore, provides considerable flexibility and adaptation to specific situations.

In summary, in light of the above considerations, we feel that the Interval Method is a more reasonable yardstick for identifying de facto public school segregation than is a static ratio. The Interval Method utilizes all of the advantages of the latter, while eliminating its major disadvantages. The Interval Method is empirically based on the ethnic composition of a given area to permit accurate classification, has the flexibility to permit adaptation to specific situations and change, and finally has equal relevance and value in all types of communities.

We note, however, that the Interval Method has a limitation that reduces its applicability in some communities. When the minority group exceeds 45 per cent of the total population of a given community (that is, as the minority group approaches majority-group status), the upper limit of our interval becomes unworkable. The 45 per cent limit serves as a meaningful cutoff point because it corresponds to the 90 per cent criterion used in many communities (the old 90-10 ratio).

Above 90 per cent, though, one approaches a situation where total segregation would be classified absurdly as "unsegregated." For example, if Negroes constitute 49 per cent of the total population, then the doubled end of the continuum would be set at 98 per cent, and a school in which as many as 98 per cent of its students are Negro would be classified as unsegregated, while obviously a situation of extreme segregation exists.

In addition, at a 50 per cent level, there is no minority group. Thus, the interval would have to be applied simultaneously to both the Negro and white communities, with only the lower level of the interval having any meaning. The internal logic of the Interval Method would then be lost.

As the minority group exceeds 50 per cent, the application of the interval would shift to the new (white) minority group, and would have to be reinterpreted in this light, modifying the conventional approach to minority-group status in our society.

This limitation of the Interval Method is a real one, but it is unlikely to limit the scale's applicability to any significant degree. Communities in the North where minority groups approach or exceed 45 per cent of the total population are extremely rare. Indeed, not more than four cities come to mind. We thus hold to our previous statement: the Interval Method is a more reasonable yardstick for identifying de facto public school segregation than is a static ratio.

We are not, however, stating that the particular Interval Method outlined in this chapter is the only measure that can be used. There are a number of ways in which this scheme may be applied. These alternatives are based upon the choice of the population base that defines the intervals. Two other bases that have been suggested are: (1) the proportion of minority children in the public school system

TABLE 4

PERCENTAGE INTERVALS FOR SEGREGATED NEGRO SCHOOLS FOR
NEW YORK CITY BY POPULATION BASE AND BOROUGH

Population Base	Borough			
	Bronx	Brooklyn	Manhattan	Queens
Community Population	26-100	31-100	51-100	21-100
Population 6-18	29-100	34-100	61-100	21-100
Population 6-12	34-100	39-100	67-100	25-100
Population 13-15	25-100	29-100	55-100	18-100
Population 6-15	31-100	36-100	64-100	23-100
School Population	49-100	55-100	77-100	35-100
Elementary School Population	50-100	57-100	77-100	41-100
Junior High School Population	49-100	61-100	77-100	39-100

of a given community (referred to as the "school specific interval");
and (2) the proportion of minority children of school age (6 to 18)
in a community (referred to as the "age specific interval"). The
"school specific interval" can be further subdivided by school division
—elementary, junior high, and high school—and the "age specific
interval" can likewise be modified to correspond to these divisions.

In an attempt to assess the value and applicability of these various
alternatives, we computed the intervals for each population base for
the boroughs of New York City and then applied these intervals to
determine the number of schools that would be defined as Negro Segregated. Tables 4 and 5 show the results of this procedure.

TABLE 5

PER CENT OF SEGREGATED NEGRO SCHOOLS FOR NEW YORK CITY
BY POPULATION BASE, TYPE OF SCHOOL, AND BOROUGH

| | Borough | | | | | | | |
| | Bronx | | Brooklyn | | Manhattan | | Queens | |
Population Base	Elem	JHS	Elem	JHS	Elem	JHS	Elem	JHS
Community Population	35	30	37	35	27	25	27	22
Population 6-18	26	30	36	35	24	21	27	22
Population 6-12	21	*	30	*	24	*	22	*
Population 13-15	*	33	*	35	*	21	*	31
Population 6-15	23	30	35	33	24	21	24	22
School Population	12	7	22	22	22	21	20	16
Elementary School Population	12	*	21	*	22	*	18	*
Junior High School Population	*	7	*	18	*	21	*	13
N of School	104	27	200	49	96	24	158	32

*This interval does not apply to this type of school.

All of the intervals presented in Table 4 represent the *two times*
end of the continuum for each population base. The "community
specific" and "school specific" intervals, however, are derived from
the respective percentage of *Negroes* in the community as a whole,
and in the school system, while the "age specific" intervals are based
on the per cent *nonwhite* in each group.

Examination of Tables 4 and 5 shows little difference in classification between the community and age specific intervals; the widest
variance appears in the classification of elementary schools in the

Bronx. It is interesting to note here that the specific cutoff points of the intervals themselves in the Bronx show only slight variation—they range from 25 to 34 per cent—while the range in Manhattan is much greater, from 51 to 67 per cent. The classification of schools in Manhattan, though, shows only slight variation; 24 to 27 per cent of the elementary schools and 21 to 25 per cent of the junior high schools are classified as Negro Segregated no matter what base is used. It seems, then, that because of the extreme Negro segregation in the public schools of Manhattan, the choice of interval makes little difference, while the more variable distribution in the Bronx is more sensitive to the change in cutoff point.

The comparison of the community specific and school specific intervals shows much less concordance in classification. Fewer schools are classified as Negro Segregated by use of the school specific intervals, especially in the Bronx and Brooklyn. This pattern results from the high public school enrollment of Negroes and the corresponding private school enrollment of whites. The influence of higher birth rates among Negroes leading to increased public school enrollment does *not* seem to be a significant influencing factor in New York City. If the latter was indeed a factor, the age and community specific intervals would also show considerable variation while the age and school specific intervals would result in a similar pattern. This is definitely not the case.

In conclusion, since the age and community specific rates result in similar classification, we feel that the community base, as outlined above, is a more useful measure. In the first place, the age specific interval method can only be derived for the "nonwhites" in a community; the census does not present data for other minority groups by age. As a result, this interval could not be applied to other minority groups such as Puerto Ricans in New York City. In addition, the "nonwhite" classification is not a precise grouping. In some communities "nonwhite" is equal to "Negro" but in other communities, such as San Francisco, the nonwhite, non-Negro population is quite large and educationally, socially, and economically different from the Negro population. If the age specific interval were used, therefore, the researcher would not be able to obtain comparable data free of compounding influences.

Secondly, we feel that another advantage of the community specific interval is its ease of application. Only one index is generated. The proper use of the age specific interval would require three separate intervals for children of elementary, junior, and senior high schools. When more than one minority group is being considered, as in New

York City, the educator, planner, or researcher would be required to handle six intervals simultaneously. The complexity introduced, therefore, would be considerable, while the advantages gained would be slight or nonexistent.

The same complexity would be generated in the use of the school specific interval method, and we, therefore, see this as a less desirable base. In addition we feel that an index based only on public school enrollment has less applicability for two reasons. First, the higher public school enrollment of minority group children is, in large part, a function of socioeconomic status. If an additional factor such as socioeconomic status is considered, however, then other important factors should also be introduced, for example, religion and fertility. This, of course, would increase the complexity of the application procedure to an unmanageable state.

Finally, the *two times* or *less than half* figures allow for variation from an ideal pattern of no segregation. This variation can be seen to be a function of, among other things, socioeconomic status, private school enrollment, and housing patterns. Therefore, to use an index that is based on some of these same factors, would compound the index and reduce its meaning for the study of de facto school segregation. This compounding would also be heightened by the considerable variation in the existence and quality of private school systems in many Northern communities. The school specific interval would, thus, have less applicability and value across all communities.

For the above reasons, we feel that the Interval Method based on the *community* proportion of minority group members is the most realistic measure to provide a meaningful new definition of public school segregation.

REFERENCES

Advisory Panel on Integration of the Public Schools ("The Hauser Report"). 1964. *Report to the Board of Education, City of Chicago.* Chicago: Board of Education.

Berkeley De Facto Segregation Study Committee. 1963. *De Facto Segregation in the Berkeley Public Schools.* Berkeley: Berkeley Unified School District.

Boardman, Richard. Unpublished paper. "The Tipping Point and Urban School Segregation."

Dodson, Dan. 1965. *A Proposal for Quality Education in Middle Grade*

Desegregation of Public Schools of Brooklyn, New York. Preliminary draft. New York: Center for Human Relations and Community Studies.

Havighurst, Robert J. 1962. *Society and Education.* Boston: Allyn and Bacon, Inc.

Massachusetts State Advisory Committee to the United States Commission on Civil Rights. 1965. *Report on Racial Imbalance in the Boston Public Schools.* Washington, D.C.: United States Commission on Civil Rights.

Public Education Association of New York City. 1955. *The Status of the Public School Education of Negro and Puerto Rican Children in New York City.* New York: The authors.

Rossi, Peter H. 1955. *Why Families Move.* Glencoe, Illinois: The Free Press.

State Education Commissioner's Advisory Committee on Human Relations and Community Tensions ("The Allen Report"). 1964. *Desegregating the Public Schools of New York City.* New York: State Department of Education.

Taeuber, Karl E., and Taeuber, Alma F. 1965. *Negroes in Cities.* Chicago: Aldine Publishing Company.

Urban League of Greater New York. 1963. *A Study of the Problems of Integration in New York City Public Schools Since 1955.* New York: The authors.

Englewood: A Northern City in Crisis

Robert La Frankie

This detailed historical examination of the efforts of Englewood, New Jersey, to desegregate its public schools should sensitize the reader to certain influences and relationships that are likely to be found, in somewhat different form, in most other cities. Any city that undertakes to desegregate its public school population is almost certain to encounter problems similar to those encountered by the Board of Education and its superintendent in Englewood. Generally speaking, the public interests which came into conflict in Englewood are indicative of the public interests that emerge in other cities facing a change of this nature (see Meyerson and Banfield, 1955, pp. 11–15).

Founded in 1859, Englewood is located two miles from the New Jersey entrance to the George Washington Bridge in the northeastern corner of the state. It is part of Bergen County, which is bordered by New York State on the north and the Hudson River on the east, and is contained in a land area of less than five square miles, extending down the western slopes of the Palisades to the northern edge of the "meadowlands" which border the Hackensack River.

Originally established as a haven for wealthy Wall Street commuters, Englewood during its early history became known as the "Bedroom of Wall Street." For the wealthy, it afforded a country environment in close proximity to New York City.

Over the course of its history, the city's population and social composition has changed considerably. First the Great Depression of 1929 took its toll. Then, in 1931, the George Washington Bridge opened to traffic, thus connecting Englewood with New York City and providing the necessary linkage for those people who wanted to flee the city (*Englewood Press Journal*, 1959). Finally, a great out-migration from New York City to Englewood occurred following World War II, when many middle-class white people flocked to the suburbs.

Between the years of 1940 and 1950, Englewood's population increased from approximately 19,000 to 23,000. This rise constituted the second greatest population increase in the history of the city (*Englewood's Schools*, 1965). A very significant transformation was taking place. Englewood had been predominantly a two-class community comprised of the wealthy and the poor, but the bulk of the new population was middle class.

24

Since the early 1920's, many of the wealthy citizens of Englewood had brought or imported Negro domestic workers from the South, mainly from South Carolina and Alabama. By 1933 the "Negro community" had increased to the point where Englewood contained the second largest number of Negro residents in Bergen County (*Englewood Press Journal*, 1933, p. 1). Some thirty years later, census reports indicated that out of Englewood's total population of 26,057 persons, approximately 27 per cent were Negroes.[1] This figure represents 40 per cent of the total nonwhite population in all of Bergen County (see Tables 1 and 2).

TABLE 1

POPULATION OF ENGLEWOOD ACCORDING TO U.S. CENSUS REPORTS
FROM 1930-1960[a]

Year	Total Population	Increase over Previous Report	Total White Population	Increase White Population	Total Nonwhite Population	Increase Nonwhite Population
1930	17,805	6,178	15,263	–	2,542	–
1940	18,966	1,161	15,939	676	3,027	485
1950	23,145	4,179	18,929	2,990	4,216	1,189
1960	26,057	2,912	18,942	13	7,115	2,889

[a]*Source: Harvard Field Study.*

TABLE 2

PER CENT OF NONWHITE POPULATION
FROM 1930-1960[a]

Year	Per Cent
1930	14.3
1940	16
1950	18.2
1960	27.3

[a]*Source: Harvard Field Study.*

The vast majority of Englewood's Negro population (approximately 90 per cent) resides in the Fourth Ward. This ward previously had experienced a pattern of successive invasions of Italian, Irish, and Jewish populations.

[1] The census reports refer to "nonwhite" population, but Negroes constitute 98 per cent of this population.

Although no religious census has ever been taken in Englewood, it is generally agreed that approximately 50 per cent of its citizens belong to Protestant denominations and that approximately one half of this group are Negroes. The remaining 50 per cent of the city's population is divided about evenly between the Roman Catholic and the Jewish faiths. For the most part, the churches still adhere to a pattern of racial segregation.

The city is subdivided politically into four major divisions. Its main street, Palisades Avenue, divides the community from east to west and in turn is bisected by the Erie Railroad tracks, which cut through the community from north to south. These "natural barriers" help separate the city into its four political wards, whose boundary lines have tended to serve as lines of demarcation between different socio-economic groupings. Ironically, the wards have numerical designations which can be equated with the level of these groups, e.g., the First Ward contains the highest priced real estate and the greatest per capita income per family, the Second Ward the next highest, and so forth.

For the last thirty years, Englewood's mayors, councilmen, and councilmen-at-large have been elected as members of the Republican Party, and have successfully maintained political control of the balance of power within the community. The only exception was the election of a Negro as Democratic Councilman from the Fourth Ward.

Englewood has a mayor-council form of municipal government, with the mayor and one councilman elected at large. Each of the four wards elects a councilman as its official representative. These are the only elective offices in the municipal government. The remaining offices of the formal power structure are appointive.

TABLE 3

PER CENT OF NONWHITE POPULATION BY WARD
1960[a]

Ward Number	Per Cent
Ward I	3.6
Ward II	7.7
Ward III	9.2
Ward IV	88.4

[a] *Source: Harvard Field Study*

The five members of the Board of Education are directly appointed by the mayor to a term of six years. They are appointed on a rotation basis so that not more than any two of them are new appointees at one time. The board does not have the power to levy and collect taxes but must rely on the Board of School Estimate, a body comprised of two members from the Board of Education (appointed by the board's president). The mayor is automatically a member of the Board of School Estimate and thereby gives the City Council control over purse strings of the school district. All in all, a total of 11 persons comprises the formal governmental decision-making body for Englewood, with the predominance of political power held by the mayor and common council. Prior to 1963, when the Englewood community reached a viable settlement concerning the desegregation of its schools, the school system consisted of five elementary schools, one in the First, Second, and Fourth Wards, and two in the Third Ward. Each elementary school was organized on a kindergarten through sixth grade plan. Table 4 presents data on the enrollment, racial, organizational, and physical characteristics of the public school complex at the height of the city's crisis in 1962.

This table makes clear the conservative policy Englewood followed in regard to school plant planning and school organization. Since 1916, the city has built only one new elementary plant, Quarles School in the First Ward, at a cost of approximately $1,000,000. (There is a serious question as to whether a school in this ward satisfied the greatest need of the city.) All this correctly suggests that Englewood is not a public-school-oriented community.

Englewood also has private and parochial school systems that currently enroll more than 1200 resident students. In addition, approximately 170 other resident students attend nonpublic schools outside the community (*Englewood's Schools*, 1965, pp. 54–57). Thus, approximately 27 per cent of the resident pupil population is enrolled in other than the public school system. The families who send their children to private schools constitute many of the wealthiest and most influential families in Englewood.[2]

For many decades, the racial imbalance in Englewood's schools amounted to a situation of de facto segregation. This pattern was the result of two factors: (a) a policy on the part of the white community to contain the Negroes in the Fourth Ward, and (b) socioeconomic

[2] The private schools of Englewood are currently involved in an expansion of their facilities. A huge building development program has been undertaken which anticipates increased enrollments at most levels. The new modern facilities will offer an increasingly attractive challenge of the public school system.

forces that compelled the growing Negro population to live where it could afford to, that is, the Fourth Ward.

As early as 1933, a delegation of white parents with children in a predominantly Negro school (Lincoln School) attended a school board meeting to request that their children be transferred to a predominantly white school (Liberty School). The Board of Education refused (*Board of Education Minutes,* September 1933). This is the first recorded reference in the minutes indicating the existence of racial segregation.

The board made no effort to change the traditional pattern of organization with the school system until 1938, when it constructed an addition to what in effect was a Negro school (Lincoln Elementary School). The primary purpose of addition was to convert the school into a combination elementary and junior high school for the residents of the Fourth Ward. A grant of $79,966 from the Federal Emergency Administration of Public Works was approved for the new addition.

The board's action led to the city's first organized protest by a Negro organization. The Urban League pointed out to the board that the number of students in the Fourth Ward was too small to support a full junior high school curriculum and that the new school would be all-Negro. The League urged that a school be built in a location that would insure integrated enrollment. In spite of this protest, the new junior high school opened its doors in February 1940, and was approved by the State Board of Education in 1941 and accredited as a secondary school of the State Department of Public Instruction, thereby establishing two separate junior high schools.

Shortly after World War II, many Negro families began an outward migration from the Fourth Ward area across the school district line into that section of the Third Ward that had been assigned attendance to the all-white Liberty Elementary School. This shift, plus an influx of many middle-class white families into the Third Ward (predominantly Jewish and principally from New York City), resulted in a loss of enrollment in the Fourth Ward's Lincoln School and placed undue pressure on the capacities of Liberty and Cleveland Elementary Schools, both in the Third Ward.

The difficulties that were gaining momentum naturally received additional force from the Supreme Court's decision on May 17, 1954, repudiating the "separate but equal" doctrine (Brown vs. Board of Education of Topeka). Within six weeks after this momentous decision, the Englewood Board of Education decided to alter the neighborhood school boundary lines to relieve overcrowding in the Third Ward's Cleveland School by increasing the size of the Lincoln School zone so as to include almost all of the Fourth Ward as part of its neighborhood district.

In June 1954, the board diverted some new kindergarteners from Liberty School to Lincoln School. Because of the change in the traditional boundary lines between the wards, Negroes who had recently moved out of the area of the Fourth Ward serviced by Lincoln School found their children nonetheless being sent to it. The NAACP, on behalf of two Negro families, filed with the State's Division Against Discrimination alleging discrimination on the part of the Englewood Board of Education. This was the first case in New Jersey in which a board of education had to appear as a defendant on charges of racial discrimination. (It may have been the first such case north of the Mason-Dixon Line.) On May 19, 1955, the commissioner of education handed down a decision declaring the Englewood Board of Education guilty of discrimination on the basis of the manner in which it had redrawn the neighborhood boundary lines. The board was ordered to redraw them in accordance with the principle that all children should be permitted to attend the school nearest their residence. The commissioner also ordered the board to eliminate the separate junior high school it had created 14 years earlier, in the Lincoln district. He charged that this school violated the 1947 Constitution of the State and, in effect, was a racially segregated junior high school. The board was ordered to eliminate the Lincoln Junior High School by September 1, 1956, or at least to have submitted by that date plans to alter these facilities.

The Board of Education thus was faced with the task of providing a new junior high school. Plans for a new junior high school had been underway prior to the commissioner's decision, but they had been blocked by the City Council and the Board of School Estimate. In 1953, the Board of Education had published a study that recommended the construction of a new junior high (*Englewood Press Journal*, May 1954). At this time, the City Council employed what appeared to be a delaying tactic by resorting to the political technique of hiring a firm of experts to conduct an educational study to determine if the board's study and proposal was adequate (*Englewood Press Journal*, May 1955). The resultant study tended to neutralize the study of the board, for the City Council rejected the board's proposal for new construction, claiming it was not sufficiently long-range. Shortly thereafter, the Board of Education itself hired a survey team from Ohio State University's Bureau of Educational Research to conduct an independent analysis of the long-range needs of Englewood. The results of this third study recommended the construction of two separate junior high schools and the construction of several new elementary schools at a cost of $7,500,000. The board then rejected these recommendations because it feared charges of discrimination would arise from the proposal to build a dual junior high school system, and also because the total cost of the program was too high. The board again proposed the construction of a single junior high school in the Third Ward at a cost of $4,898,000, but the proposal failed to pass a referendum vote. The City Council then adopted the board's proposal and appointed a committee of three engineering consultants from Englewood who pared the estimated cost of the structure down from $4,898,000 to within the community debt limit of $2,800,000. (Somewhat earlier, in March of 1957, the Board of Education, after questionable delay and under community pressures from various interest groups, also decided to construct a new elementary school in the First Ward.)

The greatest single event to challenge the static school conditions in Englewood came as a result of the "New Rochelle Case." This case involved charges of de facto segregation in the New Rochelle public schools. Referred to as *Taylor vs. Board of Education of New Rochelle,* it is often called the "Little Rock of the North" because it was the first highly publicized case concerning charges of de facto segregation in a Northern public school. In January 1961, the court decided against the New Rochelle School Board and ruled that it must "right the wrong it had previously done."

In April of 1961, the Englewood Board of Education commissioned Dr. Harry L. Stearns, the superintendent of schools, to initiate an immediate study of enrollment predictions and all factors that affected enrollment. All past surveys and studies had proven unreliable and had resulted in many inaccuracies and false enrollment predictions.

On June 12, 1961, within five months of the New Rochelle case, there occurred the first open confrontation between the Board of Education and a Negro organization—in this case the NAACP in conjunction with the "Interested Parents of the Fourth Ward." A petition was presented to the Board of Education concerning the responsibility of the board to further desegregate the Englewood public schools and Lincoln School in particular. The NAACP charged that the Board of Education was operating a segregated school system, for the enrollment in Lincoln of 532 Negro students and nine white students constituted de facto segregation.

In September of 1961, the Board of Education held a special meeting with the NAACP and the Urban League to discuss the situation at Lincoln School. The board stated its policy of opposing segregation and discrimination in all forms, but for the first time, and at the request of the NAACP, agreed to consider the matter of "racial imbalance" as part of the superintendent's depth study. Within a month following this meeting, and some three months before the publication of his report, Dr. Stearns served notice of his intention to retire as superintendent of schools, effective September 1, 1962.

The situation took on more aggressive characteristics when Negro attorney Paul Zuber entered the scene in February of 1962. Zuber had recently won the New Rochelle case for the NAACP, and he confronted the board with an ultimatum of either permitting "open enrollment" by students throughout the entire school system or facing a lawsuit in the federal courts. When the board reaffirmed its decision to abide by the neighborhood school policy, over one hundred demonstrators staged an all night sit-in at City Hall. At 8:30 the next morning 11 persons were arrested on charges of disorderly conduct. (These arrests are believed to have been the first that resulted from sit-in demonstrations north of the Mason-Dixon Line.) A suit was filed in federal court against the Englewood Board of Education, its superintendent of schools, and the state commissioner of education.

On March 12, 1962, the long awaited, controversial study by Superintendent Stearns, *Englewood, Its Schools and Its People* (1962), better known as the "Stearns Report," was released to the public. The report found that "racial imbalance" did exist in the elementary schools, and it outlined six alternate ways by which the community could deal with it. Briefly, they were: (1) to maintain a policy of drift; (2) to institute a renewal and "Higher Horizons" program; (3) to permit open enrollment; (4) to utilize the Princeton Plan; (5) to abandon Lincoln School and replace its classrooms by additions to other elementary schools; and (6) to undertake the extensive renewal and use of Lincoln School as a central intermediate school. Much community discussion and debate followed the release of the report. The Board of Education, the PTA's, and many other active community organizations debated it at length. A scheduled public meeting held by the board to consider the findings was attended by six hundred people. At this meeting, Superintendent Stearns made the first official reference to the necessity for changing the *status quo*. He said: "If we follow the American tradition, we only have one option."

At another public meeting on May 14, 1962, the board announced a plan to establish an integrated "demonstration school" from kindergarten through the sixth grade. Though attendance at the school would be voluntary and transportation left to the individual parents, the pupil population was to be based on the Negro-white pupil ratio in

the public school system, which was one-third Negro and two-thirds
white. This proposal was met by a strong negative response from
various groups. They charged that the plan meant only token integration and that it was an evasive action which failed to meet the problem "head-on."

The Urban League, NAACP, CORE, and an independent group of
citizens began a new series of demonstrations involving the picketing
of City Hall, threats of renewed boycotts against merchants in the
community, and meetings throughout the community.

On June 19, 1962, Governor Richard Hughes, the new governor of
the state, in his first official policy statement, made it clear that "flexibility" must be maintained in order to avoid "racial imbalance." More
specifically, he maintained that the neighborhood school concept was
valid but that its form had to change when conditions warranted.

On June 27, 1962, the Board of Education announced that it had
dropped its controversial plan for a "demonstration school" because
the results of a questionnaire that had been mailed to the parents of all
elementary school students indicated that the plan had failed to gain
sufficient community support. The board said it would prepare a new
plan by its July 12th meeting and issued the following statement
(*Bergen Evening Record,* June 27, 1962):

> *We can assure our citizens that the plan to be announced then will
> be in operation in September and will implement our often repeated
> intention of coming to grips with "racial imbalance" in the elemen-
> tary schools through a program that incorporates sound educational
> standards.*

The board also noted its intention to name its vice-president, John H.
Perry, a Negro, as president, replacing its then president who had suddenly and unexpectedly resigned from office.

On July 12, 1962, the board announced its new plans. It proposed a
central intermediate school that would house all the city's fifth-grade
students in a single building. The following year the complex would
be enlarged to include the sixth grade. This plan constituted an adaptation of alternates five and six proposed in the "Stearns Report." The
board, in effect, had officially recognized that "racial imbalance" existed
in the Englewood school system.

The new plan was rejected at first by the NAACP and CORE on the
grounds that it was a form of "gradualism" and did not go far enough.
Further, a group of mostly white parents from all five elementary
schools formed an organization also protesting the central intermediate
school. This group called itself SONS—"Save Our Neighborhood

Schools"—and claimed a membership of 1000. In response to SONS, other community organizations (the PTA Council, the Urban League, and the League of Women Voters) announced their qualified support of the plan on the grounds that it would be an acceptable first step.

On July 30, 1962, the Board of School Estimate voted 3–2 to refuse the additional monies needed to renovate and refurbish the building that was to house the proposed fifth-grade central school. The mayor and the two councilmen opposed the emergency appropriations, the two school board members supported it. This action incensed the Negro community. It announced plans for an "all out battle" against the mayor, the Common Council, the Board of Education, Save Our Neighborhood Schools, and "all other segregationist organizations," and issued a call to Paul Zuber to coordinate plans for action. Zuber, in turn, immediately announced that a huge rally would be held in the Fourth Ward with Negro leaders coming from all over the country to help launch the "Englewood Movement." Malcolm X and Zuber were to be the key speakers. However, Zuber's tactics to enlarge the Englewood Movement caused a split among the Negro leadership and established a rivalry between "insiders" (the traditional Negro community leadership) and "outsiders." Two community Negro ministers urged their respective congregations to boycott the rally to protest against Zuber's tactics, and on August 18th, the rally drew only about five hundred people.

On September 2, 1962, the Lincoln School PTA and parents of the children of the Fourth Ward announced their intention to boycott the Lincoln School for a period of three days, beginning on the opening day of school. On the first day of the boycott, September 5th, approximately two-thirds of the pupils stayed away from classes. The so-called "de facto segregation problem" had now reached the stage of impasse.

How had Englewood come to this impasse? It seems clear that a variety of factors were involved. The first concerns the policymakers who guided Englewood's government through the years. Eleven mayors, all Republicans, were elected and served during the period from 1930 to 1963. All had appointed boards of education that were predominantly controlled by white Anglo-Saxon Protestants. Of the 26 board members who had served during the 1930–1963 period, 13 were members of the Presbyterian Church, the oldest established church in Englewood, whose members appeared to have a controlling voice in the community's power structure. Further, approximately half of the members resided in the First Ward, even though this ward had the least number of pupils attending public school and the smallest total population of all the wards.

The clear dominance of this element of Englewood's population continued until the early 1950's, when the significant changes that had taken place in the community began to be recognized in board appointments. In 1951, the first Jew was appointed, in 1955, the first Negro. (Token representation had been granted Catholics from the earliest years, but it is safe to assume that the primary interest of most Catholics would have been to support the parochial school system and to "hold the line" against any tax increase necessary for the support of public education.)

During the same period, the Third Ward achieved a balance of political power with the First, for the first time in the history of Englewood. The First Ward had been challenged for political control of the Board of Education by elements of the middle-class liberals who, since the war, had moved into Englewood from adjoining metropolitan areas. Although the Second and Fourth Wards still only had token representation on the board, the Third gained a number of members equal to the number from the First. In the early 1960's, the Third and Fourth Wards combined forces to further challenge the "white power structure" and thus contributed to the impasse.

Another contributory element concerns the three individuals who were superintendents of the Englewood school system from 1930 to 1963. The first superintendent, a Presbyterian, can be termed a "company man." From 1930 through 1944, when he retired, there was no evidence in the minutes of the Board of Education files of any disagreement between various board members or between the superintendent and members of the board. As evidence of the tranquility within the community, only token community civic organizations appeared before the board to air their complaints. When the superintendent publicly announced his opinions on any issue, he spoke as the unanimous voice of the board.

The second superintendent was Dr. Stearns, who held office from 1944 through 1962. Unlike his predecessor, Superintendent Stearns did not project himself into issues or become personally involved in any problem. He believed that all issues should be decided by the Board of Education, which represented the people, and that the superintendent should merely carry out the program of the board. In his book, *Community Relations and the Public Schools* (1955), discussing representation on boards of education, Superintendent Stearns wrote:

There is the (type of) community with a dominant religious pattern, which keeps minority religious representation off these boards. If, in such a community, a minority group begins to grow numerically or in organization influence, there will be demands, sometimes reaching the proportion of political pressure, to place on the board representation of the minority faith. . . .

The board members are the representatives of the people, the policy makers; the schoolman is their employee and their administrator. The least he can do is to display a tolerant attitude toward each member, regardless of the religious affiliations or the balance of power between the religious groups. Occasionally, by wise leadership, he may pour oil on troubled waters.

It is ironic that Dr. Stearns, with his generally passive view of his office, found himself more and more called upon to play an active role in the integration of Englewood's schools.

The superintendent who succeeded Dr. Stearns took office in the midst of the impasse. He was working with a Board of Education that was more representative of Englewood's population than any that had preceded it. It was composed of two Presbyterians from the Second and Fourth Wards, two Catholics from the First and Third Wards, and one Jew from the Third Ward. As a result of this more adequate representation, the office of the superintendent took on a new dimension. The superintendent now was in a position to operate more freely and with such outspokenness as he felt necessary. The new superintendent considered the schools an instrument of social change. He believed that the superintendent's primary role was that of a "social engineer." Since taking office, he has proceeded accordingly.

DISCUSSION

This history from 1930 through 1963 reveals that there were seven major policy decisions in regard to the degree of integration to be allowed in the Englewood school system. The first of these, during the tenure of the first superintendent, was the decision of the Board of Education to construct an addition to the Lincoln Elementary School in the Fourth Ward, thereby establishing a complete school complex inclusive of grades one through nine, quite separate from the junior high school in the First Ward that serviced the white residents of Englewood. The board and the superintendent, in complete accord, explained that overcrowded conditions was the reason for the new junior high. Whatever the case, this decision served to promote and extend racial segregation.

The second critical policy decision did not occur until 16 years later, in 1954, when the Board of Education, again supported by the

superintendent (Dr. Stearns), decided to alter the traditional neighborhood school boundary lines for all five of the community's schools in
order to relieve the overcrowding that had developed in the schools in
the Second and Third Ward as a result of the population movement
from the Fourth—which in turn had created empty classrooms in that
ward. This decision, on June 28, 1954, led to a court action that
charged the board with racial discrimination. The court case, officially
recorded as Walker vs. Board of Education and Anderson vs. Board
of Education (*Decision of the Commissioner of Education*, 1955),
alleged that the boundary changes were "part of a consistent scheme
and plan to exclude and limit Negroes in the Liberty School [in the
Third Ward] by any illegal or extralegal device." The state commissioner of New Jersey, ruling against the Board of Education, ordered
it to establish new boundary lines. Beyond the specific issues of the
case, the court also ordered the board to eliminate the junior high it
had created in 1934.

The third critical policy decision occurred in February 1957, when
the Board of Education decided to construct a new elementary school
in the First Ward, as the major part of phase one of a proposed expansion program for the public school system.

The new elementary school was being constructed to replace the
former elite elementary school attended by the children of wealthy
families who lived in the exclusive area known as "the hill." The board
argued that the new school could be built much sooner than a junior
high (which the court had charged it to build) and that such a project
was within the bonding limits of the city.

At the public hearing seeking approval for the funds for the building
program (the cost of the new campus-type elementary school exceeded
$1,000,000), Dr. Stearns testified (*Public Hearing for State Approval
of Funds*, 1957, pp. 15–16):

> *There is more potential in the nonpublic school population of the
> city, and the tightening of the economy will have the effect of
> channeling some of this potential into the public schools. The
> construction of an attractive elementary school in the First Ward
> and the completion of an adequate and attractive junior high school
> facility will further increase the movement of present non-public
> school potential into the public school.*

This hoped-for transfer of pupils from nonpublic to public schools did
not take place. In fact, the total percentage of resident pupils who currently attend nonpublic schools in Englewood has increased from 25 to
27 per cent.

Insofar as this decision placed a new elementary school in an all-white area, it tended to perpetuate racial segregation. The construction of the new elementary school appears to have been the "price" that had to be paid to satisfy "city fathers" before gaining their support for appropriations necessary for a new junior high school.[3]

The fourth critical policy decision was made in March of the same year. After four previous years of surveys, studies, and planning (seven different studies were made), the Board of Education rejected the recommendation of the Ohio State survey team for two separate junior high schools and decided to construct only one, at a cost of $4,898,000. This figure, as already noted, was unacceptable to the Board of School Estimate, and a year and a half elapsed (during which the referendum vote was held) before a school—at the cost of $2,800,000—finally satisfied everyone's requirements.

The need for additional building construction had been a problem of long duration. The original high school was constructed in 1931, and had never been completed according to its plans, which called for an auditorium and additional classrooms. Thus, only after 27 years did Englewood, in effect, approve the construction of the auditorium.

The Board of Education made the fifth critical policy decision on February 1, 1962, when it voted to maintain the traditional neighborhood school policy and thereby denied the request of several Negro students to transfer from schools in the Third and Fourth Wards (Liberty and Lincoln, respectively).[4] Nine Negro children were involved in this attempt to push the board into adopting a policy of

[3] The junior high, built for a capacity of 1,000 pupils, and an adjacent auditorium, cost $2,800,000; the elementary school, built for 360 pupils (from the First Ward only) cost $1,000,000.

[4] It is interesting to note that approximately a year and a half later, following his retirement, Dr. Stearns testified at the State Education Department hearings concerning New Jersey's neighborhood school policy to the effect that Englewood maintained a double standard in its neighborhood school system, with one policy for white children and another for Negroes. At one point in the hearings, the result of a series of boycotts of the 98 per cent Negro elementary school, Dr. Stearns was asked by the NAACP attorney:

"Do all the public school children in Englewood attend the school nearest their home?"

"No," he replied.

He was further asked by the attorney if some students who attend the school in Englewood's wealthiest neighborhood (Quarles School) should be attending the Lincoln School in the Fourth Ward "on the basis of nearness." "Yes," answered Stearns.

It was cited that some children who attended Quarles School lived nearly two miles from it but only about one mile from the Lincoln School.

At another point, Stearns was asked, "Does the fact that a Negro child attends Lincoln School affect his performance in school?" Stearns replied, "Yes." (Smee, April 5, 1963.)

"open enrollment." The pupils were attempting to transfer to the new elementary school begun in 1957. Eventually the Board of Education modified its position, and eliminated the Lincoln Elementary School by creating a central sixth-grade intermediate school and by dispersing all the children from Lincoln to the four other elementary schools in the system.

The sixth critical policy decision in Englewood's gradual turn toward an integrated school system occurred later in 1962, when the Board of Education proposed its "demonstration school." This proposal was meant to ward off the impasse threatening to disrupt the elementary schools. With this recommendation, the board bypassed all six alternatives developed by Dr. Stearns in his report. As noted, the demonstration school, which was to include kindergarten through sixth grade, was intended to be a fully voluntary program. Even the matter of transportation was to have been left to the parents who had elected to participate in the program. The composition of the pupil population was to be based on the proportions of Negro and white students in the public school system, which was one-third Negro and two-thirds white.

The vast majority of concerned organizations in the Englewood community failed to support the board's proposal. They argued that it would lead to renewed bitterness. Many factions also felt that it was only a token offer and that another school year would go by without any real progress toward an integrated school program. Within six weeks the board rescinded its decision. On June 27, 1962, it officially dropped plans for the demonstration school.

Some two weeks later, on July 12, 1962, the board announced a new proposal—in effect, the seventh critical decision, and the one that was to become the foundation for the solution that would eventually break the impasse in which the community now found itself. The board proposed a central intermediate school which was to be modeled on the fifth and sixth alternatives in the "Stearns Report." The school would house all of the city's fifth-grade pupils in one building, and would be the first phase of a long-range program designed to create better racial balance. Ultimately, the sixth grade was chosen to be the first year of the intermediate school, so that, in accordance with better educational planning, it eventually would constitute a middle school of the sixth, seventh, and eighth grades.

An examination of these seven critical policy decisions suggests the following general conclusions and observations. First, the decisions dealt principally with aspects of school plant planning, and for the most part served to maintain the *status quo*. Second, partly as a result of the desire to maintain the *status quo,* the decisions were made on a short-range basis and lacked foresight. It was mainly as a consequence of this shortsightedness that four of the decisions were reversed or rescinded at a later date, either through the fiat of an outside governmental agency, such as the commissioner of education or the courts, or by the pressure of numerous community organizations that arose to challenge the decisions.

During the period from 1930 through 1963, as many as nine different studies were undertaken to aid the Board of Education in its planning and decision-making processes. An analysis of the various studies reveals a consistent lack of comprehensive planning. Until 1961, the problem of racial segregation as such was never officially recognized by the different boards of education and superintendents. The problem was recognized only after the NAACP had confronted the Board of Education in June of 1961 with the charge that one of Englewood's schools, having 98 per cent Negro enrollment, was racially segregated. Even then, after the board consented to include this concern as a part of the depth study then being prepared by Dr. Stearns, it did so only under the designation of "racial imbalance" rather than that of racial segregation. Finally, although the "Stearns Report" did acknowledge that "racial imbalance" existed in the Englewood public schools, the Board of Education refused to accept its findings and recommendations—until, in effect, it was forced to accept them by public pressure. (It is interesting to note that between 1960 and 1962, some sixteen organizations, a number newly activated for the purpose, took stands to influence the board to seek an integrated school system. For Englewood, this was an unusually high degree of public participation.)

Today, Englewood lives precariously in the shadow of its immediate past. Although a temporary settlement has been achieved in the community through the closing of the basically all-Negro school and the establishment of a sixth-grade intermediate school, the "truce" that prevails is an uneasy one. The students from the Negro elementary school in the Fourth Ward have been absorbed into the central sixth grade and the four other elementary schools. Table 5 shows the present racial composition of the schools. But the problems that cause, and follow in the wake of, racial segregation cannot be solved simply by a mechanical reassignment of students. These problems require, first of all, a program of urban renewal that will change the housing patterns that are at the root of segregation in the schools. Further, new concepts in curricula must be developed to break the present lockstep educational program that tends to maintain and perpetuate patterns of segregation

TABLE 4

BACKGROUND DATA AND RACIAL COMPOSITION OF ENGLEWOOD
PUBLIC SCHOOLS, OCTOBER 1961[a]

School	History	Size of Area in Acres	School Organi- zation	Opera- tional Seating Capacity	White Enroll- ment	Negro Enroll- ment	Total Enroll- ment	% White and Negro
Lincoln	1870-Original 1916-Fire Des. 1917-New Const. 1925-West Add. 1927-East Add. 1938-Addition	2.1	K-6	624	7	531	538	1.3-W 98.7-N
Liberty	1902-Original 1912-South Add. 1927-North Add.	2.26	K-6	432	161	275	436	36.9-W 63.1-N
Cleveland	1909-Original 1930-Gym Add. 1949-Addition	5.51	K-6	480	496	1	497	99.8-W .2-N
Roosevelt	1925-Original 1949-Addition	3.28	K-6	336	324	43	367	88.3-W 11.7-N
Quarles	1959-Original	10	K-6	336	353	17	370	95.4-W 4.6-N
Franklin and Engle St.	1905-Original 1916-Altered 1915-Original	4.26	Vacant	Vacant	Vacant	Vacant	Vacant	Vacant
TOTAL ELEMENTARY				2208	1341	867	2208	60.8-W 39.2-N
Englewood Junior High	1960-Original	34	7-9	950	510	332	842	60.6-W 39.4-N
Dwight Morrow Senior High	1931-Original		10-12	825	525	184	709	74.0-W 26.0-N
TOTAL SECONDARY				1775	1035	516	1551	66.7-W 33.3-N
TOTAL SCHOOL				3983	2376	1383	3759	63.2-W 36.8-N

[a] *Adapted from Stearns, 1962, pp. 40-112.*

even within "integrated" schools. One example of such patterns is the practice of homogeneous grouping. This practice alone tends to perpetuate the discrimination that the schools now officially oppose.

The settlement in Englewood has bought time, but the time is running out. The elementary schools are overcrowded (see Table 5), and one of them—Liberty School, with a Negro enrollment of 67 per

TABLE 5

BACKGROUND DATA AND RACIAL COMPOSITION OF ENGLEWOOD
PUBLIC SCHOOLS, OCTOBER 1, 1964[a]

Name of School	School Organization	Operational Seating Capacity	White Enroll-ment[b]	Negro Enroll-ment[c]	Total Enroll-ment	% White and Negro
Lincoln	Pre K	624	94	81	175	53.7-W 46.3-N
Liberty	K-5	432	148	309	457	32.4-W 67.6-N
Cleveland	K-5	480	416	251	667	62.4-W 37.6-N
Roosevelt	K-5	336	248	156	404	61.4-W 38.6-N
Quarles	K-5	336	288	59	347	83.0-W 17.0-N
Engle Street	Central Sixth Grade	550	165	118	283	58.3-W 41.7-N
TOTAL ELEMENTARY			1359	974	2333	58.3-W 41.7-N
Englewood Junior High	7-9	950	467	363	830	56.3-W 43.7-N
Dwight Morrow Senior High	10-12	825	485	325	810	59.9-W 40.1-N
TOTAL SECONDARY		1775	952	688	1640	58.1-W 41.9-N
TOTAL SCHOOL			2311	1662	3973	58.2-W 41.8-N

[a]*Adapted from* Englewood's Schools, *1965, p. 44.*
[b]*Includes all pupils not referred to as Negro.*
[c]*Includes the small per cent of other nonwhite pupils who reside in Englewood.*

cent—appears to be on the way to becoming another all-Negro school.
A Study of Racial Distribution in the Englewood Public Schools
(Commissioner of Education, New Jersey, 1962, p. 27), completed
during the height of the crisis in 1962, before the closing of Lincoln
School, had already reported the following:

> *The committee must conclude that the housing patterns, land acquisi-*
> *tion for school sites, [and] elementary school boundary lines have*
> *contributed to the containment of Negro families in the Fourth*
> *Ward and a resultant racial imbalance in the elementary schools. A*
> *further result of these conditions is the growing degree of imbalance*

*in the Liberty School that may soon counteract the achievements
made by boundary changes between Lincoln and Liberty schools
required by the decision of the Commissioner of Education.*

The problem facing Englewood is two-fold: a steadily increasing
Negro population within the total community and a rapidly increasing Negro enrollment in the public school system. The Negro school
population has increased from 19.4 per cent of the total in 1930 to
well over 40 per cent of the 3,900 students from prekindergarten
through grade twelve in 1965. To help offset the problems created by
this growth, the Board of Education and the superintendent of schools
have made a contractual arrangement with a district contiguous to
Englewood (Englewood Cliffs) which has no secondary school of its
own to utilize those in the Englewood school district. The newly signed
ten-year agreement will bring approximately four hundred additional
white students into the high schools.

For all that Englewood has not yet developed a full solution to its
educational problems and for all that the past decade has been one of
strife and conflict, it would be grossly misleading not to observe that
this period also has provided the opportunities for important changes
and as a result has helped establish a certain degree of affirmation. The
strife and conflict have forced a conservative community to modify its
total educational philosophy. The superintendent of schools has become a "social engineer of change" and has been able to operate, more
than ever before, as a free agent. New teaching techniques have been
introduced with the creation of the central school. Such innovations as
team teaching and large group and individualized instruction have been
instituted as part of the entire school program. The schools have been
awarded a Ford Foundation grant for $250,000 to be used in revising
the curriculum to help overcome the problems associated with de facto
segregation. Finally, as the problem of school segregation came to a
head, it forced the Englewood community to develop long-range planning for the first time in its history. It is in large part on the intelligence and implementation of this planning that the achievement of
quality desegregation in Englewood depends.

REFERENCES

Bergen Evening Record (Bergen, New Jersey). June 27, 1962.
Board of Education Minutes (Englewood School District). September, 1933.

Brown vs. Board of Education of Topeka. May 17, 1954. Decision of the Supreme Court of the United States.

Commissioner of Education (New Jersey). October, 1962. *A Study of Racial Distribution in the Englewood Public Schools.* State of New Jersey.

Englewood Press Journal. 1933; May, 1954; May, 1955; Centennial Edition, 1959.

Englewood's Schools. 1965. President and Fellows of Harvard College. Mimeographed.

Meyerson, Martin and Edward C. Banfield. 1955. *Politics, Planning and the Public Interest.* Glencoe: The Free Press.

Public Hearing for State Approval of Funds (Trenton, New Jersey). March, 1957.

Smee, Jack. April 5, 1963. UPI News Memorandum.

Stearns, Harry L. 1955. *Community Relations and the Public Schools.* Englewood Cliffs: Prentice-Hall.

Stearns, Harry L. 1962. *Englewood, Its People and Its Schools.* Englewood School District.

Walker vs. Board of Education and Anderson vs. Board of Education. May 19, 1955. Decision of the Commissioner of Education, Trenton, New Jersey.

Resistance to School Desegregation:
A Case Study of Backlash Among Jews*

Kurt Lang and Gladys Engel Lang

Every social movement toward major social reform is bound to generate some opposition, some counterreaction, from those who see their position adversely affected by the changes sought. No one was surprised, therefore, when whites in the South resisted the desegregation of public schools and public facilities. Nor was it entirely unexpected that some Northern white groups would seriously seek to obstruct Negro progress toward the attainment of full civil rights. What did occasion some surprise—and, in some circles, bewilderment—was the unexpectedly strong resistance among groups of whites who, by virtue of their past minority-group status, were expected to be active in the struggle against intolerance and discrimination or who, at the very least, were counted upon not to oppose and resist legitimate Negro demands. It is among these groups, previously judged liberal and tolerant, that one now looks to find evidence of a new opposition to the political and moral crusade for equal civil rights, a phenomenon popularly dubbed "backlash."

The resistance of population groups traditionally hostile to the Negro does not constitute, in the literal sense, a "backlash" phenomenon. That term applies rather to a broadening of the base of opposition among whites as a direct reaction to the gains and demands of the civil rights movement. Conflict has sharpened as an increasing number of whites, hitherto shielded by social status and residential location from direct involvement, have suddenly found themselves directly affected by desegregation measures. The stand people have to take in this situation goes beyond generalized expressions of sympathy with the victims of Birmingham bombers and of Mississippi lynchers; they

* This is a slightly altered version of an article that originally appeared in *Sociological Inquiry*, Winter 1965. The authors gratefully acknowledge financial assistance from the American Jewish Congress, whose officers recognized early the significance of the opposition by Jews to school desegregation and the need for research as well as for community action. Without this aid, the survey data could not have been collected. Queens College helped us to hire Richard Ofshe as a research assistant. We are also deeply indebted to Donald Gelfand, Michael Goldstein, and others who volunteered coding help and to other students, too numerous for listing, who undertook some of the rather difficult interviewing assignments.

have to stand up and be counted. Nowhere has this confrontation been more direct than where the public schools are concerned. In the large metropolitan cities of the North with their sizable Negro (and Puerto Rican) slums, measures designed to relieve overcrowding in ghetto schools and to ameliorate racial imbalance in individual schools here and there have frequently touched off violent opposition. The number of such incidents, plus the call by some Negro leaders for nothing less than citywide school desegregation, have contributed to the coalescence of scattered and sporadic resistance into a countermovement of some significance.

The particular school desegregation controversy discussed here grew out of a proposal to pair two elementary schools, located some five city blocks or .24 miles apart, so that together they could serve their school populations as a single area. As in Princeton, which lent its name to such pairing plans, this one applied to two schools close to one another but serving two quite different neighborhoods. In 1963, according to official estimates (State Education Commissioner's Advisory Committee on Human Relations and Community Tensions, 1964), about 87 per cent of the children in one school (P.S. 149Q) were white, while about 99.5 per cent in the other (P.S. 92Q) were Negro and Puerto Rican, mostly Negro. Junction Boulevard, a moderately busy thoroughfare, separates predominantly white Jackson Heights from predominantly Negro Corona, and until the late 1950's—when an adjustment explicitly aimed at sending more Negro children from Corona to the "white" school was made in school zone boundaries—it also marked off one school population from the other.

The initial proposal for the pairing came from a group of white parents with children in the local public school. Their suggestion followed the summer, 1963, issuance by Dr. James E. Allen, state commissioner of education, of a general policy directive to local school boards that they reduce "racial imbalance." It anticipated by nearly six months the New York City Board of Education's announcement of its own intentions for the school year 1964–5. Because the proposal helped pave the way for similar suggestions elsewhere, the area of Jackson Heights became one of the first testing grounds in the city which measured the strength of forces for and against steps in the direction of better "balance." Several leaders on both sides of the local controversy quickly rose to citywide leadership in the struggle, as it spread throughout New York City.

The two authors of this paper, former residents in the area, have been engaged in systematic participant observation since September 1963, that is, from the time the existence of a local pairing proposal first became public knowledge. In November 1963, we undertook to supplement these observations through intensive interviews with a systematic sample of the population nearest the "white" school, specifically in a four-block apartment cooperative where the "battle" mostly raged.[1] At that time, there had been no official commitment to any plan; yet almost all the residents in the area, whether or not they had children likely to be affected, felt strongly enough to take a definite stand on the proposal to pair the schools. In this paper we have limited ourselves to an analysis of this early resistance to the plan, based mainly on the interview data supplemented by such other observations as seem pertinent. Though the study concerns one single locality, an examination of the social characteristics and general attitudes that discriminate between protagonists and opponents should help to identify the social base on which much of the Northern resistance to school desegregation proposals rests.[2]

THE PLAN AND ITS SETTING

The plan for pairing the schools was actually approved and put into effect with only minor modifications in September 1964, just about a year after its proposal set off the neighborhood controversy. As finally worked out, all first and second graders in the high-concentration "white" school were transferred to the "Negro" school, while third through sixth graders attending the "Negro" school were sent to the "white" school. Thus, one school building now serves all children in grades one and two; the other, all children in the third through sixth grades. Kindergarteners, as before, continue to attend the school nearer

[1] Interviews averaging forty minutes were obtained from respondents in 188 households, selected on a random systematic basis from a list of all households in a four-block cooperative where roughly half the school population of the high-concentration white school resided, with a deliberate over-sampling of large apartments to increase the proportion of respondents with children. Respondents were predesignated, and substitutions permitted in only very special circumstances. Callbacks, sometimes as many as six, produced a 70 per cent coverage. For many reasons—such as the character of the neighborhood and the circumstances of the controversy—we experienced unusual difficulty in obtaining completed interviews. Though a quota sample would evidently have produced a larger number of interviews, we are certain that it would have resulted also in a serious misestimate of the degree of support for the plan, and of the educational level of the population.
[2] The dynamics of attitude change in response to the controversy, the hardening of positions taken early in the controversy, and their possible erosion in the face of new experience, shall be taken up on the basis of data to be collected, following the implementation of the pairing proposal.

their home. A minimum of bussing has been required; only some two to three dozen children in the combined school zone as redrawn lived beyond the legally prescribed walking distance.

While this paper makes no attempt to evaluate the plan and its effects, it is nevertheless important to note that the proposal was not simply a plan to end racial imbalance in what was de facto a Negro school. Included in the package were provisions for upgrading the educational facilities in *both* schools. The "Negro" school, housed in an older building, was completely renovated before the plan went into effect. It had for some time been designated a "special service school" and as such received certain extra resources and personnel for which the "white" school had heretofore not qualified. For instance, classes with nearly forty children (and sometimes more) had not been atypical of the "white" school. As a result of the pairing, average class size was reduced to twenty-seven students, and the school obtained a number of very much needed teaching specialists.

Jackson Heights, where the previously "white school" was located, can be considered a middle-class apartment house area, even though in 1960 one-third of its population still lived in one- and two-family dwellings. The population grew steadily from 1940 to 1960, many of the apartment houses having been built after World War II. Where not long ago lots stood vacant in the area surrounding the "white" school, modern six-story apartment houses now directly face Corona—with its smaller and mostly much older buildings—across Junction Boulevard. There, Negroes have been steadily replacing whites, mostly of Italian and Eastern European stock, so that Corona, together with East Elmhurst to the north, now is the second largest enclave of Negroes in the borough of Queens.

Yet, when indicators of social status other than race are considered, the discrepancies between the two populations in the immediately adjacent areas—where the controversy centered—are not as great as some might believe. Certainly Corona ranks lower in income, education, proportion employed in the so-called middle-class occupations, etc., than does Jackson Heights. But it is hardly a lower-class Negro area. Despite some very obvious contrasts in the physical characteristics of the two communities and disparities to the disadvantage of Negroes, the whites in the recently settled blocks nearest the Negro district are more nearly similar to their nonwhite neighbors than are the whites living in that part of Jackson Heights farther away. There is a fairly continuous decline in a variety of socioeconomic indicators, based on census tracts, as one moves from the center of Jackson Heights toward the Negro area. For example, median years of schooling completed

in the census tract containing the "white" school is 11.2; in the tract
with the "Negro" school, it is 10.1. Given the imperfect overlap of
tracts with school zones, inferences with regard to school populations
are open to challenge. Still, we mean to convey the idea that this is no
"Gold Coast and Slum" situation with the two adjacent communities
worlds apart.[3]

Though a few nonwhite families have moved into Jackson Heights,
there is little chance in the near future of a massive invasion by lower-
class Negroes. Occupancy, as measured by persons per room, is at
present just about as dense in the white tracts as in the Negro tracts,
where buildings are older and rents consequently lower. The four-
block cooperative apartment development that borders on Junction
Boulevard and surrounds the "white" school, together with other cooperatives in the area, constitutes a special barrier. Carrying charges
in these apartments, completed in 1958 and 1959, are modest by New
York City standards, but a cash purchase of stocks at a price beyond
the reach of most Negroes is an additional requirement for occupancy.
While the directing boards of the cooperatives directly control occupancy on the basis of the financial solvency of applicants and limit
the number of persons occupying a given apartment, this power, as far
as is known, has not been used deliberately to exclude nonwhites. A
few Negroes (Negro-white married couples), Orientals, and Puerto
Ricans live in the cooperative.

The white residents living near the school are a "minority group"
population.[4] Nearly three-quarters of the respondents in the survey
identified themselves as Jewish, another fifth as Catholic. Though
locally dominant, more Jews than not still considered themselves members of a minority group.

Most of the people in the area studied are part of the continuing
"middle income" exodus from the center of the city outwards. Many
(40 per cent) had moved in from deteriorating areas of Brooklyn and
the Bronx; only 10 per cent were prior residents of the surrounding
neighborhood and just 6 per cent had come from outside New York
City limits. The move into the cooperative development was generally
an "upward" move in one or more of several senses—as a first "home"
after marriage, as an investment to secure sufficient living space for a
growing family, or as a refuge from "overrun" neighborhoods with
their multiple problems.

[3] That "equal status" contacts are a condition favorable to the reduction of intergroup tensions has been amply confirmed by empirical research.
[4] Strictly speaking, the generalizations based on the sample survey apply only to
the population of the cooperative development. Still, half the white school population resided there, and it was the hub of the controversy.

These residents in the aggregate are best characterized as middle mass, not middle class, insofar as many are hardly secure in status or solidly established economically, even though the income and ambition of most differentiate them clearly from the real lower classes. Of all adults in our sample only two out of five said they had continued their schooling beyond high school.[5] A fourth were college graduates, and it was primarily the latter who expressed openly their desire to be on their way up and out of the neighborhood into a more solidly middle-class milieu. The fact that only 17 per cent of the heads of households were in the professional, technical, and managerial category (including 5 per cent who were teachers) must be viewed in the light of the city's unusual occupational structure. (In 1960, 23 per cent of the male labor force fell into this occupational category. So the 17 per cent figure is unexpectedly low.) Business and white-collar supervisory occupations, not in any sense managerial, together with semiprofessional jobs not protected by licensing, account for an additional 16 per cent. All of the 15 per cent who were self-employed in "business" owned small family-run establishments. The rest, excluding a few who were retired, were in sales, delivery, and a variety of skilled and semi-skilled blue-collar jobs, which, as 45 per cent of the total, made up the largest group. Finally, despite the high proportion with children, 40 per cent of all women held jobs, two-thirds of these full time.

MINORITY GROUP IDENTIFICATION

Discussions of conflict and controversy over racial imbalance in the public schools of New York City cannot gloss over the fact that in many areas, such as this one, the white public school population is made up to a large degree of Jewish children. Catholics, in greater proportions than twenty or thirty years ago, are receiving their primary education in parochial schools, and white Protestants cluster in the suburbs and in the independent schools of the better residential areas. For some years now, the city's public schools have been officially closed on Jewish holidays as well as on traditional Christian holidays. To what extent, then, can one rely on what is essentially a confrontation between Negroes and Jews (with an assist from Catholics) as a reflection of the presumably liberal attitudes of Jews on ethnic and racial issues?

[5] The reader is reminded that the deliberate oversampling of large apartments inflated both occupational status and education, as well as the degree of support for the plan.

In this particular neighborhood, Jews expressed no greater readiness to accept the pairing proposals than did their Christian neighbors. Actually the proportion of Catholics favoring the plan (33 per cent) was slightly larger than that of Jews (28 per cent). It is true that fewer of the Catholics interviewed had children going to the public school or preschool children whom they expected to enroll someday. But whether or not his children were involved had no statistical relationship to the side of the issue that any person was likely to favor. This *did* make a difference, however, as to whether or not the person had done something specific to support or oppose the plan, such as joining an organization, giving money, or attending a meeting. In keeping with this, the 74 per cent of the sample that was Jewish made up 88 per cent of all the "activists" on both sides. Jews were more vocal *pro* and *con*.

Racial and ethnic attitudes were gauged by a series of questions, essentially a social distance scale, where each respondent was asked whether he "would mind" being in certain types of situations involving either members of another religion or Negroes. The items, adapted from the battery employed by Louis Harris on a national sample of whites (Brink and Harris, 1964), were: (1) giving preferential treatment in job opportunities to Negroes; (2) having your own teenager date a Negro; (3) having a close friend or relative marry a Negro; (4) living in a neighborhood where *a good many* of your neighbors are Negroes; (5) sitting in a restaurant where *the majority* are Negroes; (6) having your child go to a school where *about half* are Negroes. Items one, two, four and six were duplicated to apply to contact between Jews and non-Jews, with slight variations in the wording to take account of whether the respondent was Jewish or not.

An index indicating group acceptance of "outsiders" was constructed from responses to these hypothetical situations. The possible range is from 0 to 1, with 0 designating where nobody "minds" contact in any of the situations and 1, a condition where all in the group "mind" every one of the situations cited.[6] Though it is quite probable that these responses underestimate the actual degree of avoidance between groups, the index seems useful for group comparisons (see Table 1).

Judged by this index, Jews indeed turn out to "mind" contact with Negroes less than do non-Jews. But a difference of .023 is not at all meaningful, especially when compared to the difference of .233 that

[6] The formula for the index is a simple one: $\frac{\Sigma \text{Rpos}}{\text{I} \times \text{N}}$ where Rpos = a response to the effect that the person "minded"; I = number of items (6 concerning Negroes, 4 concerning Jews or non-Jews), and N = number of respondents.

TABLE 1

"SOCIAL DISTANCE" INDEX TOWARDS MEMBERS
OF OTHER RACES AND RELIGIONS

Respondent	Other Races Index Value	Other Religions Index Value
Pro-Pairing	.296	.162
Anti-Pairing	.529	.268
Jews	.459	.295
Non-Jews	.482	.106

separates proponents and opponents of the plan. Despite their many public protestations that the plan was being rejected solely because it was educationally unsound, opposition seems to have been based on, or at least related to, underlying attitudes concerning contact with outgroups. Measured by these stated attitudes, Jews turned out to be rather less tolerant of their Christian neighbors than the latter were of Jews. Yet, one must assume that non-Jews in this predominantly Jewish apartment house development were self-selected with regard to their sentiments about close contact with Jews. Indeed, this self-proclaimed tolerance among a predominantly Catholic population extended even to "not minding" close friends and relatives intermarrying.

What seems most telling is that the responses signifying a rejection by Jews of non-Jews, as their rejection of Negroes, are significantly associated with being against the pairing plan. The inference to be drawn is that the opposition by Jews represents a form of ethnocentrism, directed not solely against Negroes but reflecting, in part, a pro-ghetto outlook. The Jewish ingroupishness is dramatically expressed by the woman who phoned the local city councilman, after he had publicly endorsed the pairing, to scold him: "How could you, Mr. Councilman, do this to us, a nice Jewish boy like you?"

Minority groups living in a hostile environment find some measure of protection by sticking to "their own kind." It stands to reason that even where an individual lacks the ghetto experience there may have been ample opportunity for attitudes generated in the ghetto to have been communicated down to him by his elders. Hostility and distrust between Negroes and Jews is far from novel; one is not surprised to find opposition to the pairing proposal greatest among those who moved into the neighborhood from the now overrun Jewish sections of the Bronx and Brooklyn. Among those *against* the plan, the proportion coming from these two boroughs was nearly twice as great as

among those *for* the plan. Clearly the nearness of the Negro community in Corona and the dilution of racial homogeneity in the local
school was to many a potential threat.

SOCIOECONOMIC STATUS

Socioeconomic status had a considerably greater influence on individual attitudes towards the pairing proposal than did ethnic identification.
Larger proportions of managerial, professional, semiprofessionals, and
small business owners were found among those who favored the proposal than among those opposed. An even more sensitive indicator of
attitude is educational level (Table 2). Most likely to oppose the plan
were those who had failed to complete high school and most likely to
support it were the college graduates. Note, however, that only the
barest majority of college graduates endorsed the proposal.[7] Since the
issue concerns the welfare of children, it is not altogether unexpected to
find that the educational achievement of wives in the households (even
where males were respondents) was even more closely associated with
the stand taken. Finally, the contrast between the educational level of
the two groups was most marked where the active participants in the
controversy were concerned. Half the activists on the "pro" side were
college graduates. This alone made them somewhat unrepresentative of
the residents in the area. In this respect, the activists on the "anti" side
were much closer to being a cross section of the community. It is
characteristic that two-thirds of the women working actively against
the proposal had no schooling beyond high school.

Respondents who favored the plan revealed in a variety of ways
greater sensitivity to the *quality* of education their children were
receiving. A larger number had been active in the local Parents
Association of the school and a larger number were themselves enrolled
in courses and continuing their own education. The two groups exhibit differences in their current style of life and in the ambitions most
of the parents harbor for their children. Parents on both sides were
interested in "advancement" and "education," but whereas the interest
of most pairing supporters was sustained and continuous, that of the
opposed was more likely to focus on problems and specific dissatisfac-
tions or difficulties their children were encountering in the school, with
teachers, or with other children. The difference in orientation can perhaps be illustrated by the typical educational aspirations of parents in

[7] The relationship between education and increase in tolerance has been documented in such studies as Tumin (1958) and Hyman and Sheatsley (1956).
Some doubt has been thrown on the clarity of this association by Stember (1961).

TABLE 2

ATTITUDE ON PAIRING BY EDUCATION

	% College Grad.	% Some College	% H.S. Grad.	% Less than H.S. Grad.	% Total
All Respondents					
Pro-Pairing	51	32	26	20	32
Anti-Pairing	49	68	74	80	68
N = 171	100	100	100	100	100
Female Respondents and Wives of Male Respondents					
Pro-Pairing	57	35	28	13	32
Anti-Pairing	43	65	72	87	68
N = 168	100	100	100	100	100
"Activists"					
Pro-Pairing	61	35	29	0	38
Anti-Pairing	39	65	71	100	62
N = 74	100	100	100	100	100

the two opposing factions. Most respondents said they intended to send their children to college. Asked where they would send them, most of those opposed to the plan indicated their children would go to a city college (if eligible) because they were "free" and the children could live at home. Those in favor were more likely to name specific colleges where they "hoped" their children might be accepted or, if they named one of the city colleges, said their children could get a good education there.

These orientations are generally linked to the occupational status of parents and to the education they themselves had received. In this respect socioeconomic status seems to operate as a critical determinant of the stand taken on the pairing proposal. The image of the white liberal —Jewish or not—torn between liberal "instincts" and an overriding concern for the educational welfare of his own child, ultimately opposing the drive toward school desegregation when the issue becomes salient, simply does not fit this situation. The "backlash," for the most part, does not represent a selfish resolution of a moral dilemma. The more "liberal," the more sensitive to the ingredients that enter into a good educational milieu, the more likely was the respondent to favor this particular proposal.

The above data suggest a simple conclusion: class was more important than ethnicity in determining the likelihood that a person was on one side or the other of this school desegregation controversy. They lend no support to the proposition that Jews, just because they are Jews, will necessarily behave differently from other whites. On the contrary, Jews frequently divide along class lines, very much as other groups do.

CLASS AND MINORITY GROUP STATUS

The attitudes of a minority formed in response to past experiences are always mediated through the perspectives of current social position and often are profoundly modified as a result. Hence, ingroup solidarity assumes a new and different meaning when it is turned against an outgroup clearly lower in prestige and inferior in economic standing. Whether or not, and in what way, a person carried the traditional attitude to the present was, to a large degree, a function of his orientation to the neighborhood, which was influenced in turn by the characteristic pattern of residential and social mobility associated with occupational status and education.

For many of the Jews against the plan, the neighborhood was in certain respects an upgraded version of the familiarly comfortable but shabby and rundown ghetto from which they had escaped. Many respondents stressed the fact that they (and others) had worked hard to get here; it was a good neighborhood and they wanted nothing to spoil it. Though surrounded by a mass of brick buildings with playgrounds completely paved and with only the smallest patches of greenery in sitting areas, respondents frequently spoke about the neighborhood as if it were a part of suburbia. The low carrying charges, the modest down payment, and the soundness of the investment were almost unanimously given by the "antis" as the reason for moving into and liking the cooperative. But primary ties also exerted an attraction. Many more of those opposed to the plan than those for it had either friends or relatives (or both) living within the immediate vicinity *before* they moved in, and at the time of the interviewing more said their "three closest friends" all resided within the four-block area of the cooperative. They were more involved in informal visiting with their neighbors and they had participated more frequently in a variety of social affairs under the formal sponsorship of the cooperative. They were, in short, neighborhood oriented.

Thus, insisting that they were not "prejudiced," opponents repeatedly proclaimed their welcome of any Negro who enrolled "naturally" as a *bona fide* resident within the school zone as redrawn before the pairing. "If they want to go to *our* school, let them move into our neighborhood" came to be a familiar cat call at turbulent meetings as soon as any speaker rose to support the plan. But the queries of our interviewers revealed that the number who "minded living in a neighborhood where *a good many* of your neighbors" were Negroes was actually more than twice as great as those who "minded having their child go to a school where *about half* the children were Negroes" (52 per cent compared with 24 per cent). Negroes in small numbers could evidently be assimilated; in large numbers they were considered a threat to the character of the neighborhood.

Finally, there is the issue of the "neighborhood school," a matter of very real concern. Any investment in housing within a given locality is, for those with children, in large part, however indirectly, an investment in the schools that serve the area. The public school in socially homogeneous neighborhoods is in a very real sense a substitute for private schooling. More than ever before, the aspirations and hopes of urban masses—just as those in suburban areas—rest on the adequacy of the schooling they receive. Far from being indifferent, the residents in this area are very concerned about the progress their children make through the grades, about possibilities for acceleration, about admission to special programs and to college, as partial insurance against future insecurity. Among this highly urbanized population, schooling is viewed as a "free" social service that is valued not so much for its content as for its marketability. Education is a necessity if children are to retain the same relative position as their parents, but some of the magic appeal education once had for ghetto children seems to be lost as a consequence.

Supporters of the pairing, being better educated, were on the whole more socially mobile. Asked directly and early in the interview (before its main purpose had become apparent) about their plans for moving out of the neighborhood, more supporters than opponents said that for a variety of reasons (none of which had anything to do with the pairing of the schools) they intended to move out into a larger home, a better neighborhood, and so forth. They felt much less tied to the particular neighborhood and expressed much less satisfaction with their cooperative living arrangements. Despite their lower participation in the formally sponsored cooperative activities, this group, paradoxically, more frequently cited "living in a cooperative" as one of the reasons for moving into the development in the first place. Their primary group contacts were more apt to extend beyond the immediate neighborhood and they appeared much more selective with regard to the neighbors with whom they chose to be friendly. In fact, general disappointment with the people in the area was a topic they frequently discussed among themselves; their awareness of social differences with their neighbors was sharpened by the controversy and operated as a stimulus to their desire to move out. Though any residential exodus on their part is likely to be cited as proof of hypocrisy, there is no question that being socially more mobile they were psychologically on their way up and out of the neighborhood some time before the proposal to pair the schools was initiated.

The greater cosmopolitanism of the supporters expressed itself in still another way, namely in the matter of minority group identification. As far as the "practice" of Judaism was concerned, a larger proportion of those against the plan, according to their own claim, "belonged to or regularly attended" a synagogue. In spite of this, it was the "pros," though less likely to be practicing Jews, who, on being asked whether they considered themselves members of a minority group, were more likely to say "yes." Again, their response was not in terms of the immediate neighborhood, where Jews are dominant, but in terms of the society at large, where they make their way as individuals, and thus continue to be aware of the incapacities of minority group status.

The position of the mass of Jews has certainly undergone a drastic change over the past forty years: Jewish opposition to this (or any other) desegregation proposal might be attributed simply to their rise in the status system of ethnic groups. How, then, can we account for the fact that the individuals enjoying the higher socioeconomic status were less opposed to the pairing plan? The point here is the distinction between *structural mobility,* the result of general prosperity and technological advance that upgrades whole groups, and *individual social mobility,* which requires that an individual free himself from his former group affiliations and leave them behind. The two types of mobility differ in their social-psychological import. Structural mobility is compatible with parochialism, but individual social mobility provides a strong impetus towards cosmopolitanism. This mentality facilitates a loosening of particular ethnic identifications and tends to transform them into a more universalistic concern with minority group status as such. Even where Jewish affiliations are retained, as is frequently the case, their content is reinterpreted and broadened.

A last point to be brought out is the difference between the attitudes of the groups toward education. Until voted out of office over the issue of school pairing, the pro-group had dominated the Parents Association and provided the school with most of its community support.

When they spoke of the "quality" of education, they were much less inclined than their opponents to refer to grade achievement, promotions, and getting into special progress programs or college. Rather, the definition of quality centered on the skills and values their children were acquiring.[8] They felt some confidence that they knew what type of education their children should have, and were loath, as a result, to entrust this entirely to school officials and teachers. To a much greater degree, they felt that education had not only an instrumental value for the achievement of material advantage but also a terminal value that assured entry into the world of intellect and culture. Still, the high valuation placed on learning by these second-generation Jewish parents is essentially that of the middle class; education for them is not the magic key to the kingdom sought by the children of immigrant parents before them.

[8] The distinction here is in some way akin to that made by Bernard C. Rosen between achievement-motivation and achievement-oriented values. (Cf. Rosen, 1957, for a discussion of their relationship to social mobility.)

REFERENCES

Brink, William, and Harris, Louis. 1964. *The Negro Revolution in America.* New York: Simon and Schuster.

Hyman, Herbert H., and Sheatsley, Paul B. 1956. "Attitudes Towards Desegregation," *Scientific American.* 195: 35–39.

Rosen, Bernard C. 1957. "The Achievement Syndrome: A Psycho-Cultural Dimension of Social Stratification," *American Sociological Review.* 22: 67–73.

State Education Commissioner's Advisory Committee on Human Relations and Community Tensions. 1964. *Desegregating the Public Schools of New York City.* New York: State Department of Education.

Stember, Herbert. 1961. *Education and Attitude Change.* New York: Institute of Human Relations Press.

Tumin, Melvin. 1958. *Desegregation—Resistance and Readiness.* Princeton, New Jersey: Princeton University Press.

PART II

The Intergroup Relations of Urban School Children

As citizens and schoolmen engage the question of Northern urban school desegregation in a school district, they inevitably ask, to what purpose? Certain parts of the answer are self-evident. For example, a constitutional imperative exists, based upon the moral principle of equal opportunity. Further, the student of urban ecology and the student of administration note that, regardless of legal dictates, public services are apt to be distributed *unequally* across a public school system as a result of racial determinants. Unequal services ordinarily entail unequal opportunities for the clientele.

This answer is particularly salient for public education. Public education, as originally organized, was intended to be universal, with interchangeable components being modifiable to guarantee free, universal inclusiveness. Thus, citizens and schoolmen sometimes surmount special interests and the inertia that maintains things as they are. They sometimes conclude that school desegregation is necessary because, in the language of the report from the State Board of Education, Massachusetts, "it is right educationally."

This constitutional, moral, and egalitarian view, however, is handicapped by a lack of clear evidence about the pragmatic effects of desegregation upon academic performance and *social* learning. Schoolmen want to assign weights of relative importance to desegregation on the basis of educational costs and benefits.

This evidence is hard to come by. Districts that decide to desegregate (as we observed in the introduction to Part I of this book) neither plan adequately for changes in their programs of instruction nor plan to evaluate the outcomes of their policy decisions. Having committed themselves to some movement on the issue, their energies are given over to administrative implementation. They rarely remain experimental in spirit or evaluative in disposition once change has been agreed upon.

The papers in this section explore some aspects of the pragmatic question, particularly those involving relations between the social attitudes of schoolchildren, their school performance, and the ethnic composition of student populations. These papers were prepared prior to the publication of James Coleman's major national survey, *Equality of Educational Opportunity*.* They lack the authoritative as well as large-scale significance of his report. Yet, by treating problems within a limited system, these papers reinforce and qualify his conclusions.

The paper by Dentler and Elkins, for example, distinguishes between events in naturally segregated as against naturally unsegregated urban schools. It warns that attitudes and achievement in naturally unsegregated schools do not indicate what to expect in a school that has been *planfully* desegregated. In addition, it offers some benchmarks for planners, by describing the state of intergroup attitudes among young urban school children.

Dorothy Jessup, in her paper "School Integration and Minority Group Achievement," offers data that go beyond the Coleman report, particularly on self-concept. In addition, she attends closely to specific differences in the administrative and instructional conditions peculiar to the big-city elementary schools from which her small samples were drawn.

Both Dorothy Singer and Dorothy Schaefer amplify our understanding of the relationship between intergroup relations and individual intelligence. Singer, in her paper "The Influence of Intelligence and an Interracial Classroom on Social Attitudes," demonstrates that the unsegregated student group does benefit in its social learning in ways that cannot occur in the racially isolated group. Intergroup contact, under certain conditions, has a clear contribution to make to the social maturation of the child. This contribution is not uniform, however, as her analysis of the effect of intelligence upon attitudes makes clear.

Dorothy Schaefer's study, "Prejudice in Negro and Puerto Rican Adolescents," adds to the research evidence on this question two important considerations. She examines the intergroup attitudes of *two minority* groups instead of emphasizing the traditional Negro versus white relation. And her analysis attends to the attitudes of educably *retarded* youths, while the previously available literature is limited to studies of normal gifted students.

* Supt. of Documents, U.S. Government Printing Office, Washington, D.C., 20402.

Intergroup Attitudes, Academic Performance, and Racial Composition*

Robert A. Dentler and Constance Elkins

THE PROBLEM

Most of the literature on school desegregation argues that under certain social and psychological conditions, desegregation will improve learning. In its most rudimentary form, the thesis is that increased intergroup exposure will enhance academic achievement as well as social learning, given conditions where the exposure has been effectively patterned, that is, where the staff welcomes all groups equally and where the contact has been designed so as to reduce perceived threat or other modes of conflict.

Verification of this proposition requires longitudinal study of changes of exposure, and changes in attitudes and mental abilities or school performances, before, during, and after a program of desegregation. Although large scale, rigorous, and sustained studies of this kind have not thus far been completed, Katz (1964), Pettigrew (1964), Long (1964), and Singer (1966), have summarized the work that has been done. No research published to date contradicts the proposition, though most work qualifies the thesis by way of identifying selected programmatic conditions under which school desegregation seems to be more or less contributive to growth.

Unfortunately, in the absence of longitudinal studies, many investigators have treated naturally unsegregated schools in educationally "unprogrammed" circumstances as if they were examples of *desegregated* settings. We say "unfortunately" because this substitution ignores two ways in which naturally unsegregated school settings may actually amplify intergroup conflict. Ecologically, they may be the only public schools within a community and may be so located in a racial fringe area that, for example, both Negro and white pupils may perceive it as socially undesirable. Educationally, these schools may be ones undergoing the greatest internal social change in an area at a time when

* The authors are grateful for the support from the New World Foundation which made this work possible. They also acknowledge the vital help of their associates, particularly the late Theresa M. Barmack, and Bernard Mackler, Dorothy Singer, Mary Ellen Warshauer, and Richard P. Boardman.

the school district as a whole has *no* programmed response to problems of student and staff intergroup relations, so that the school is forced to shift for itself in a comparatively unnatural condition.

Preparatory to the necessary longitudinal research to examine this thesis, therefore, we felt it would be helpful to measure the relatively static relation between intergroup attitudes, mental abilities, and a school's ethnic composition, in a Northern city where no program of school desegregation had been inaugurated. Not only would the findings prepare us for better work when occasions of planned change did present themselves, but the analysis of data from a fairly large urban school district would enable exploration of differences between naturally segregated and naturally unsegregated settings.

Thus, this study was conducted in order to answer three questions:

1. What are the characteristic intergroup attitudes of a large sample of Northern urban elementary school children?

2. Are intergroup attitudes associated with measures of school-related ability?

3. Are attitudes and abilities patterned in their distribution in terms of the ethnic composition of student bodies?

PROCEDURES

A student population of approximately 2,230[1] third, fourth, fifth, and sixth-grade children in 11 elementary schools completed three tests of abilities and one attitude questionnaire, administered by a visiting team of university field researchers. This population comprised more than 95 per cent of the pupils in the four grades of one particular public school district of the city.

About 19 per cent of the participating students were Negroes. Unfortunately, no ethnic identification was permitted in the course of the data collection, although we did know with precision the proportion of Negro students in each of the 11 schools. This proportion ranged from 0 to 64 per cent. Five of the schools were 99 to 100 per cent white. Another five ranged from 10 to 35 per cent Negro. One school was 64 per cent Negro.

One of the three school ability tests used was Science Research Associates Test of General Ability (TGA), developed by John C. Flanagan. This instrument was selected because it was designed in an effort to avoid biasing or cultural limitations and because it is nicely suited to group testing conditions.

[1] Number of students varies from test to test because not all students completed all portions of the work.

Of the other two tests, the Circles Creativity Test, developed by Paul Torrance, offers a meaningful index of originality, is brief in form and intelligible to younger children; and the Gates Reading Survey provides a measure of the task most relevant to school success.

The intergroup attitude questionnaire contained three instruments. One was a version of the Bogardus Social Distance Scale (SDS), adapted after pretesting by Singer (1966). A typical item from this scale reads as follows:

Put a check (√) next to the people on this list that you would like to have live on your block. Check the ones you wish. You may check all of them, or some of them, or none.

.... *Chinese*	.... *Jewish*
.... *Russian*	.... *Japanese*
.... *Italian*	.... *Polish*
.... *Negro*	.... *African*
.... *German*	.... *Turkish*
.... *Irish*	.... *Puerto Rican*

A check was given a positive score of one. First, the number of positive responses per ethnic group per question was summed. Then, each child received an overall score on the number of positive responses, and also subscores on responses to three selected groups: Negro, Jewish, and Puerto Rican. The five criteria used to determine distance are shown in Table 1.

The second attitude instrument we labelled the Racial Opinions Index (ROI). It provided a measure of group stereotyping and was limited to tapping anti-Negro or pro-white sentiments in their simplest forms of expression. The items, selected through item analysis from a larger group, were:

Most Negro children are not as smart as white children.
Many Negro children like to use bad words.
Negro boys are tougher than white boys when they get mad.
White children are more polite than children of other colors.
White children are smarter in school than Negro children.
A lot of Negro children don't do their homework at all.

A forced choice listing of these items within a series of statements involving opinions about other groups and beliefs, revealed that 60 per cent of all of the children *agreed* with these six statements. The items were of course deliberately slanted to explore the extent to which children responded to unparticularized, unconditional, and thus unjust stereotypes under conditions where the stereotype could be rejected directly by simple disagreement.

The third intergroup attitude instrument, designed and pretested by Singer (1966), was intended as a device for probing more projective dimensions of social attitudes. This device was called the Make Believe Bus Test (MBB). Students were given a drawing of a school bus with the faces of four pupils looking out of separate windows—a Negro boy and a white boy, and a Negro girl and a white girl. Each was given a name. Students were asked to fill in the blank lines on a page of 24 statements following the picture with these names. The statements were balanced to reflect judgments and social preferences cued to academic performance, aggressive conduct, and peer association. For example:

> . . . . *works hard in arithmetic.*
> . . . . *is the one I like to sit next to on the bus.*
> . . . . *always gets sent to the principal's office.*

Eight items were provided on a randomized list for each of the three areas of judgment or preference (school performance, aggression, and peer association). Each listing of a white child's name received a score of one, where the preference was stereotypically *desirable,* while each listing of a Negro child's name received a score of one, where the preference was stereotypically *undesirable.* Scores thus ranged from 24 for an extremely pro-white, anti-Negro pattern of responses, to zero for an extremely anti-white, pro-Negro attitude.

Singer (1966) found in her pretesting a split-half reliability coefficient for the instrument of $r = .95$. In this inquiry, the three subscales of school performance, aggression, and peer association, were so very highly intercorrelated ($r = .90, .91, .92$), that only the overall scores were used.

RESULTS

Table 1 summarizes by grade level the proportions of children who responded affirmatively to the statements that they would welcome specific ethnic groups as citizens of the United States, as residents of their block, as members of their club, as best friends, and as individuals to invite home to dinner. The table reflects stable orders of preference and consistency across the five categories of distance. These patterns, as well as the high preferences shown for the Irish, Italian, and Jewish groups in a city composed predominantly of these groups, indicate that the responses have a high degree of validity.

TABLE 1

PER CENT "WELCOMING" RESPONSES OF CHILDREN ON BOGARDUS SOCIAL DISTANCE SCALE

(By Grade Level)

Group	As U.S. Citizens				To Live on My Block				As a Club Member				As Best Friend				Home for Dinner			
Grade	3	4	5	6	3	4	5	6	3	4	5	6	3	4	5	6	3	4	5	6
Irish	60	69	80	85	56	67	74	81	51	62	71	78	51	60	70	74	49	59	67	75
Italian	60	73	79	86	53	64	71	75	52	63	69	75	49	63	67	74	46	61	65	71
Jewish	63	63	78	78	58	58	68	65	58	58	68	65	56	56	68	66	51	52	62	58
Japanese	54	64	74	78	42	59	65	70	46	60	66	72	49	57	63	68	44	56	60	64
Chinese	57	63	68	73	51	56	61	66	51	55	64	66	49	56	56	61	47	54	57	60
Negro	55	63	81	80	40	52	63	63	42	54	66	69	40	52	59	62	35	44	52	56
German	49	54	61	69	39	40	49	60	43	45	52	62	43	43	47	56	39	42	49	57
Puerto Rican	43	50	66	64	39	43	50	50	36	41	52	53	32	39	45	46	33	37	44	45
Polish	38	47	63	70	28	38	50	55	28	38	51	56	29	36	47	51	26	36	45	51
African	46	46	60	68	35	41	44	50	38	40	49	53	35	36	40	48	33	35	38	45
Turkish	43	46	58	66	28	36	44	52	32	36	45	53	31	32	36	45	32	32	39	46
Russian	34	36	44	52	20	27	33	44	24	30	39	48	23	27	33	40	23	29	32	41

Total Enrollment: Grade 3 – 538; grade 4 – 569; grade 5 – 535; grade 6 – 582.

The effects of both social growth and formal schooling on the responses of the students are implied in the increases in the extent of social inclusiveness from third to sixth grade. Social acceptance of Negroes "as citizens," for example, tends to be restrictive at each grade level, if contrasted with acceptance of the Irish and the Italian groups. Even so, the acceptance of Negroes increases from 55 per cent for third graders to 80 per cent for sixth graders. In all cases each of the 12 ethnic groups receives a 10 to 20 per cent increase in extent of acceptance across the three grades, including the generally excluded Russians.

One clue to the effect of family as against school influences may possibly be found in the departure of the children's responses from those characteristic of adults in similar urban communities. Where adults tend rather uniformly to be most discriminating in welcoming groups as best friends, the children in this study were most distant about bringing a group member home to dinner. Fifty-four per cent of all the children responded that they would welcome a Negro as a best friend, for example, while 47 per cent would invite a Negro home to dinner. On the whole, it is true, these two criteria of acceptance converged, but there appears to be some effect resulting from the fact that children probably do not invite anyone home to dinner without parental permission. Incidentally, one might also see in the data evidence of the limits of positive school influences. Even after three years of conditioning about civically desirable responses, only 56 per cent of the sixth graders, contrasted with 35 per cent of the third graders, would invite a Negro home to dinner. The school's effect on social learning may be inferred as distinctive but it is also seriously limited.

TABLE 2

INTERCORRELATION OF
SOCIAL DISTANCE AND ABILITIES

(N = 2,221 Students)

Scale or Test	*IQ*[a]	*Reading*[b]	*Creativity*[c]
Social Distance, Total	−.29	−.26	.00
Social Distance, Negroes	−.15	−.09	.03
Social Distance, Jews	−.32	−.33	.03
Social Distance, Puerto Ricans	−.19	−.16	.01

[a]*Science Research Associates General Mental Abilities.*
[b]*Gates Reading Survey Average Percentile.*
[c]*Circles Test of Creative Originality.*

The Bogardus Social Distance Scales are associated significantly with intelligence and level of reading ability in a statistical sense *but very weakly in degree*. The greater the tendency toward social distance, the lower the intelligence and the lower the reading ability. However, no measure of social distance was associated with an index of creative originality, nor was creativity correlated with intelligence or reading ability (see Mackler, 1965).

Further analysis revealed that the social factors of sex and socioeconomic status were more strongly associated with social distance than were intelligence or reading ability. Girls at all age levels were more uniformly accepting of diverse ethnic groups than were boys. Similarly, students attending schools located in relatively higher income and occupational census tracts were significantly more accepting than those from lower income tracts. Further, students reporting continuous attendance at a single primary school were significantly more accepting.

The Racial Opinions Index measured anti-Negro stereotyping. The possibility of establishing noteworthy correlations between this index and mental abilities was limited by the fact that at least 60 per cent of all of the children responding *agreed* with all six items listed above. The uniformity of agreement is especially striking in view of the obviously biased properties of the items. The general directional validity of the index is suggested, nonetheless, by its significant correlation with the Social Distance Toward Negroes Scale (r = .38), and with the Bus Projective (r = .46).

TABLE 3

CORRELATIONS OF
OPINIONS INDEX WITH ABILITIES[a]

(N = 2,221 Students)

Scale	IQ	Reading	Creativity
Opinion Index	−.18	−.18	−.02

[a]*See Table 2 for Ability Tests.*

As with the social distance scales, the Racial Opinions Index is significantly yet weakly associated with intelligence and with level of reading. It is not associated with creative originality. Age and sex effects were identical with those noted in the case of the distance scales.

The projective instrument, the Make Believe Bus, associated significantly with the Social Distance Toward Negroes Scale (r = .45) and

with the Racial Opinions Index ($r = .46$). Mean score on the Bus Test
was 11.7 (the scale, as noted, ranging from 24 to zero) with a standard
deviation of 7. In spite of the fact that the three intergroup measures
clearly assessed different aspects of social disposition, each correlated
significantly yet weakly with intelligence and reading ability and not at
all with creative originality.

The Make Believe Bus instrument correlated -.19 with intelligence,
-.04 with reading ability, and .01 with creativity. We suspect that the
lower association with reading ability is in part a function of the nonverbal task involved in the Make Believe Bus instrument. (The subscales for achievement-oriented, associational, and aggression-oriented
choices on the Bus instrument yielded no correlational effects that differed from those characteristic of the relations already reported.)

Although individual ethnic identification of students could not be
obtained, it was possible to designate each pupil in terms of the per
cent of Negro students attending his school. Thus, the coefficients presented in Tables 4 and 5 are based on individual scores, with per cent
Negro treated as a unit variable attributed to individuals.

TABLE 4

CORRELATIONS OF ATTITUDES
WITH PER CENT NEGRO PER SCHOOL

| Variables | Correlation with % Negro Students | |
	Boys	Girls
Social Distance	.10	.21
Opinions	.09	.17
Bus Instrument	.00	.05
I.Q.	−.27	−.28
Reading Ability	−.41	−.38
Grade Level	−.01	−.01
	N = 1175	N = 1045

For both boys and girls, but more distinctively for girls, intergroup
attitudes are associated significantly but not strongly with per cent
Negro students, except in the instance of the Bus Test. Prejudice as
indicated on the Bogardus Social Distance Scale and the Racial Opinions Index increases as per cent Negro increases. Intelligence and reading ability are clearly and negatively associated—that is, they increase
as per cent Negro decreases.

Table 5 is representative of a series of multiple regression analyses we conducted in an attempt to isolate the relative effects upon inter-group attitudes of grade level, reading achievement, intelligence, and ethnic composition of the school. Although the multiple R's obtained ranged to $R = .39$ for the overall Bogardus Scale, the effect of the percentage of Negro students was in every instance very negligible when the other variables were held constant. Indeed, at this individual level of correlation analysis, the attributed unit variable made no significant contribution to the observed variance.

TABLE 5A

BOY'S REGRESSION TABLE WITH OPINION SECTION OF THE ATTITUDE TEST AND THE FOUR SELECTED VARIABLES

Variable Used	Beta Weight	Addition to Multiple	Zero Order R
Grade	−.273	.16	−.16
Achievement	−.009	.21	−.15
% Negro	.005	.22	.09
I.Q.	.003	.22	−.05

TABLE 5B

GIRL'S REGRESSION TABLE WITH OPINION SECTION OF THE ATTITUDE TEST AND THE FOUR SELECTED VARIABLES

Variable Used	Beta Weight	Addition to Multiple	Zero Order R
Achievement	−.011	.21	−.21
Grade	−.246	.26	−.18
% Negro	.009	.28	.17
I.Q.	.000	.28	−.13

To explore further the possible group effects of ethnic composition, we pooled the mean scores of students by type of school. In turn, the pooled means were transformed into (comparable) scores of "per cent anti-Negro and pro-white stereotyping" for three of the attitude indicators and into average percentile reading achievement scores for the Gates Reading Survey. The results are graphed in Figure 1. (Pooling was acceptable because there were no statistical differences between the variances on these scores for the 11 schools.)

Three student group means are shown on each of the indices. One

FIGURE 1

MEAN ATTITUDES AND READING ABILITY
BY ETHNIC TYPE OF SCHOOL

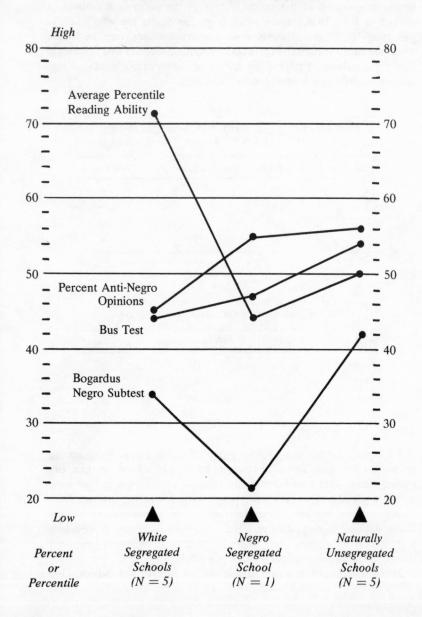

group contained 237 third through sixth graders in the one city elementary school defined as Negro segregated, with a student population
that was 64 per cent Negro. Another group included third through
sixth graders from five segregated white schools, each of which was
99 or 100 per cent white. The third group contained students in five
naturally unsegregated schools, which were 10, 16, 31, 34, and 35
per cent Negro in student composition.

On the Bogardus Scale of Distance Toward Negroes, the greatest
distance was reflected in the unsegregated settings. The striking result
of this treatment of the data is that anti-Negro sentiments are *highest*
on all three indices for students in the naturally unsegregated schools.

Another interesting finding is that social preferences and stereotyping as measured by the Bus Test and the Racial Opinions Index were
substantially lower in the white segregated than in either the Negro
segregated school *or* the unsegregated settings.

We infer from the data that the only children in this city not subjected to extensive conditioning in anti-Negro stereotypes are the white
children who have not been exposed to Negro schoolmates. Even in
the segregated Negro group, projective judgments (on the Bus Test)
favoring association with Negro peers are less favorable than the level
struck for such judgments among the segregated white students—and
while we are unable to make an individual-level analysis, it is obvious
that the group means in this school must have been determined primarily by its two out of three respondents who were Negro.

Group level analysis is extended in Figure 2. Here, nine elementary
schools are graphed in clusters of two or three each, according to a
combined typing by the ethnic composition and socioeconomic character of the census tract in which the school is located. The Negro
segregated school has been excluded as has been one socially heterogeneous school which contained too intermediate a socio-economic
status (SES) to allow for classification as high or low. As an example,
the three "high SES" segregated white schools were those in tracts
where a majority of families had incomes of more than $10,000 a year
and where 60 per cent of the labor force was in professional or managerial occupations.

Although the grouping was necessarily crude, obtaining the expected
inverse relation (between reading achievement and student groups typed
by SES and ethnicity) demonstrates the power of these demographic
variables. White segregated schools are more precisely differentiated
than the naturally unsegregated schools with respect to intergroup
attitudes. When SES is added, anti-Negro or pro-white stereotyping
is *lowest* in the highest SES group. The introduction of SES is very

FIGURE 2

MEAN ATTITUDES AND READING ABILITY
BY SES AND ETHNIC TYPE OF SCHOOL

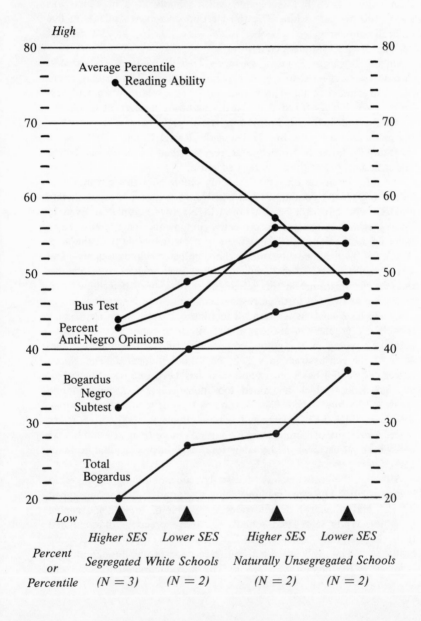

negligible in effect upon the unsegregated schools, suggesting the primacy, for intergroup relations, of ethnic exposure as against status conditioning.

Mean scores on the overall Bogardus Scale are included in Figure 2 to show that the ethnic grouping and SES effects are not associated solely with anti-Negro prejudice. Rather, expressed social distance toward all 12 ethnic groups on the scale (summed across five criteria) is greatest in the lower SES unsegregated school, where the mean is 37 per cent "exclusionist" in disposition as contrasted with 20 per cent for the higher SES white segregated schools.

DISCUSSION

Aware as we are of the limitations inherent in this study—including group rather than individual testing of abilities, crude indices of intergroup attitudes, and the great difficulty of coping with the data in the absence of ethnic designations of individual respondents—we still believe the results are worth some disciplined speculation. At the very least, they challenge the notion that the distribution of Negro and white pupils in a school district in a Northern city has any simple or direct consequences for academic performance or for social learning.

The findings suggest to us that the case for school desegregation cannot be made on the basis of evidence about intergroup relations among individual students within naturally unsegregated schools. It appears to us that intergroup prejudice is highest in these five unsegregated schools in our study because they are located in neighborhoods undergoing (most) rapid ethnic residential change. Children in these schools experience intergroup exposure in an educationally unplanned, unregulated fashion. Distance scores on the Bogardus in all schools are reduced for sixth as compared to third graders, for instance, but the reduction in distance is greater in the white segregated than in the unsegregated schools. Civically desirable responses are apparently easier to make under the condition of no intergroup exposure than under the condition of unplanned, residentially determined exposure within school settings.

Mean creativity scores did not differ across schools, but children in the white segregated schools were substantially superior in reading achievement to the children in both the unsegregated and Negro segregated schools. One implication seems to be that the ecology of neighborhood school distribution of students in this city necessarily operates to reinforce at least two aspects of the community *status quo.* The materially most and least advantaged elementary school children are grouped homogeneously, strengthening the quality of teaching and learning in the advantaged (or white segregated schools) and weakening them most profoundly in the Negro segregated setting. Conditions for intergroup learning of a haphazard type parallel this distribution of pupils, so that anti-Negro opinions are more common *even* in the Negro segregated setting than in the white segregated. Finally, those white children situated in once-white segregated but now naturally unsegregated schools read less well and express greater social prejudice.

On the basis of these data, then, it follows that a desegregation process could affect achievement as well as social attitudes *indirectly* yet rather powerfully if it aimed at interrupting these "ecological reinforcements" under planned conditions. If status, as well as ethnicity, were consciously mixed in all schools, for example, the staff could expect to take advantage of the more uniform presence of students who are both high achievers and "high transmitters" of civically desirable attitudes. But unless this possibility was prepared for and utilized educationally, mixing alone could enlarge the patterns embodied in our naturally unsegregated schools.

We believe that, with few exceptions, improved achievement and greater social learning of desirable attitudes will tend not to occur unless and until planned desegregation is introduced to break the basic ecological condition. Its introduction, moreover, will set in motion no simple process, but rather a set of serious, but instructionally very stimulating, challenges.

One unresolved question springs from our finding that the most segregated, higher status white students reflect the most desirable intergroup attitudes. Will intergroup exposures not challenge and reduce this trend? This requires longitudinal assessment, of course, but our hypothesis would be that advantaged, previously segregated white students would consolidate and deepen their positive attitudes under integrated school conditions of guidance and instruction. In any case, it should be noted that without strategically reinforced social exposure, their current attitudes will remain untested and are likely to be vulnerable to negative change under any future threats of status loss.

CONCLUSION

This study reported on school test and attitude data received from 2,230 Northern metropolitan children in third through sixth grade.

Three associated yet different indicators of intergroup attitudes showed pervasive trends toward exclusion and disapproval of selected ethnic groups. Negro students, as well as white students, were consistently prejudiced toward disapproval of Negroes and toward biased preferences for whites. This pattern was correlated significantly with school grade level, I.Q. level, reading achievement, and SES. Correlations between attitudes and a test of creativity revealed no association.

Among individuals, attitudes were only weakly, if significantly and positively, associated with per cent of Negro students per school. In a multiple regression analysis, ethnic composition failed to contribute significantly to the relation between grade level, I.Q., reading achievement, and intergroup attitudes. When students were grouped by school ethnic composition, however, important mean differences between attitudes were disclosed. Students in white segregated schools expressed *less* anti-Negro prejudice than pupils in Negro segregated or naturally unsegregated schools. When SES of school neighborhood was added, this difference between white segregated and naturally unsegregated schools increased.

We concluded that the ecology of ethnic and status distribution of students plays a noteworthy yet indirect role in affecting academic as well as social learning, and that the educational success of Northern school desegregation efforts will probably depend heavily upon thoughtful and well-planned staff responses to the challenges inherent in changes in a *status quo* situation—changes grounded in restructured community residential patterns, yet permeating the public school.

REFERENCES

Katz, Irving. 1964. "Review of Evidence Relating to Effects of Desegregation on the Intellectual Performance of Negroes," *American Psychologist.* 19: 381–399.

Long, Herman. 1964. *New York State Commissioner's Conference on Race and Education.* Albany, New York: State Education Department.

Mackler, Bernard. 1965. "Creativity: Theoretical and Methodological Considerations," *The Psychological Record.* 15: 217–238.

Pettigrew, Thomas F. 1964. *A Profile of the Negro American.* Princeton, N.J.: Van Nostrand.

Singer, Dorothy. 1966. *Interracial Attitudes of Negro and White Fifth Grade Children in Segregated and Unsegregated Schools.* Doctoral dissertation, Teachers College, Columbia University. Also see Singer article in this collection.

TABLE 6

CORRELATION MATRIX

	SRA			GATES				CREATIVITY				BOGARDUS				OPINION	BUS PATTERN				N
	1	2	3	4	5	6	7	8	9	10	11	12	13	14	15	16	17	18	19	20	
SRA 1	—																				2013
2	.59	—																			1787
3	.77	.77	—																		1702
GATES 4	.43	.38	.47	—																	2213
5	.64	.46	.63	.60	—																2215
6	.58	.48	.62	.60	.77	—															2215
7	.62	.50	.65	.82	.88	.89	—														2213
CREATIVITY 8	-.18	-.15	-.15	-.04	-.20	-.22	-.18	—													2214
9	-.16	-.14	-.14	-.04	-.19	-.21	-.17	.97	—												2214
10	-.05	-.04	-.05	.05	-.07	-.08	-.04	.78	.76	—											2214
11	-.12	-.09	-.10	.00	-.14	-.16	-.12	.94	.92	.77	—										2205
BOGARDUS 12	.32	.27	.32	.23	.32	.31	.33	-.08	-.07	-.03	-.06	—									2220
13	.21	.19	.15	.04	.11	.10	.09	-.05	-.05	-.03	-.05	.38	—								2218
14	.24	.19	.19	.10	.16	.17	.16	-.04	-.04	-.01	-.02	.41	.46	—							2220
15	.34	.30	.29	.19	.26	.25	.26	-.06	-.06	.00	-.03	.61	.61	.74	—						2220
OPINION 16	-.23	-.21	-.18	-.14	-.19	-.16	-.18	.03	.03	-.02	.00	-.18	-.38	-.20	-.26	—					2221
BUS PATTERN 17	-.12	-.12	-.10	-.02	-.04	-.03	-.03	.04	.04	.01	.02	-.13	-.38	-.19	-.25	.41	—				2221
18	-.12	-.10	-.08	-.01	-.03	.00	-.01	.04	.03	.01	.03	-.12	-.46	-.22	-.28	.40	.71	—			2221
19	-.14	-.13	-.12	-.02	-.07	-.04	-.05	.03	.03	.00	.01	-.14	-.39	-.20	-.25	.45	.78	.74	—		2221
20	-.13	-.13	-.19	-.02	-.06	-.02	-.04	.04	.04	.01	.02	-.14	-.45	-.22	-.28	.46	.91	.90	.92	—	2221

TABLE 6

CORRELATION MATRIX[a]

Variable

1. T.G.A. Verbal Grade Expectancy
2. T.G.A.
3. T.G.A. IQ (normed)
4. Gates Speed Percentile
5. Gates Vocabulary Percentile
6. Gates Comprehension Percentile
7. Gates Average Percentile
8. Creative Fluency
9. Creative Flexibility
10. Creative Originality

11. Creative Elaboration
12. Bogardus Jewish Subscale
13. Bogardus Negro Subscale
14. Bogardus Puerto Rican Subscale
15. Bogardus Total Distance
16. Racial Opinions Index
17. Make Believe Bus Test (Achieve)
18. Make Believe Bus Test (Associate)
19. Make Believe Bus Test (Aggress)
20. Make Believe Bus Test TOTAL

[a]*Base (N = 2,221) varies slightly per factor because of noncompletion.*

School Integration and Minority Group Achievement*

Dorothy K. Jessup

The following study is an attempt to shed light on the question of whether classroom integration itself contributes to the achievement patterns of minority group children. The exploratory nature of the study cannot be overemphasized. Limited to a few months' time, conducted on an informal basis without any official sponsorship, it depended for its information entirely upon the cooperation of individual principals and teachers within the schools being investigated. A major purpose of the study was to determine the desirability of pursuing its line of inquiry in a larger investigation.

PROCEDURE

The Schools

The following considerations were the basis for the selection of the three schools in which this study was conducted. First, to make a valid comparison between children exposed to segregated and integrated school situations, it was necessary that the groups be ethnically similar and that they live under approximately equivalent socioeconomic conditions. Second, to study the effects of integration, the sample within the integrated classroom had to be relatively heterogeneous. Third, to study the effects of segregation properly (since educational facilities in schools servicing minority groups often are inferior to the facilities provided in middle-class neighborhoods), the facilities of the segregated school had to be equal or superior to those in the integrated school.

The necessity of selecting an appropriate *integrated* sample proved

* This study would not have been possible without the cooperation of a number of people—teachers, principals, a district supervisor, and parents—many of whom went out of their way to provide me with necessary data, improve my insights, or just be helpful. To those to whom I promised anonymity, I cannot make this acknowledgement personal, but I would like to extend my appreciation to each. In addition, I am particularly indebted to District Superintendent Maurice Mehlman for his support, and to my teacher, Robert Dentler, for his advice and encouragement.

to be the most difficult criterion to meet. Most schools in New York City, where this study was conducted, follow the practice of grouping students by their abilities. Since this practice generally results in socio-economic and racial segregation by classroom units, many racially mixed schools were ruled out where the minority group sample might, in other respects, have been more ideal for study than the one finally selected.

The "integrated" school used in the study is located in a predominantly middle-class neighborhood, referred to here as "Hillside." It is a small school, serving about 450 children, a population which is 75 per cent white (primarily middle class), 15 per cent Puerto Rican, and 10 per cent Negro.

The school building is 60 years old, and lacks many of the facilities found in newer schools. There is no gymnasium. Plumbing, heating, and cafeteria provisions are antiquated. Lighting in many of the class-rooms is poor. Because of its size, the school does not qualify for a full principal. Its administrative head is a junior principal, with no assistant principals or special personnel. (From 1958 to 1965, the school changed principals three times.) There are no guidance services in the school, no remedial reading services, and, except for a music program, no other special activities. There is no librarian in the school. In addition, from the third through the sixth grades, each grade level has two classes. They each average well above thirty students. In spite of these deficiencies and handicaps, the school has a good reputation in the community. Pupil and teacher turnover are moderate.

In recent years, following a period of physical rehabilitation in some sections of the community, the ethnic character of the school has undergone substantial changes. Because the school is small, the loss of several Puerto Rican children from each grade meant a shift in balance for a time from "racially mixed" to predominantly white. In the course of these changes, the school followed a very flexible policy with regard to its grouping procedures. The older children in the sample (which consists of students in the second and fifth grades), who for the most part have been in Hillside School since the first grade, have experienced a variety of arrangements. During their first two years, before the shift in the school population, they had been separated according to language ability, which resulted in complete segregation from the Puerto Rican students. Starting in the third grade, however, during the school's period of transition, it became necessary to con-solidate classes, and children in the first, second, and third grades were grouped heterogeneously. Following a change in school administration and a general increase in student population, the usual grouping procedures were restored. By this time, however, growth in the white population was such that the lower ability groups in several grades retained a heterogeneous character. All minority group children in the study's sample are still in predominantly white classes.

To match the integrated minority group population represented in Hillside school, it was important that the segregated population include both Puerto Rican and Negro children. Further, since most of the Negro and Puerto Rican students in Hillside had lived in the surrounding neighborhood for a period of years and had attended the school since first grade, it was desirable that the segregated group show the same pattern of residential stability.

These criteria were met by the selection of a school which served, almost exclusively, the population of a low-income housing project. Referred to here as "Project School," it is comparable in size to Hillside, with a student population of 466. The ethnic distribution is 65 per cent Negro, 31 per cent Puerto Rican, and 4 per cent other. School personnel report pupil mobility to be low. Records showed that most of the children in the two grades selected for the sample (the second and the fifth) had attended the school since first grade.

Like Hillside, Project School is too small to qualify for a full principal, and is run by a junior principal. The building is over eighty years old, and physical facilities are poorer than at Hillside. However, classes are smaller, averaging less than twenty-six students. A limited number of additional personnel is provided during part of the school week for remedial reading, guidance, and library services.

It is difficult to assess real differences in the quality of education offered by any two given schools. In many ways Hillside and Project seem to differ only slightly, if at all, in the education they provide. The administration, supervision, and curriculum are basically similar, though Project has a few additional staff positions. However, in their physical plants, general reputation, and "tone" the two schools *are* significantly different. In such a context, Project School might be classified as a "typically inferior slum school."

Thus, for the purposes of this study, to hold constant any important factors of the student population in addition to ethnic and social class composition, it became necessary to include another group of children from a segregated school whose facilities and programs were superior to those in the integrated school.

A Higher Horizons school in the Bedford-Stuyvesant area of Brooklyn was selected to meet these criteria. The school serves a child population of twelve thousand, 93 per cent of which is Negro. The building plant is, in effect, brand new (six years old), with a complete gymnasium, cafeteria, library, intraclass television, and many other modern facilities. In addition to a full-time Higher Horizons staff, the school has a guidance team, remedial reading services, a school volunteer program (under the Public Education Association), and a full-time librarian. According to members of the staff, the school has a pleasant and stimulating atmosphere, due to the calibre of its personnel and its general administrative tone. The principal is fully experienced, and has served in the school since its opening. He has two assistant principals, who spend almost their full time in assisting and guiding the teachers. Teacher turnover is reported to be minimal. Average class sizes are below 30. (Though the school has a small population of middle-income Negro students and also some white students [7 per cent], there was not enough time to follow through on the various possibilities for study that these groupings suggest.)

The Sample

The original sample included all children in the second and fifth grades in Hillside and Project School. In the Higher Horizons School, where there were six to eight classes on each grade level, the sample was limited to the top, middle, and bottom ability groups of the second and fifth grades.[1] Children who were absent from school on the day of the testing, or for whom school achievement records could not be obtained, were eliminated. It was also deemed necessary to eliminate children who attended Hillside School under the Open Enrollment program, which meant that they lived outside the district and attended the school by special request (a selective factor that might tend to prejudice the results).[2] Two Chinese children were also dropped from the sample rather than include them under the heading of other ethnic groups.

The final sample included 349 children. One hundred and eight attended Hillside School (87 white, 5 Negro, and 16 Puerto Rican), 95 attended Project School (4 white, 56 Negro, and 35 Puerto Rican), and 146 attended the Higher Horizons School (13 white, 133 Negro, and 1 Puerto Rican). One hundred ninety six were in the second grade, 153 in the fifth.

Determination of Socioeconomic Status

None of the three schools kept records showing the occupations of the students' fathers. If time had permitted, this information could

[1] The school grouped children according to their reading ability and IQ test performance. Scores were obtained for the entire second and fifth grades in order to determine whether the sample adequately reflected the total achievement range and distribution, which it did.

[2] Data on the patterns revealed by the Open Enrollment students can be found in footnotes 7 and 8.

have been obtained through interviews or similar means. Under the circumstances, the following method of determination was used. Though liable to a high probability of error and considerable overlap among the children, it nonetheless allows for a more objective means of classification than the teachers' judgments.

Each child's address was obtained from the school. The addresses were then classified according to census tract and block numbers. The census data revealed a high correlation between median rents above $90, median income above $5500, high educational attainment, low rates of unemployment, and low rates of deterioration and crowding. But correlations of rents below $90 with other factors showed more variation. Since it was possible for rents from $70 to $90 to accompany high rates of crowding and deterioration and actually reflect worse socioeconomic conditions than lower rents where other factors are more stable, a socioeconomic index was computed for each block by cross tabulation of four demographic characteristics: median education of adults (by census tract), median rent, per cent crowding, and per cent deterioration.

The tabulation of block data fell into three groupings. Group A reflected median rents above $90, median education of adults above the twelfth grade, and median incomes ranging from $5500 to $10,000. This group may be said to represent a range of economic and occupational statuses that falls within what is generally referred to as the "middle class." The sample included 100 children from this group— 22 Negro and 78 white.

Group B reflected median rents from $55 to $80, low rates of deterioration (below 20 per cent), and moderate rates of crowding. Where data for B blocks were uniform within a given tract, median education was shown to be approximately at the tenth-grade level, and median income was between $4000 and $4500. Group B included, in many cases, the blocks where casual observation revealed substantial differences in housing characteristics. It also included all the Negro and white residents of the public housing projects that fed into the two segregated schools. Group B may be said to represent a fairly wide range of occupational and economic statuses, including both "white collar" and "working class" categories. The sample included 151 children from this group—125 Negro and 26 white.

Group C reflected median rents from $18 to $70, high rates of deterioration (above 30 per cent), and high rates of crowding (30 to 70 per cent). Where data for C blocks were uniform within a given tract, census data showed the median education of adults to be approximately at the eighth-grade level for Negroes and at the seventh-grade level for Puerto Ricans. The median family income was $3000 to $3500. Unemployment rates tended to be considerably higher in the C than in A or B tracts. Rates of marital separation were also higher, and within the group tended to be somewhat higher for Negroes than for Puerto Ricans. Residential instability was also perhaps somewhat higher for Negroes.

The C group may be said to represent a lower-class population— that is, low educational attainment and occupational status, low income, and high rates of crowding and unemployment. There were 98 students from the C group—46 Negroes and 52 Puerto Ricans.[3]

Measurement of Achievement

Where school records were available, achievement scores from reading, math, and intelligence tests were obtained for each child. For the most part, these scores were the results of tests administered in the spring of the previous school year. (The IQ test scores for fifth-grade children had been obtained at the end of the third grade.[4])

[3] Census data for the public housing project serviced by the Project School showed substantial differences in median education, income, and employment status for Negro and Puerto Rican residents, in spite of the fact that the two groups were mixed within the project. Negroes living in the housing project fell into the B grouping, as did the whites, while Puerto Ricans fell into the C grouping. The demographic characteristics of the Puerto Rican population in the project showed close similarity to the characteristics of the Puerto Rican population in the Hillside district.

DEMOGRAPHIC CHARACTERISTICS OF NEGRO AND PUERTO RICAN
POPULATIONS WHOSE CHILDREN ATTEND
PROJECT AND HILLSIDE SCHOOLS

| | Project School | | Hillside School[a] |
Tract Data	Negro (B)	Puerto Rican (C)	Puerto Rican (C
Education	10.1	7.3	7.9
Family Income	$4036	$3506	$3236
Per Cent Unemployment	7	10	7

[a]*Separate data are not available in census reports for Negroes residing in the Hillside district. Those classified as C Group lived in blocks where the bulk of the population was Puerto Rican, and where rates of crowding and deterioration were high. Whether they were strictly comparable to the Puerto Rican residents might be questioned. But for the purposes of this study, since their absolute number was so small, it was assumed they were.*

[4] Standardized reading and math tests are generally given in New York City schools at the end of each school year. IQ tests are given in the spring of the first, third, and sixth grades. The Pintner-Cunningham IQ test is used in the first grade, and the Otis Quick Scoring IQ test in the third.

Math scores were available only for fifth graders in the Hillside and Higher Horizons schools. In Project School, neither math nor reading tests had been administered at the end of the fourth grade the previous year. However, teacher estimates of individual reading levels made at that time were available in school records. On the basis of these estimates and the results of tests administered a year earlier, it was possible to compute a reading score for most of the children.

Through cross tabulation, indexes of *high, middle,* and *low* achievement—25, 50, and 25 per cent of the sample, respectively—were derived by using all the achievement scores available for each child.

Measurement of Self-Concept: The Drawing Test

Previous studies (Clark, 1963; Clark and Clark, 1962; Deutsch, 1960) have indicated there is a relationship between racial status and self-concept. To get at the effects of integration upon self-concept, each child in the sample was asked to make a freehand drawing of himself, using crayons.

Drawings of the human figure provide clues to several dimensions of personality. Apart from demonstrating his artistic ability, the child also reveals his intelligence or conceptual ability through the accuracy and range of his perceptions (Goodenough, 1926). In addition, through the emotional *tone* of his drawing, the child often indicates his personality traits and self-attitudes (Goodenough and Harris, 1950; Machover, 1949). In his depiction of the figure, he may also disclose his awareness and evaluation of certain personal, cultural, or racial characteristics.[5]

Standard white paper and crayon sets were distributed to the children. The crayon sets had the usual assortment of colors, including

[5] The drawing test, as used in this study, is perhaps too unconventional and too undirected to be considered a precisely reliable method of evaluating individual personality factors or mental ability. As a test of group tendencies, however, it served a number of useful purposes that standardized written tests fail to fulfill. First, it took a short time to administer, and the directions were simple. This meant that a great many children could be reached in a limited period of time, without undue disturbance of classroom and administrative routines. Second, performance bore no relation to verbal ability, and in this sense, the drawing may be considered more "culture free" than written tests. Third, the nondirective approach reduced the likelihood of "cueing" children as to what was desired.. Finally, the test permitted the children to reveal unconscious attitudes and values to a far greater extent than would have been the case with written tests, especially in the instances of very young children. The scheme for the test was derived from three sources: the Goodenough "Draw-a-Man" test (Goodenough, 1926), the Clark crayon tests (Clark and Clark, 1962), and the Dennis use of the "Draw-a-Man" test (Dennis, 1963).

black and brown, to which had been added white, tan, and "flesh."
Each child was then asked to draw a picture of himself. No further
instructions were given.

The drawings, labeled with the children's names to permit their correlation with other information, were then analyzed according to three
criteria:

(*1*) Accuracy of perception of the human figure (*"intelligence,"
according to the Goodenough scale [Goodenough, 1926]). Meas-
urements provided an IQ score for each drawing, based upon
the subject's chronological age. The scores were then divided
into* high, middle, *and* low *categories—25, 50, and 25 per cent
of the sample, respectively.*

(*2*) Self-concept, *as revealed by the general tone of the drawing
and presentation of the figure. Evaluations in this area were
more subjective, and two other persons were used to confirm
judgments. In general, the drawings fell into five categories: (a)
realistic and positive portrayals; (b) conventional or stereotyped
portrayals that avoided depiction of personal characteristics;
(c) fantasy portrayals; (d) portrayals with undue distortion
or mutilation; and (e) drawings which avoided depictions of
the human figure altogether. These categories were classified
into three groups, representing positive, neutral, and negative
self-concepts, with 25 per cent of the sample in each of the
extreme categories, and 50 per cent in the middle category.
Realistic, positive drawings fell into the positive or* high *category; conventional and fantasy portrayals into the neutral or*
middle *category; and distortion, mutilation, or refusal to depict
self into the negative or* low *category.*

(*3*) Racial concept, *as indicated by representation of skin color.
Performance, most significant in relation to Negro and Puerto
Rican children, was measured in accordance with the child's actual skin coloration (i.e., dark or light). Coloring patterns fell into
four categories: (a) realistic depiction of skin color—brown or
tan for dark-skinned children, "flesh" or pink for light skinned;
(b) depiction of color distinctly lighter or darker than own skin
—pink for a dark-skinned child, or black or white for* any
*child; (c) avoidance of skin color (blank); and (d) bizarre
color—red, purple, green, etc.*

The IQ scores derived from the drawings were regarded as a dimension of achievement, and were included along with standardized IQ

scores, reading, and math achievement scores in computing an achievement index for each child. Ratings for self-concept and racial concept, however, were treated separately.

FINDINGS

Granting the full limitations under which this study was conducted, it is nonetheless the case that conspicuous patterns in the findings suggest that school integration in itself makes an important difference in the performance of minority group children.

In analyzing the data, it was first necessary to take into account the influence of achievement on socioeconomic background (recognized by other investigators as powerful) before the effects of integration could be clarified. Table 1 examines the relationship between these two variables for the entire sample.

TABLE 1

PUPIL ACHIEVEMENT AND SOCIOECONOMIC STATUS[a]

| | *Pupil Achievement* | | | |
SES Groups	High	Middle	Low	Total N
Group A	53	42	5	100
Group B	18	54	28	151
Group C	2	55	43	98
TOTAL	82	178	89	349

[a]*The relationship between socioeconomic status and pupil achievement is significant at the .01 level, using the chi-square test.*

Children from higher status locations showed a consistent advantage over others from locations that reflected a lower income and lower occupational status. Wherever class distinctions were evident within racial groups, achievement in the four areas tested—IQ, math, reading, and self-concept—tended to be highly related to social class for both age groups.[6] This held for all three schools.

For the purpose of making a valid comparison of children in segre-

---

[6] Children generally showed consistent levels of performance in the four achievement areas. While a close relationship between reading and IQ test results might be expected on the basis of their dependence upon language, it is important to note that strong relationships were also evident between these and the nonverbal areas—math and drawing test scores.

gated and integrated schools, the sample, as noted before, was limited to low status Negro and Puerto Rican children actually residing within each school district. The total number in the integrated Hillside School (18) is therefore small, and when the second and fifth grades are considered separately, the numbers are even smaller. However, the patterns among these children are at such variance with those that emerge for children in the two segregated schools that their possible significance cannot be overlooked.

Comparison of low status Negro and Puerto Rican children in Hillside School with those in the Higher Horizons and Project schools reveals that the children in the integrated school show a better total performance. The most conspicuous difference occurs in the varying proportion of low achievers found in integrated and segregated situations (see Table 2).

TABLE 2

EFFECTS OF INTEGRATION
UPON ACHIEVEMENT OF LOW-STATUS
NEGRO AND PUERTO RICAN CHILDREN (C GROUP)[a]

Schools	*Pupil Achievement*			
	High	*Middle*	*Low*	*Total N*
Integrated	0	95	5	18[b]
Segregated	3	45	52	80[c]
TOTAL	2	54	42	98

[a]*The relationship between integration and achievement is significant at the .01 level, using the chi-square test.*
[b]*C group in Hillside School included 16 Puerto Rican and 2 Negro children.*
[c]*C group in the Higher Horizons and Project Schools included 36 Puerto Rican and 44 Negro children.*

The significance of this difference is underscored in the patterns of change from the second to fifth grade. They are summarized in Table 3. Low status Negro and Puerto Rican children in a segregated situation showed a decline in achievement levels between the two grades in *both* the Project School and the Higher Horizons School, in spite of the distinctly superior program and services of the latter. In contrast, children of similar status at the socially integrated Hillside School showed a relative improvement in their level of performance between the same grades.

In order to determine whether these effects could be attributed to integration, the possible influence of two additional factors was ex-

The Urban R's

TABLE 3

PATTERNS OF ACHIEVEMENT IN 2nd AND 5th GRADES AMONG
LOW-STATUS CHILDREN (C GROUP) IN INTEGRATED
AND SEGREGATED SCHOOLS

| | | Pupil Achievement | | |
Schools	*High*	*Middle*	*Low*	*Total N*
Integrated				
2nd Grade	0	90	10	10
5th Grade	0	100	0	8
Segregated				
2nd Grade	5	56	39	43
5th Grade	0	33	67	37
TOTAL	2	54	42	98

amined: (1) differences in school quality, and (2) the fact that the
C group of children in Hillside School was predominantly Puerto
Rican. To weigh the influence of these factors, the integrated group
was compared with the two segregated control groups, one of which
had equal or superior educational facilities and the other of which
included a substantial number of Puerto Rican children. Comparisons
were also made among children attending the two segregated schools,
to determine whether the differences in the school had a visible effect
upon achievement patterns, and whether a further breakdown of the
segregated group would show any change in the apparent superiority
of the integrated group.

If school quality were the significant factor, it would follow, other
things being equal, that children in the Higher Horizons School would
show a performance superior to that of the children in the Project
School and at least equivalent to the low status children in Hillside
School. This was not the case. Table 4 shows, moreover, that whether
the integrated group is compared with a segregated group under conditions of superior school facilities or with a segregated Puerto Rican
group, the former maintains a superior level of performance.

It is also apparent from Table 4 that in comparing the children
from the two segregated schools, there was a higher relation between
achievement and status than between achievement and school or race.
Achievement patterns in the Higher Horizons and Project schools are
almost identical for both the B and the C groups, despite both the

TABLE 4

ACHIEVEMENT PATTERNS OF B AND C GROUP NEGRO AND
PUERTO RICAN CHILDREN IN THREE SCHOOLS

A. Higher Horizons School[a]

Achievement	Negro — B Group (67)	Negro — C Group (44)
High	12	2
Middle	54	47
Low	51	34

B. Project School

Achievement	Negro — B Group (56)	Puerto Rican — C Group (35)
High	7	3
Middle	61	44
Low	32	53

C. Hillside School

Achievement	Negro — B and C Group (4)	Puerto Rican — C Group (16)
High	0	0
Middle	94	100
Low	6	0

[a]*The one Puerto Rican child from the Higher Horizons School, with an achievement level of low, is not included here.*

more adequate facilities in the Higher Horizons School and the ethnic differences between Negro and Puerto Rican C group children.

The slight difference in the proportion of high achievers in each school for B groups may reflect the influence of superior conditions in the Higher Horizons School, or possible slight variations in socio-economic characteristics within the B groups. It is important to note that the number of B pupils in Hillside School is very small (2). This may account for the absence of high achievers among minority groups there.[7]

The conspicuous difference to emerge from Table 4, as from Tables

---

[7] High achievement patterns were evident among Open Enrollment children in Hillside School. Of the 12 Negro and Puerto Rican children in this group, 54 per cent were high achievers, 38 per cent middle, and 8 per cent low.

2 and 3, is the greatly reduced proportion of low achievers among C group children in Hillside School. These C group children do better than B group Negroes in the two segregated schools, a difference that cannot be attributed to ethnic differences, since in the segregated schools Puerto Rican performance does not surpass Negro performance.

Unquestionably, there are a host of factors that contribute to the relationship between integration and achievement. As already discussed, this study chose to focus on the possible effects of integration on a minority child's self-image. Through analysis of the drawings made by the sample, it was possible to devise indexes of both a child's self-concept and his racial concept. The indexes were then examined in relation to race, achievement, and integration. Table 5 shows the first of these relationships, between self-concept and race.

TABLE 5

SELF-CONCEPT AND RACE[a]

| | Self-concept | | | |
Race	High	Neutral	Low	Total N
White	53	39	8	104
Puerto Rican	14	63	23	52
Negro	9	54	37	193
TOTAL	80	178	91	349

[a]*Relationship significant at the .01 level, using the chi-square test.*

Self-images by Negro children, as compared to those of white children, tended to be extremely low. Even middle-class Negro children rarely showed a positive concept of self, whereas white children in general were positive. Low status Puerto Rican children were in general less negative than low status Negro children, but were more often neutral than positive.

Striking differences were revealed between Negro and white children in their depiction of racial characteristics. These differences were most conspicuously brought out in relation to skin color. In terms of the color chosen to *outline* the figures, there was an almost universal recognition of accurate skin color among all groups. While 68 per cent of the white children colored the skin realistically, Negro children showed an overwhelming tendency to avoid a realistic self-portrayal in this area. Only 24 per cent of the Negro children colored the skin brown or tan, while 64 per cent failed to color it at all, and 12 per cent used

a shade distinctly lighter than their own. This last pattern was exhibited for the most part among middle-class Negro children. Puerto
Rican children who were light-skinned tended to show greater freedom
in coloring the skin than dark-skinned Puerto Rican children, but altogether, only 25 per cent of the Puerto Rican children colored their
figures realistically. It is perhaps worth noting that a number of light
Puerto Rican children actually colored the skin *white*, although the
paper was white and the crayon didn't show up.

Is the negative self-concept of minority group children a contributing factor to their patterns of low achievement? In view of the fact
that fewer middle than lower-class Negro children showed negative
self-attitudes, it would appear that self-concept may be partially related to social status. Some variations in overall achievement patterns, however, indicate that these are separate factors, each of which
may also play an independent role.

As shown in Table 6, middle-class children with a *low* self-concept

TABLE 6

SOCIO-ECONOMIC STATUS, SELF-CONCEPT,
AND ACHIEVEMENT

	Achievement			
Self-Concept	*High*	*Middle*	*Low*	*Total N*
A Group Children				
High	79	21	0	47
Middle	33	62	5	38
Low	20	60	20	15
TOTAL	53	42	5	100
B Group Children				
High	54	42	4	24
Middle	16	61	23	86
Low	0	49	51	41
TOTAL	27	82	42	151
C Group Children				
High	9	91	0	11
Middle	2	67	31	52
Low	0	26	74	35
TOTAL	2	54	42	98

were performing below the level of other middle-class children, but rarely fell into the lowest achievement group. Children in the lowest social class (C group) with a *high* self-concept generally performed above the level of other lower-class children, but rarely attained high achievement ratings. *Low* self-concept among lower-class children was highly related to low achievement. Middle-class children with *high* self-concepts invariably showed high achievement.

It appears from findings presented earlier that a positive relationship exists between school integration and pupil achievement. There is also the possibility that self-concept, as an independent factor, helped to account for variations in achievement levels. Table 7 examines the relationship between integration and self-concept.[8] The effects of integration upon self-concept are revealed in the contrasting percentages in the *high* and *low* categories of the integrated and segregated groups.

TABLE 7

INTEGRATION AND SELF-CONCEPTS OF MINORITY GROUP CHILDREN IN B AND C GROUPS[a]

Schools	*Self-Concept*			
	High	*Middle*	*Low*	*Total N*
Integrated	25	65	10	20
Segregated	9	55	36	203
TOTAL	24	125	74	223

[a]*Relationship significant at the .05 level, using the chi-square test.*

The relationship between integration and self-concept is even better demonstrated by charts showing how the latter develops between the second and fifth grades for children in the integrated and segregated situations, and how the development relates to school achievement.

Low status minority group children in the segregated schools showed a tendency to maintain relatively low ratings in self-concept at both grade levels. Children of the same status in the socially integrated Hillside School showed a distinct improvement in their ratings from the second to the fifth grade. In each case, the self-concept ratings are reflected in distinct achievement trends. In the integrated school, the improvement in self-concept is accompanied by the complete absence of low achievers in the fifth-grade group. In the segregated schools,

8 Self-concepts of Open Enrollment children (12) in Hillside School broke down as follows: *high,* 50 per cent; *middle,* 50 per cent; *low,* 0.

where self-concept remains depressed, achievement scores in the fifth grade show a sharp decline.

DISCUSSION

The effects of integrated schooling are most clearly demonstrated in the dramatic reduction of low achievement patterns among low status minority group children. It would appear that the improvement in self-concept associated with social integration may be a significant factor in accounting for this result.

TABLE 8

COMPARISON OF TRENDS FROM 2nd TO 5th GRADE AMONG
MINORITY GROUP CHILDREN (B AND C GROUPS) IN
SEGREGATED AND INTEGRATED SCHOOLS

	High	*Middle*	*Low*	*Total N*
Children Attending Segregated Schools:				
Self-Concept				
2nd Grade	12	52	36	114
5th Grade	6	60	34	89
Achievement				
2nd Grade	8	58	34	114
5th Grade	6	45	49	89
Children Attending Integrated Schools:				
Self-Concept				
2nd Grade	20	60	20	11
5th Grade	38	62	0	9
Achievement				
2nd Grade	0	90	10	11
5th Grade	0	100	0	9

It will be noted from Table 8, however, that the changes in self-concept and achievement ratings are not parallel. While, in the integrated group, the improvement in self-concept was impressive, achievement improved only slightly. On the other hand, while for the segregated group self-concept ratings remained the same, achievement ratios dropped noticeably, with almost half of the fifth-grade children in the lowest category of achievement.

It seems logical to assume that the lag between self-concept and achievement among low status children can be attributed to socio-economic factors. Where self-concept remains weak, the child is powerless to compete with the negative forces in his environment which act to depress achievement. When self-concept is strengthened, however, his motivation to achieve is enhanced, and he is in a better position to compete with such forces. The fact that children in the lowest socioeconomic groups rarely attained high achievement levels, even when self-concept was high, indicates the potent influence of other factors. Indeed, it would be foolish to expect that improved social conditions in a school would be sufficient to enable a child to overcome the many handicaps imposed upon him by the circumstances of low socioeconomic status.

But the findings of this study reveal not only the empirical relationship between integration, self-concept, and achievement. They reveal, as well, some clues as to the underlying processes that connect these three variables—the way in which integration leads to a higher self-concept and improved school performance.

The Effects of Segregation upon Self-Concept

The findings suggest that social segregation has the effect of reinforcing a concept of social inferiority and a feeling of racial rejection among minority group children. Some further observations in the cause of the study support this conclusion. While administering the drawing test in the two segregated schools, it became evident from the remarks of Negro and Puerto Rican children that their tendency to avoid coloring the skin represented a deep-seated recognition of the negative valuation society placed upon dark skin coloring.

After the test had been administered and the drawings collected, some attempts were made to raise the issue explicitly among the fifth-grade Negro children in the Higher Horizons School. Individual children would be asked: "Do you mind telling me why you didn't use the crayons?" or, "I wonder why you colored practically everything else on the page, but left the skin blank?" Some of the children took the question as a sign of permission, and, taking the picture back, would color the skin appropriately. But more often they responded with questions that revealed their mixed feelings: "What color would you want me to color it, *black?*" or, "You mean I should color it *brown?*"

Deutsch (1960), Clark (1963), the Ausubels (1963), and others have noted the anxiety with which segregated Negro children regard their relationship to the larger white world and the expectation they have that it will be fundamentally rejecting and critical. Deutsch points out that to the Negro child this is a world with which he has had practically no personal contact, and that, thus, the experience of segregation, with its consequent anxieties, plays a vital role in the development of a negative self-image. It also appears (Ausubel and Ausubel, 1963) that children in segregated neighborhoods use idealized models (taken from the mass media, absorbed through hearsay, and so forth) as a basis for comparison with themselves. Thus, the gap between what they perceive to be their own potential and what they assume to be the standards of the larger society is far greater than the differences that exist in actuality.

The Effects of Integration upon Self-concept

During an informal discussion with a group of parents at Project School, after the research there had been completed, one young mother commented on her own childhood experience.

> *I lived in Harlem until I was in about the fifth or sixth grade. All of the children in the school were Negro, of course. Sometimes we used to go down to 110th Street to look at the white kids. We just stared at them, and thought how wonderful they were, and how they could do everything so well. Later, my family moved to the Lower East Side. I went to school with a lot of white kids. And then I found out that they weren't so much better than we were, after all!*

Children who are exposed to a socially heterogeneous situation are in a position to perceive individual differences *within* racial or social groups. Minority group children (as well as lower-class white children) who attend racially and socially mixed schools are thus in a more favorable developmental situation than those who attend lower-class or segregated schools. They are able to compare themselves with actual individuals, instead of idealized models—individuals as prone to human error and inadequacies as anyone else. Minority group children thus are able to develop a sense of personal identification—and a more realistic sense of self—apart from their racial status.

The Relationship of Self-concept to Achievement

The relationship of self-concept to achievement can perhaps be best understood in terms of motivation. Motivation has long been recognized as a key factor in school performance (Davis, 1955). When one con-

siders the almost universal reluctance with which children view academic tasks, it is important to bear in mind that their willingness to
undertake such tasks depends to a large extent upon the degree to
which a child is oriented toward future goals. If a child perceives that
his own status group is alienated from the larger society and, hence,
from its opportunities, it is understandable that he may be discouraged
from pursuing either immediate academic tasks or more ultimate future
goals.

Under segregated conditions, the minority group child identifies his
social potential with his racial status. Under integrated conditions, however, the child is able to develop a sense of self based upon other dimensions. His perception of his potential is not tied to the potential attributed to his racial group. The realization that one can compete and make
one's way in the larger society marks a giant step in the reduction of his
feeling of alienation from that society. A positive identification with
society and the feeling that socially approved goals are obtainable are
crucial to the development and sustenance of the motivation necessary
to achievement in school.

Other Related Factors

In addition to providing more favorable conditions for the development of a positive self-concept and the motivation to compete, the
integrated school situation leads to improvements in student performance in other ways. The diversity in the classroom allows for a greater
stimulation and sharing of perceptions than is otherwise possible.[9]
Moreover, children who have the advantages of receiving positive
educational stimuli at home may assist in providing a school environment that is conducive to intellectual achievement. Peer values regarding
school achievement are especially significant in regard to the lower-
income child (Goldberg, 1963, p. 88).

Further, in spite of attempts to improve teaching programs in many
segregated schools, such as the Higher Horizons School included in this
study, the classroom atmosphere in such schools is rarely conducive to
learning. During visits to the two segregated schools in the course of the
present study, classrooms were frequently disrupted by children who
appeared to become restless or were easily distracted. In the integrated
school, however, few such problems arose. Deutsch (1960) observed
this phenomenon in his comparison of lower-class Negro and white
schools. He reported that in the Negro school as much as 80 per cent

[9] Frances Minor of New York University made this suggestion in a speech to
the Farragut-Heights Community School Committee, in Brooklyn, New York,
May 6, 1964.

of the school day was channeled into maintaining discipline and into organizational concerns, while in the white school such activities never amounted to more than 50 per cent of the day. Deutsch attributed this disorganization in the minority group school to a general lack of motivation among the children.

In the socially integrated school situation, the academic problems posed by the lower-income or minority group child become more manageable. When the classroom atmosphere is generally conducive to a learning situation, the teacher can develop his energies more effectively to teaching.

In summary, the central finding of this study is that low achievement patterns among low status minority group children are noticeably reduced by attendance in an integrated school. This improvement appears to be the result of the more positive self-concept (and perhaps the other changes) that occur in an integrated school situation. If these findings are valid, the first and most urgent task to be accomplished in raising the educational level of disadvantaged children is to resolve the problem of segregation. Improved techniques and school programs can only be effective when this has been done.

REFERENCES

Ausubel, David P., and Ausubel, Pearl. 1963. "Ego Development Among Segregated Negro Children," in *Education in Depressed Areas,* ed. A. Harry Passow. New York: Teachers College, Columbia University.

Clark, Kenneth B. 1963. *Prejudice and Your Child,* 2nd Ed. Boston: Peter Smith.

Clark, Kenneth B., and Clark, Mamie P. 1958. "Emotional Factors in Racial Identification of Negro Children," in *The Child,* ed. Jerome M. Seidman. New York: Holt, Rinehart and Winston.

Davis, Allison. 1955. *Social Class Influences Upon Learning.* Cambridge.

Dennis, Wayne. 1963. "Values Expressed in Children's Drawings," in *Readings in Child Psychology,* ed. Dennis. Englewood Cliffs, N.J.: Prentice-Hall.

Deutsch, Martin. 1960. *Minority Group and Class Status as Related to Social and Personality Factors in Scholastic Achievement.* Monograph #2.

Goldberg, Miriam. 1963. "Factors Affecting Educational Attainment in Depressed Urban Areas," in *Education in Depressed Areas,* ed. Passow.

Goodenough, Florence. 1926. *Measurement of Intelligence by Drawings.* New York. World Books.

Goodenough, Florence, and Harris, D. 1950. "Studies in the Psychology of Children's Drawings II, 1928–1949," *Psychological Bulletin.* 47: 369–433.

Machover, Karen, 1962. *Personality Projection in the Drawing of the Human Figure.* Springfield, Ill.: Charles C. Thomas.

The Influence of Intelligence and an Interracial Classroom on Social Attitudes

Dorothy Singer

The three investigations discussed in this paper represent an initial exploration of whether the interaction of intelligence and classroom contact is a factor in determining ethnic attitudes. More specifically, the investigations are concerned with the following questions: 1) Will children who have classroom contact with a minority group reveal greater differentiation in ethnic attitudes than children without such contact? 2) Does intelligence alone, or in conjunction with classroom contact, lead to such greater differentiation?

In the following studies, it was assumed that change toward the extremes of either more positive or more negative attitudes (or toward both) on the part of one group in regard to another indicated the development of greater differentiation. It was assumed further that proximity and intelligence together would have a stronger effect in producing attitude change than either alone.

INVESTIGATION I

The first study explored the attitudes of white children toward Negroes of the same age. Its hypotheses were:

1. White children who had several years of association with Negro children in integrated classrooms (termed the *high* exposure group) reveal a more differentiated cognitive structure concerning Negro children than do comparable white children in unintegrated classrooms (the *low* exposure group). Specifically:

   a. *high* exposure children reveal more positive attitudes towards Negroes than *low* exposure children.
   b. *high* exposure children reveal more positive attitudes towards foreign peoples, e.g., Africans and Asians, and towards the United Nations, than do *low* exposure children.
   c. *high* exposure children reveal less acceptance of social stereotypes concerning Negro children and foreign nationalities than do *low* exposure children.

99

2. *High* exposure children reveal less social distance between themselves and Negro children than do *low* exposure children.

3. *High* exposure children reveal less social distance between themselves and foreign peoples, e.g., Africans and Asians.

4. From a list of popular sports, entertainment, and political figures, *high* exposure children will show greater cross-ethnic familiarity and admiration than *low* exposure children.

Subjects

Subjects included 27 *low* exposure fifth-grade pupils (12 boys and 15 girls) from a school with no Negro students, and 28 *high* exposure fifth-grade pupils (15 boys and 13 girls) from an integrated school. Both schools are located in a suburban area near New York City and are within three miles of each other. All the subjects were white, although in the integrated school the Negro children took the tests along with their classmates.

Ratings based on the dwellings and parental occupations of the students were obtained from the school psychologist in the *low* exposure school and from the principal in the *high* exposure school. The subjects were rated as middle class, with relatively little range within this grouping.

The mean IQ of the *low* exposure group (based on the Henmon-Nelson test given in April 1962) was 118.3. The score for the *high* exposure group (based on the Kuhlman-Anderson test given in October 1963) was 118. There is no significant difference in IQ functioning.

The mean reading achievement score for the *low* exposure group (based on the Stanford Elementary K reading test given in June 1963) was 5.6 years. For the *high* exposure group (based on the Metropolitan Achievement Test given in May 1963) it was 6.5 years. Both groups are reading at their proper grade level or better, and the difference is not significant.

The children were cooperative, interested, and showed no difficulties in comprehending the materials.

Procedure

Four separate measures were administered to both groups.

1. *Attitude Questionnaire.* This measure consisted of 35 items drawn from a larger list of 100 questions devised by the researcher. Two judges selected the final 35 items after the entire set of 100 was administered to ten fifth graders who were not included in the actual study. The questions were selected to fit into five categories, with seven ques-

tions in each category. The categories were *neutral, pro-Negro, anti-Negro, pro-generalized groups* (positive attitudes towards minorities and foreign countries), and *anti-generalized groups* (negative attitudes).[1] After each item were the choices "Yes, I agree" and "No, I do not agree." Pupils were asked to circle one. The questions on the test were randomly arranged to avoid sequence effects.

2. *Cultural Stereotypes.* The second of the four measures was a list of cultural stereotypes based on the Katz and Braly study (1933). Stereotypes were given for six groups: Chinese, German, Negro, native white American, Jewish, and Italian. (The language of the original was modified for children. For example, the phrase "work hard" was substituted for "industrious.") Seven adjectives were presented for each of the six groups. Both positive and negative stereotypes were listed. For example, the adjectives for the Chinese included both "sly" and "loyal to the family." The subjects were told to circle as many of the adjectives as they thought were necessary to describe the group.

3. *Social Distance.* The third was based on the Bogardus Social Distance Scale (Bogardus, 1925). This scale, originally used for adults, was also adapted by the researcher. The object was to test the degree to which a subject would create social distance between himself, on the one hand, and Negroes and other national groups, on the other. The children were given a list of 12 groups of people (Chinese, Russian, Italian, Negro, German, Irish, Jewish, Japanese, Indian, African, Turkish, Puerto Rican) and five items representing degrees of social distance (from the least distance to the greatest: best friend, home to dinner, live on your block, belong to your club or scout troop, and be citizens of the U.S.A.) and were told to put a check next to the groups that each particular item would characterize. Next, the children were told to put a cross by the group they would *not* want to describe by the particular item. The items were presented in random order.

4. *List of Celebrities.* The last measure was a list of prominent Negroes and whites from the sports, entertainment, and political worlds. The list included such figures as Martin Luther King, Willie Mays, Eleanor Roosevelt, Mickey Mantle, etc. Each name was slowly read out loud by the researcher. The subjects were asked to circle any of the names with which they were familiar. They then were asked to check

---

[1] Examples of each category: *neutral*—"I would like to see the United States get to the moon before Russia"; *pro-Negro*—"I would like to have a Negro teacher as my classroom teacher"; *anti-Negro*—"I think that a lot of Negro children like to sing and dance but don't do their homework at all"; *pro-generalized*—"I would like to invite a student from a foreign country to be my guest"; *anti-generalized*—"Jewish people talk too much."

the names of the people they liked and admired. This produced a measure of familiarity and one of popularity.

Administration of the four measures took 40 minutes in each class. The students were told not to sign the test booklets, each of which was coded by the researcher with a number corresponding to the pupil's name. In addition, the teachers and the researcher were available to answer questions, clarify items, or give definitions when needed. The following statement was read to each class before the booklets were distributed:

> *I am doing a survey dealing with children's attitudes concerning many topics in the world. We think boys and girls in fifth grade are able to think about many issues and are able to form their own opinions. Today I would like you all to participate in this study. We want you to think for yourself, and answer all the questions truthfully. Please do not put your name on any of the papers. We do not need to know who you are. Work quickly, by yourself, and be truthful.*

Results

1. *Attitude Scale Findings.* The attitude scale as a whole did not reveal sufficient discrimination between the two groups of subjects, but on an item analysis the data leaned in support of corollary (a)—that *high* exposure children reveal more positive attitudes toward Negroes than *low* exposure children. For example, Item 30, "I would like to have a Negro teacher as my classroom teacher," yielded significant results at the .03 level on a chi-square test. When Item 26 was analyzed —"I would like all my teachers to be white"—there were no *high* exposure subjects and nine *low* exposure subjects in agreement. This result was significant at the .001 level on a chi-square test. In addition, the *high* exposure children more generally thought of Negro boys as "rougher . . . than white children," and were still willing to have a Negro teacher.

The attitude scale, on the basis of a median test, did not reveal any significant difference between *high* and *low* exposure subjects concerning their attitudes towards foreign groups, e.g., Africans and Asians, or towards other minority groups, such as Jews. The *high* exposure subjects were only slightly more in favor of extra-national groups than the *low* exposure subjects.

2. *Cultural Stereotype Test Findings.* No significant difference was found between the two groups of subjects in regard to the mean number of positive and negative stereotypes each assigned to Negroes. The

high exposure children, however, attributed a slightly greater number of positive than negative stereotypes to Negroes than did the *low* exposure children. Also, the *high* exposure group differs significantly beyond chance expectancy in attributing more positive and fewer negative stereotypes to foreign and other minority groups, e.g., Jews, than the *low* exposure group (P < .01). This supports the last section of corollary (c)—that *high* exposure children reveal less acceptance of social stereotypes concerning nationalities than do *low* exposure children.

3. *Social Distance Scale Findings.* The results of the Social Distance Scale partially support hypothesis 2 (*high* exposure children reveal less social distance between themselves and Negroes than do *low* exposure children). The *high* exposure group ranks Negroes higher than does the *low* exposure group—in eighth and eleventh place, respectively. There also was a narrower range of rankings among the *high* exposure group (from the Irish at 3.3 to the Russians at 12.3) than among the *low* exposure group (from the Italians at 3.7 to the Russians at 18.8).

Weights from one to five were assigned to the five statements indicating degrees of social distance. "Best friend," the least distant, was rated *one,* "citizen of U.S.," the most distant, was rated *five.* Rank orders were determined by a mean of all the ratings for each national group on each statement.

The items were separately analyzed to determine which group of subjects was more favorably disposed towards Negroes. In regard to the first item, there were 21 *high* exposure children willing to have a Negro as "best friend," but only 11 *low* exposure children. Results were significant as P < .02 > .01 on a chi-square test. In regard to the item dealing with willingness to have Negroes as "citizens of the U.S.," there were 12 *low* exposure subjects who were not willing to give Negroes "citizenship" as compared to only four *high* exposure subjects. This item was significant at P < .02 > .01 on a chi-square test. The other three items were not significant for the two groups together.

When rank orders of social distance of the five items are examined, the ratings of the *low* exposure group more or less approximate the anticipated order, that is, this group is most willing to admit Negroes as "citizens" and least willing to admit them to its homes or to engage in personal relations with them as "best friends." However, the results for the *high* exposure group deviate in a most interesting fashion from the anticipated order. This group, while most willing to admit Negroes as "citizens" and "best friends," shows its greatest reluctance in having them "live on the block" or "home for dinner." One possible interpretation of this pattern is that while the *high* exposure subjects can envision friendship with Negro children whom they see regularly in school, in barring them from "block" and "home," they reflect the concerns and prejudices of their parents. It should also be noted that the overall range of denial of acceptable proximity to Negroes is narrower and at a consistently more negative level for the *low* exposure group, suggesting that it feels more threatened by such a possibility. In short, *high* exposure children place less distance between themselves and Negroes than do *low* exposure children.

4. *List of Famous People.* Hypothesis 4, concerning cross-ethnic familiarity with and admiration for prominent figures from sports, entertainment, and politics, is supported by the results of the investigation. *High* exposure subjects tend to be more familiar than their *low* exposure counterparts with Negro figures and tend to admire them more as well. The *high* exposure subjects are also familiar with more white figures and admire more white figures than do the *low* exposure subjects, but there is no significant difference between the two groups in this regard.

A frequency count was made to determine which figures were most familiar and most popular for both groups. Qualitatively, the count shows some interesting results. Mickey Mantle (the white baseball star) ranked first in familiarity with both *high* exposure and *low* exposure subjects, but Willie Mays (the Negro baseball star) ranked higher than Mantle in the popularity scale of the *high* exposure group.

There is little difference in the rankings of the two groups, although the *high* exposure subjects included six Negroes among its first eight choices in regard to familiarity, while the *low* exposure subjects included only three. It is interesting to note also that of the 12 lowest rankings for both groups, almost all were Negroes. Finally, both groups were equally more impressed by sports figures and entertainers than by political figures.

Summary

The results indicated partial support of the general notion that white children with several years of integrated classroom experience would have a more differentiated view of Negroes than would white children with no such interracial experience. On the attitude questionnaire, even though the instrument was not particularly discriminating, *high* exposure subjects showed significantly more positive attitudes toward Negroes than did *low* exposure subjects. Again, although mean differences concerning the acceptance of social stereotypes were not significant, *high* exposure children attributed a slightly larger number of positive than negative stereotypes to Negroes than did the *low* exposure children. In addition, the *high* exposure group indicated a willingness to have greater proximity with Negroes (particularly in terms of personal friendship), and indicated also greater familiarity with and positive feeling for Negro celebrities. Only one of the hypotheses dealing with foreign minority groups received support: *high* exposure children attributed significantly more positive and fewer negative stereotypes to foreign and minority groups than did *low* exposure subjects.

These results were interpreted as suggesting that the interracial classroom experience may well lead to greater affective warmth on the part of white children towards Negroes but does not completely counteract negative parental attitudes.

INVESTIGATION II

The second investigation explored the attitudes of Negroes towards whites. The hypotheses were the same as for the first investigation except with Negroes and whites reversed.

Subjects

Subjects included 30 *low* exposure fifth-grade pupils (eight boys and 22 girls) from a school whose population was only 25 per cent white, and 29 *high* exposure fifth-grade pupils (15 boys and 14 girls) from an integrated school. The schools were not the same as those used in the first experiment, though again they were located in suburban areas near New York City. Information on dwellings and occupations was obtained from the principals in each school, and the subjects were rated as lower class, with relatively little range within this category.

All the subjects were Negroes, although the white children in each classroom also took the tests. The mean IQ for the *low* exposure subjects (based on the Otis Quick Scoring test given in June 1963) was 99.0, with a range of 83–118. For the *high* exposure subjects (based on the Kuhlman-Anderson test given in October 1963) it was 95.5, with a range of 71–123. There is no significant difference in the IQ functioning of the two groups.

The mean reading achievement score for the *low* exposure group (based on the Iowa Test of Basic Skills given in December 1963) was 4.8 years, with a range of 3.9 to 7.2 years. For the *high* exposure subjects (based on the Metropolitan Achievement Test) it was 4.0 years, with a range of 2.2 to 6.8 years. In terms of averages, both groups are reading one year below their grade level. Although both groups have a four year difference between their lowest and highest reading score, there is no significant difference between the groups when their means are compared. The range for the *low* exposure subjects is one year higher. This difference may be due to the fact that the *low* exposure group contained more girls.

The children were cooperative, absorbed in their booklets, asked for help when needed, and, in general, seemed to comprehend the materials.

Procedure

The same procedure and materials were used in this investigation as in the first.

Results

1. *Attitude Scale Findings.* The attitude scale was originally designed to measure attitudes of whites toward Negroes. Nine questions, however, could be rephrased to tap Negro attitudes towards whites, and these questions were separately analyzed. On the whole the scale did not yield significant discrimination between the two groups, but several items indicated a negative self-concept on the part of Negro subjects in both schools. For example, Negro children in both *high* and *low* groups were reluctant to agree that "some Negro children are smarter than some white children" and that Negroes are "better athletes than whites." In the *high* exposure group of the first experiment, the white children granted this ability to the Negroes (on the basis, probably, of actual knowledge, since Negro boys are the star athletes in that school).

There was no statistically significant difference between the two groups with regard to a median test of the number of positive attitudes concerning Negroes. But the *high* exposure subjects were slightly more favorably disposed toward their own race than were the *low* exposure subjects.

To get at attitudes toward whites, the questions on the attitude scale relating to foreign and other minority groups (e.g., Jews) were examined. *High* exposure subjects are slightly more favorably disposed towards foreign or other minority groups than are *low* exposure subjects, but the results are not statistically significant by a median test.

Two further questions indicate the effects of interracial contact. In reply to "Some white children that I know are pretty sloppy in the way that they dress," *high* exposure subjects were more in agreement than were *low* exposure subjects (P < .03 on a chi-square test). They also were more in agreement with the statement, "Some whites are snobbish or unfair to children of other colors." These items support the notion that *high* exposure subjects reveal a more differentiated cognitive structure than their *low* exposure counterparts. The former were more willing to see negative as well as positive aspects of the whites.

2. *Cultural Stereotype Test Findings.* Per subject, both groups gave approximately the same number of positive and negative stereotypes toward Negroes. With regard to positive and negative stereotypes of whites, there was no statistically significant difference between the groups, although the *high* exposure group gave slightly more negative stereotypes than did the *low* exposure group. *High* exposure subjects also assigned more negative stereotypes to themselves than did *low* exposure subjects. This suggests that the Negro child in the integrated school may experience some feelings of low self-esteem. Finally, although each subject selected approximately the same number of stereotypes toward whites, the total number of positive and negative stereotypes was higher for the *low* exposure group than for the *high* exposure group. (This possibly means that the latter are using phrases that are less cliché or pat.)

Results indicated that both groups assign almost the same number of stereotypes to groups such as Italians, Germans, and Jews. Although the *low* exposure subjects tended to give more positive stereotypes, no statistically significant difference was found between the two groups of subjects.

The responses concerning the Jewish minority were selected for further analysis to test the hypothesis that proximity and contact lead to more favorable attitudes. There are no Jewish children in the *low* exposure school, and about three Jewish families in the town, while the *high* exposure students have contact with Jewish classmates and teachers, and a Jewish principal. These students checked 56 positive and 26 negative stereotypes for Jews, while the *low* exposure students checked 45 positive and 34 negative stereotypes. Some of the positive words were "religious," "work hard," "close family ties," and among the negative were "like money," "talk loud," "are shrewd." While the differences between the two groups are not statistically significant, they lean in the direction of supporting the hypothesis.

3. *Social Distance Scale Findings.* The results of the Social Distance Scale support hypotheses 2 and 3: *high* exposure subjects reveal less social distance between themselves and other groups than do *low*

exposure subjects. Negroes rank themselves first for both groups (as might be expected). The range of scores among the *high* exposure group is a slightly narrower one, from an average of .71 for Negroes down to 19.6 for Russians, as compared with the range of the *low* exposure group, from .13 for Negroes down to 20.1 for Russians. (The scale goes from 0, which indicates the least distance, to 30, which indicates the greatest.)

The *high* exposure group ranks highest the groups with which it is most familiar (or perhaps identifies). Chinese are first after Negro, followed by Puerto Ricans, Jews, and Africans. Actual contact is important in terms of Jews and Chinese (popular Chinese restaurants are located in the *high* exposure area—one especially is frequented by Negroes for "take home" food). The *low* exposure group also appears to be influenced by contact. For example, it ranks Jews in tenth place while the *high* exposure group ranks them in fourth place. Similarly, although Italians are familiar to both groups, they are the major white population in the *low* exposure school, which also has an Italian principal. Accordingly, the *low* exposure students rank Italians third, and *high* exposure students rank them eighth.

The Negroes in both schools, similar to the whites in the first investigation, place the Russians at the bottom of the list. The Negroes rank the Russians even lower than the whites ranked them. (Negroes in the *low* exposure group also ranked Indians and Turks higher than other more familiar national groups. This ranking may reflect identification with minority groups of color, since Jews were ranked lower than Indians, Turks, Chinese, and Africans.)

For further analysis, three groups were chosen from the list to determine how each group would rate them on the separate items. In regard to Jews, it was found that *high* exposure subjects were more willing than *low* exposure subjects to have a Jew as a "best friend" and to "admit a Jew to citizenship." Results were statistically significant for both items. In regard to Germans, the data indicated that each group was negative on all five items. Both groups were more accepting of Italians, but the *low* exposure group was most willing to accept them on its block, as members of its club, and as citizens (χ^2 sig. $P < .01$ for all three). These responses support the central thesis of this investigation, that proximity and contact lead to greater acceptance of other groups.

4. *List of Famous People.* The data indicate that there are no significant differences between *high* and *low* exposure subjects in their ratings of familiar and popular white and Negro celebrities. Both groups were more familiar with white than Negro celebrities, and the popularity

rankings of both listed more white figures higher than Negro figures. As in the first investigation, more Negro figures were found in the last six ranks of both familiarity and popularity. It may be that one factor influencing these choices is the greater publicity that white personalities receive. It is interesting, however, that even in the predominantly Negro school, the Negro subjects were more familiar with, and had a higher admiration for, the white personalities on the list.

Summary

The results of the attitude questionnaire indicated that the *high* exposure students have a more differentiated cognitive structure than the *low* exposure students. The former were willing to designate white children as "sloppy" and "snobbish" and yet held positive attitudes towards them.

The cultural stereotype test indicated that both groups gave more stereotypes to themselves than the whites in Investigation I gave to Negroes. The groups did not differ significantly in the number of positive and negative stereotypes they attributed to other national groupings. *High* exposure subjects assigned fewer negative stereotypes to Jews than did *low* exposure subjects, who had no classroom contact with Jews.

Data from the Social Distance Scale demonstrated again the importance of proximity and contact. The *high* exposure group ranked Jews higher than Italians, while the *low* exposure group ranked Italians higher, in accord with their differing daily experiences. On a *List of Famous People,* both *high* and *low* exposure students generally rated Negroes below whites. More whites than Negro personalities were familiar to and popular with Negroes in both schools.

INVESTIGATION III

The third investigation was an attempt to study the effect of intelligence in shaping ethnic attitudes, and to ascertain the influence of the interaction between intellectual capacity and interracial proximity. The hypotheses were:

1. Among *high* exposure white children in integrated classrooms, those with high IQs should have a more differentiated cognitive structure than children with low IQs. Specifically, among the *high* exposure children, those with a high IQ will reveal:

   a. more positive attitudes toward Negroes on an attitude scale than those with a low IQ;

    b. more positive attitudes towards foreign nationalities, e.g., Africans and Asians, and towards the United Nations, than those with a low IQ;

    c. less acceptance of social stereotypes concerning Negro children and foreign nationalities than those with a low IQ;

    d. less social distance between themselves and Negro children than those with a low IQ;

    e. less social distance between themselves and foreign nationalities, e.g., Africans and Asians, than those with a low IQ;

    f. greater cross-ethnic familiarity with and admiration of a list of popular sports, entertainment, and political figures than those with a low IQ.

2. High or low IQ white children in an integrated (*high* exposure) classroom should have a more differentiated cognitive structure than either high or low IQ white children in a comparable unintegrated (*low* exposure) classroom.

3. Among *low* exposure children, those with a high IQ will be more favorably disposed towards Negroes, other minority groups and foreign nationalities than those with a low IQ.

4. In general, differences between high and low IQ subjects will be more marked in the *high* exposure group than in the *low* exposure group, since it is postulated that the combination of IQ and proximity will lead to greater cognitive differentiation.

Subjects

Subjects included 23 *low* exposure fifth-grade white pupils (ten boys and 13 girls) in a school in which there were no Negro students, and 29 *high* exposure fifth-grade white pupils (16 boys and 13 girls) in an integrated school. Both schools were located near New York City in suburban areas that are within three miles of each other. Ratings based on dwellings and parental occupations were obtained from the school psychologist in the *low* exposure school, and from the principal in the *high* exposure school. In addition, census tract information was secured concerning the ethnic composition, income, and general level of education in the two areas. Subjects were rated as middle class, with relatively little range within this grouping.

The IQ and reading scores among both the high and low IQ subjects in these two groups are shown on page 111.

As Table 1 shows, there were no significant differences between the low or high IQ groups in either school on the IQ or reading means.

TABLE 1

IQ[a] AND READING SCORES[b] AMONG HIGH AND
LOW IQ SUBJECTS, BY EXPOSURE

| | High Exposure | | Low Exposure | |
Variable	Low IQ	High IQ	Low IQ	High IQ
Mean IQ Score	104.3	122.2	110.0	124.5
Range of IQ Scores	86-115	116-133	98-115	116-132
Mean Reading Score	5.7	7.1	5.4	6.0
Range of Reading Scores	2.8-7.9	6.1-7.9	3.5-7.0	4.3-7.6
N	14	15	12	11

[a] *IQ was determined by means of the Henmon-Nelson test for the low exposure group (given in April 1962) and by the Kuhlman-Anderson test for the high exposure group (given in October 1963).*
[b] *Reading level was determined for the low exposure group by the Stanford Elementary K reading test (given in June 1963) and for the high exposure group by the Metropolitan Achievement Test (given in May 1963).*

The children were cooperative, interested, and showed no difficulties in handling the materials. The *high* exposure school had a male teacher, the *low* exposure school a female. Both were white.

Procedure

Procedure for the third investigation followed the same employed in the first two and used the same material and instructions.

Results

1. *Attitude Scale Findings.* The attitude scale revealed that in the *high* exposure group, high IQ students were more favorably disposed towards Negroes than low IQ students. The results were significant on a chi-square test ($P < .01$). Twelve of these high IQ students were above the median on the scale of positive attitudes towards Negroes, as compared with only three of the low IQ students.

No significant difference was found between the low and high IQ students in the *low* exposure group. Hypothesis 4—that differences between high and low IQ subjects will be most marked in the *high* exposure group—is therefore supported. Where there is contact with Negroes, IQ plays the role of a "sensitizer" and so, generally speaking, the higher the IQ, the more differentiated the response. Where there is no contact, as is the case with the *low* exposure group, there is nothing, in effect, to differentiate.

High IQ students in the *high* exposure group were also more favorably disposed than the low IQ students towards minority groups other than Negroes, thereby supporting hypothesis 1(b) (P < .05 > .01, on a chi-square test).

No significant differences (by a chi-square test) were found in the numbers of *low* exposure students in the two IQ categories who were favorably disposed towards minority groups, a result that supported hypothesis 4.

An item analysis was made to determine whether certain of the questions on the scale were more sensitive than others in picking up attitude differences. Item 30, "I would like to have a Negro teacher as my classroom teacher," was chosen by high IQs in both *high* and *low* exposure groups. In the integrated school, the differences between the high and low IQs were significant on a chi-square test (P < .01). Fourteen high IQ students were in favor of a Negro teacher and only one was against. Of the low IQ students in this school, six were in favor and eight against. However, these low IQs were more favorably disposed than the low IQs in the segregated school. In the latter school, there was no significant difference on this item (on a chi-square test) between high and low IQs, although the trend of the former is in favor, wanting a Negro teacher. Three other pertinent items were analyzed. On the first two—dealing with a teacher's color and the acceptance of people of different races on one's block—statistically significant results were found between the high and low IQ students of the *high* exposure group, and no significant differences were found between subjects in the *low* exposure group. On the third item, dealing with the intelligence of Negro and white children, there was almost total agreement among *high* and *low* exposure groups, whatever the IQ. But it is worth noting that *all* high IQ students of the *high* exposure group agreed that "some Negro children are smarter than some white children."

In general, the attitude scale yielded differences between both high and low IQ subjects in the *high* exposure group and between all *high* exposure and all *low* exposure subjects. High IQ children in the *high* exposure group are more favorably disposed towards Negroes than any of the other three categories of subjects. However, among the *low* exposure group, high IQ subjects indicated the most positive feelings towards Negroes. In sum, the results of the attitude scale support hypothesis 1(a) and (b), and hypothesis 4.

2. *Cultural Stereotype Findings.* Using a t test, no significant differences were found between high and low IQ subjects in the integrated school in terms of the positive and negative stereotypes they attributed to Negroes, although the low IQ students held slightly more stereotypes

than their high IQ counterparts. Similarly, no significant differences were found in the *low* exposure school. Of the four groupings, the high IQ students among the *high* exposure subjects gave the least number of stereotypes per individual.

In regard to data concerning foreign students, among the *high* exposure group the high IQ students attributed fewer stereotypes to other nationalities than the low IQ students. Results on a chi-square test were significant (P < .05 > .01) and supported hypothesis 1(c). No significant differences were found on a chi-square test between the subjects in the *low* exposure school.

An examination of the total number of stereotypes attributed to foreign groups reveals that high IQ students in both the *high* and *low* exposure groups gave more positive stereotypes to foreign groups than did the low IQ in the *low* exposure group. This finding suggests that, in the case of the high IQs in the *low* exposure group, contact and IQ are interacting in regard to foreign nationalities and such minority groups as Jews. While these students did not give more positive than negative stereotypes to Negroes (due perhaps to lack of contact), contact with Jewish children and children of German and Italian descent seems to have enabled them to differentiate among individuals. The result is more positive attributes. In short, the brighter children with contact can differentiate more readily than low IQ children with contact. This supports hypothesis 4.

3. *Social Distance Scale Findings.* The results of the Social Distance Scale supported hypothesis 1(d) and (e). High IQ students in the integrated school ranked Negroes higher than did the low IQ—in fourth and seventh place, respectively. The high IQs also had a narrower range for all 12 groups, starting from Jews with a rank of 1.9 down to Russians with a rank of 13.0. The low IQs also ranked Jews first and Russians last, but with respective ranks of 4.0 and 22.6.

In general, all foreign groups were ranked closer by high IQs, a finding that supports the central notion of this paper—that contact and intelligence interact to lead to more favorable attitudes with regard to foreign groups and minorities. There were also statistically significant differences between high and low IQ students with regard to all but one item concerning Negroes (as "members of a club"). The former students were more favorably disposed than the latter. (The high IQs also had a narrower range of distance between Negroes and other groupings than did anyone else.)

The data for the *low* exposure group supported hypothesis 3. The high IQ students among this group rank Negroes higher than do the low IQ students—in seventh and eleventh place, respectively (paralleling the fourth and seventh place ranking of the *high* exposure group).

4. *List of Famous People.* No statistical difference was found on a t test between the means for either high or low IQ students in the *high* exposure group as concerns the number of white celebrities with whom they were familiar and whom they admired. The data revealed that the high IQ students were more familiar with and admired more Negro figures than the low IQ students. Results leaned in favor of hypothesis 1(f).

In the *low* exposure school, both high and low IQ subjects were familiar with, and admired, about the same number of white celebrities, with no statistically significant difference. However, the low IQ students were more familiar with and admired more Negro celebrities than did high IQ subjects. This finding may be due to less discrimination on the part of the former or perhaps to a greater involvement with sports and television figures.

Results of this test are consistent with the results from the other three measures. The high IQ students in the *high* exposure group were both more familiar with and admired more Negro personalities than all other experimental subjects. This great cross-ethnic familiarity again may be explained by the interaction of contact and intelligence.

Summary

Results of this investigation indicated support for the central thesis of the study. On the attitude scale, the high IQ, *high* exposure students were significantly more favorably disposed towards Negroes and towards foreign nationalities than the other three categories of students. Although no significant differences were found between *high* and *low* exposure subjects in terms of the social stereotypes they attributed to various groupings, the high IQ, *high* exposure students did attribute more positive and fewer negative stereotypes to Negroes and to foreign groups than the other categories. On the social distance measures, these students also indicated willingness for a greater proximity with Negroes, and had the narrowest range of distance for the twelve groups. These students also indicated greater familiarity with and positive feeling for Negro celebrities.

DISCUSSION

The central notion behind these investigations has been supported by the results. Contact of white children with Negroes does appear to lead to more favorable attitudes on the part of the former. The third investigation also indicated that there is an interaction between intelligence and contact in regard to such attitudes. The high IQ, *high* exposure students were generally more favorably disposed towards Negroes on all four measures than the other subjects.

The evidence further suggests that intelligence alone is not significantly influential in shaping children's attitudes towards Negroes or other minority and foreign groups. For example, the high IQ students in the *low* exposure (segregated) school did not show as much cognitive differentiation in regard to Negroes as the high IQ students in the *high* exposure (integrated) school. However, with regard to the national groups with whom the high IQ, *low* exposure students had contact, these students were able to differentiate and consider group members as individuals. They were more positive towards foreign groups than towards Negroes, and were less threatened by the former than the latter.

The second investigation provided dramatic evidence of the effects of contact. Negro children who had no school contact with Jews and very little outside contact with them were more prejudiced towards Jews than were the Negro children in the integrated school, where there had been contact not only with Jewish children but with Jewish staff members as well. Similarly, Negro children in the segregated school were more favorably disposed towards the Italians, who were the major group of whites in the community, than were the Negroes in the integrated school, which contained fewer Italians.

The most striking results of the investigations related to the Social Distance Scale. This measure was a more subtle one than the attitude scale and reflected most dramatically the effects of contact. In Investigations I and II, the integrated subjects, both Negro and white, tended to be more willing to associate with each other and admit each other into closer contact than were either the whites or Negroes in the segregated schools. In addition, in the third investigation, four of the five items revealed statistically significant differences between the high and low IQ students of the *high* exposure group—indicating more favorable attitudes on the part of the former—which again points to the role of intelligence as a sensitizer. In contrast, high and low IQ students in the *low* exposure school showed no significant differences. In other words, where there were no Negroes, the more intelligent students acted very much like the less intelligent in their desire for social contact with Negroes. In the integrated school, the intelligent student was able to differentiate among the Negroes and see them as individuals with whom he would like to associate.

These investigations represent a beginning approach to the study of the effects of school integration upon the attitudes of whites and Negroes. They indicate that the school can play a vital role in helping children to develop more tolerance and understanding.

In addition, the analysis suggests the value of attitude measurement in assessing the effects of integration, and might well be useful in pointing to changes in the curriculum that would enhance the likelihood of greater mutual respect among children from different ethnic backgrounds.

REFERENCES

Bogardus, E. 1925. "Measuring Social Distance," *Journal of Applied Sociology.* 9: 299–308.

Katz, D. and Braly, K. W. 1933. "Racial Stereotypes of 100 College Students," *Journal of Abnormal Social Psychology.* 28: 280–290.

Prejudice in Negro and Puerto Rican Adolescents

Dorothy Schaefer

The purpose of this study was to investigate the effects of intelligence and minority group status on the prejudice of Negro and Puerto Rican adolescent boys. The study attempted to determine: (1) whether there were any significant differences between Negroes and Puerto Ricans in their attitudes toward their own and other minority groups; (2) whether there existed significant differences in these attitudes at varying levels of intelligence (the mentally retarded, average, and bright); (3) whether there was any significant interrelationship between intelligence and minority group status in determining the attitudes; and (4) whether, statistically speaking, the attitudes of the Negroes and the Puerto Ricans, treating them as two separate groups, departed significantly from "zero—zero," representing neutral feelings.

SAMPLE, PROCEDURES, AND EXPERIMENTAL DESIGN

The Negro and Puerto Rican boys employed in this study were all enrolled in a Northeastern city school system near New York City. The mentally retarded group was selected from classes for the educable mentally retarded, while the boys of average and bright levels of intelligence were selected from regular public school classes. All the boys were from 14 to 16 and lived in low socioeconomic areas of the city. The entire sample population totaled 90.

The population was delimited by a variety of factors. To insure that the sample would be able to read the test material, it was necessary to establish a minimum reading level of third-grade ability. At two of the IQ levels, the range of intelligence quotients was sharply limited: from 65 to 75 for the *mentally retarded* group, and from 95 to 109 for the *average* group. The *bright* group was permitted to range above 115 without restriction.[1] However, since the highest IQ score was 122, this

[1] The Peabody Picture Vocabulary Test was used to obtain the intelligence levels of the boys. The Stanford Achievement Test, Intermediate Level, was administered to those for whom there was no achievement test score in the school file, and the reading sub-test scores were used to select boys with a third grade or better reading level.

TABLE 1

MEANS AND STANDARD DEVIATIONS OF INTELLIGENCE QUOTIENTS
IN 90 MENTALLY RETARDED, AVERAGE, AND BRIGHT
NEGRO AND PUERTO RICAN BOYS

	Mentally Retarded		Average		Bright	
	Negro	P.R.[a]	Negro	P.R.	Negro	P.R.
Mean I.Q.	70.6	70.4	100.9	99.5	117.4	117.0
Standard Deviation	3.26	3.12	3.49	3.19	2.06	1.95
Range	66-75	65-75	96-105	95-105	115-121	115-122
Number	15	15	15	15	15	15

[a]*Puerto Rican.*

group approximated the ranges of the other two. The means and standard deviations of intelligence levels for Negroes and Puerto Ricans used in the study are shown on Table 1.

The socioeconomic level of the sample was determined by the occupation of the father or mother. These occupations included jobs in the manual, the service, the unskilled, and the semiskilled areas. The distribution of the occupations appears in Table 2.

TABLE 2

DISTRIBUTION OF PARENT OCCUPATIONS OF 90
NEGRO AND PUERTO RICAN ADOLESCENT BOYS

Occupational Area	Negro	Puerto Rican
Manual Worker—Unskilled	4	5
Manual Worker—Skilled	3	4
Factory Worker	6	16
Mechanic—Unskilled	3	2
Domestic	3	2
Construction Worker	6	8
Truck Driver	5	1
Cook (Short Order)	3	0
Building Superintendent	3	4
Welfare Recipient	·6	2
Unknown	3	1
Number	45	45

The Trait Attribution Test was used to test the attitudes of the boys toward their own individual group and toward other ethnic groups. The test was administered to all 90 subjects after a pilot study had determined its suitability as a measure for the mentally retarded boys. The pilot study was also utilized to assess how well the different intelligence groups understood the traits listed. (On the basis of responses by ten mentally retarded, ten average, and ten bright boys, substitute words were inserted for traits handled correctly less than seven times out of ten, in each intelligence group. The adjusted set of 28 traits was given to a new group of 30 and found acceptable.)

This investigation was designed in the form of a two by three factorial, with minority group status (Negro and Puerto Rican) representing the "two" category and the intelligence factor (*mentally retarded, average,* and *bright*) representing the "three" category. The design was applied to what hereafter will be called self-group and other-group attitudes. The 5 per cent level of confidence was used to evaluate the significance of differences.

RESULTS

Table 3, derived from the responses to the Traits Attribution Test, contains a statistical summary—in terms of means and standard deviations—of how the Negro and Puerto Rican boys rated their own ethnic groups. It will be observed that there is an ordered trend in the means

TABLE 3

MEANS AND STANDARD DEVIATIONS OF SELF-GROUP RATINGS
ON THE TRAITS ATTRIBUTION TEST FOR NEGRO
AND PUERTO RICAN ADOLESCENT BOYS
(N = 15 in Each Cell)

	Negro		Puerto Rican	
Intelligence Level	*Mean*	*S.D.*	*Mean*	*S.D.*
Mentally Retarded	+0.8	5.24	+3.1	5.23
Average	+1.6	5.64	+3.0	7.64
Bright	+2.1	4.62	+1.2	8.71

and that they move in opposite directions for the two ethnic groups. In the Negro sample, the means run from +.8 to +2.1, the lowest figure having been obtained from the *mentally retarded* group. In contrast, in the Puerto Rican sample, the range goes from +3.1 to +1.2, where the highest mean was derived from the *mentally retarded* group. Since the score is an indicator of degree of acceptance, it is thus clear that as the intelligence level in the Negro sample increased, so did positive group feelings. With the Puerto Rican sample, the reverse was the case. That is, as the intelligence level increased, self-acceptance declined.

From Table 4, which is derived from the other-group ratings of the Traits Attribution Test, it is apparent that both the Negro and Puerto Rican groups rejected each other. In the Negro sample, the mean scores showed less acceptance (a larger negative score) as the intelligence level increased. The trend was the same for Puerto Ricans, with the exception of the *average* group, which manifested the least rejection (the lowest negative mean score).

TABLE 4

MEANS AND STANDARD DEVIATIONS OF OTHER-GROUP RATINGS
ON THE TRAITS ATTRIBUTION TEST FOR NEGRO
AND PUERTO RICAN ADOLESCENT BOYS
(N = 15 in Each Cell)

	Negro		*Puerto Rican*	
Intelligence Level	*Mean*	*S.D.*	*Mean*	*S.D.*
Mentally Retarded	−2.5	4.22	−2.0	6.54
Average	−4.2	5.43	−0.4	6.33
Bright	−4.5	8.13	−3.3	6.32

To determine the significance of the sample means—the extent, that is, of their departure from zero (neutral feelings)—the t test was administered. The results with regard to self-attitudes are given in Table 5, which indicates that just one t score was significantly different from zero. This appeared in the Puerto Rican *mentally retarded* group. All

TABLE 5

SIGNIFICANCE OF MEANS OF SELF-GROUP RATINGS
ON THE TRAITS ATTRIBUTION TEST FOR NEGRO
AND PUERTO RICAN ADOLESCENT BOYS
(T TEST)

Intelligence Level	*Negro*	*Puerto Rican*
Mentally Retarded	0.6	2.3[a]
Average	1.1	1.5
Bright	1.7	0.5

[a]*Significant at .05 level (degrees of freedom = 14).*

TABLE 6

SIGNIFICANCE OF MEANS OF OTHER-GROUP
RATINGS ON THE TRAITS ATTRIBUTION TEST
FOR NEGRO AND PUERTO RICAN
ADOLESCENT BOYS
(T TEST)

Intelligence Level	Negro	Puerto Rican
Mentally Retarded	2.2[a]	1.1
Average	3.0[a]	0.4
Bright	2.1[a]	2.0

[a]*Significant at .05 level (degrees of freedom = 14).*

other scores for both ethnic samples did not approach significance. Table 6 lists the results in regard to attitudes toward other groups, and indicates that at each intelligence level, the Negro population differed significantly from zero.[2] With the Puerto Rican sample, only the mean for the *bright* group appeared to be nearing significance.

To evaluate the impact of intelligence and minority group status, the data were subjected to the two by three factorial design already noted. As a preliminary step, the homogeneity of variance was evaluated by the Bartlett test (Edwards, 1950, p. 211) in order to justify the use of the analysis of variance as a suitable statistical technique. For the self-group data, a chi-square of 7.30 was obtained; for the other-group data, a chi-square of 6.21. With five degrees of freedom, neither of these figures was statistically significant. On the basis of the Bartlett test, then, it was concluded that the variances were homogeneous and that the analysis of variances was a suitable measure of the significance of appropriate differences.

The results of this analysis in regard to self-group attitudes of the sample are summarized in Table 7; in regard to other-group attitudes in Table 8.

For self-group attitudes, the difference between the means of the two minority groups and the three intelligence levels was not significant. Nor was there any significant interaction of the variables in determining the attitudes. The results were much the same with other-group attitudes.

[2] These three ratings constitute the only significant expression of prejudice uncovered by the Attribution Test. It may be that they are as much the product of general public concern with civil rights as of the deeper feelings of this part of the sample population. See Langer (1953) for a discussion of the "superficial level of consciousness" reached by the Attribution Test.

TABLE 7

ANALYSIS OF VARIANCE OF SELF-GROUP ATTITUDES ON
THE TRAITS ATTRIBUTION TEST OF NEGRO AND
PUERTO RICAN ADOLESCENT BOYS OF THREE
DISCRETE INTELLIGENCE LEVELS

Source of Variation	Sum of Squares	df	Mean Square	F
Between Minority Groups	19.59	1	19.59	—
Between Intelligence Levels	6.02	2	3.01	—
Interaction	42.47	2	21.24	—
Within Groups	3655.88	84	43.52	
TOTAL	3723.96	89		

TABLE 8

ANALYSIS OF VARIANCE OF OTHER-GROUP ATTITUDES
ON THE TRAITS ATTRIBUTION TEST OF NEGRO AND
PUERTO RICAN ADOLESCENT BOYS OF THREE
DISCRETE INTELLIGENCE LEVELS

Source of Variation	Sum of Squares	df	Mean Square	F
Between Minority Groups	72.90	1	72.90	1.72
Between Intelligence Levels	54.59	2	27.29	—
Interaction	44.95	2	22.03	—
Within Groups	3556.96	84	42.34	
TOTAL	3728.50	89		

Again there was no significant difference between the two minority groups and the three intelligence levels. Although a slightly higher F value (1.72) was found for the minority group variable, the interaction did not prove to be significant. Since the values of F did not meet the requirements of significance for the intelligence and minority group variables, it may be inferred that the differences between them can be accounted for by random sampling from a common population.

As a further test, the hypothesis concerning the relationship between intelligence and ethnic prejudice was evaluated by the Product-Moment correlation technique. The matrix of correlations for all groups is shown in Tables 9 and 10. Of the four correlations obtained, none was statistically significant.

Thus, in confirmation of the analysis of variance findings, the results

TABLE 9

PRODUCT-MOMENT CORRELATION COEFFICIENTS
BETWEEN INTELLIGENCE AND SELF-GROUP
ATTITUDE RATINGS ON THE
TRAITS ATTRIBUTION TEST
(N = 45 in Each Cell)

Ethnic Group	Correlation Coefficient[a]
Negro	+.09
Puerto Rican	−.02

[a]*Neither of the correlation coefficients was significant at the .05 level.*

TABLE 10

PRODUCT-MOMENT CORRELATION COEFFICIENTS
BETWEEN INTELLIGENCE AND OTHER-GROUP
ATTITUDE RATINGS ON THE
TRAITS ATTRIBUTION TEST
(N = 45 in Each Cell)

Ethnic Group	Correlation Coefficient[a]
Negro	−.17
Puerto Rican	−.06

[a]*Neither of the correlation coefficients was significant at the .05 level.*

of this second evaluation indicate that the ratings of self- and other-group feelings are independent of the intelligence scores. This hypothesis of the study, then, was not substantiated.

DISCUSSION AND IMPLICATIONS

Other-Group Attitudes

There are a number of studies which generally support the hypothesis that this research did not confirm: that the less-prejudiced individual is one who possesses higher intelligence. However, all these studies—Minard (1931); Zeligs and Hendrickson (1933); Rokeach (1943); Else Frankel-Brunswick (1948); Kutner (1958)—used the dominant white majority as the experimental population. In each case, white pupils rated the Negro minority group. It may be that the white majority is psychologically freer to use its intelligence in the area of prejudice, since it does not experience the frustration of belonging to one ethnic group and knowing that another has a superior position in society. Perhaps this type of frustration and the emotional impact of being a member of a less favored racial group offsets such ameliorative effects as derive from an increase in intelligence.

On the other hand, it should be said that these studies did not consider intelligence in terms of IQ, as the present research did. They were concerned with the quality of mental functioning or the analysis of thinking processes, and focused on the way prejudiced individuals solved intellectual problems. Moreover, Minard (1931, p. 62) cautions that although he found intelligence to be a factor in race attitudes, it was not a strongly determining one and its effect was "probably due in part to the individual's developing consciousness" and to the conditioning effect of the values held by the group to which the individual belonged. Further, in the findings of Kutner (1958), Rokeach (1943), Frankel-Brunswick (1948), and Zeligs and Hendrickson (1933), though there was a slight positive correlation between intelligence and desirable attitudes toward different racial groups, the power of influence of intelligence was rather indefinite.

Self-Group Attitudes

In light of the rather uniformly positive self-group feelings expressed by both ethnic samples, it is relevant to note Jersild's belief (1952) that a child's self-concept depends on how he is treated as he grows up and that this self-concept is positive or negative in terms of his feeling of being accepted or rejected. The Negro and Puerto Rican adolescents in this study attend well-integrated junior high schools where growth in developing a worthwhile educational milieu has been constant. They are recognized for their achievements in sports, academic studies, and extracurricular activities. In addition, classes are so arranged that an unwholesome competitive stress is avoided. The school also provides remedial services, a guidance program, and special educational facilities for pupils and their families; and an active Parent Teacher Association unit encourages the participation of parents in school programs.

The findings that these groups are mildly, though not differentially, rejecting of one another points to the fact that although the Negroes and Puerto Ricans are both minority groups, they share little sense of unity or identification. This may be explained by their differing histories, and the different sense of aspiration to which these histories give rise. Each group appears to view itself as having unique problems, and each attempts to respond to these problems in its own way. Further,

Jenkins (1958) has reported that better-educated Negroes are resentful of Puerto Ricans and feel that they represent a strong competitive threat in economic terms and any rise in their status would be achieved at the expense of the Negro population.

REFERENCES

Edwards, Allen L. 1950. *Experimental Design in Psychological Research.* New York: Rinehart and Company, Inc.

Frankel-Brunswick, Else. 1948. "A Study of Prejudice in Children," *Human Relations.* 1: 295–306.

Jenkins, Shirley. 1958. "Intergroup Empathy: An Exploratory Study of Negro and Puerto Rican Groups in New York City." Unpublished Ph.D. thesis. New York University.

Jersild, Arthur T. 1952. *In Search of Self: An Exploratory Study of the Role of the School in Promoting Self-Understanding.* New York: Teachers College, Columbia University.

Kutner, Bernard. 1958. "Patterns of Mental Functioning Associated with Prejudice in Children," *Psychological Monograph.* Vol. 72, No. 7, pp. 1–47.

Langner, Thomas S. 1953. "A Test of Intergroup Prejudice Which Takes Account of Individual and Group Differences in Values," *Journal of Abnormal and Social Psychology.* 48.

Minard, Ralph D. 1931. "Race Attitudes of Iowa Children," *University of Iowa Studies: Studies in Character.* Vol. 4, No. 2.

Rokeach, Milton. 1943. "Generalized Mental Rigidity as a factor in Ethnocentrism," *Journal of Abnormal and Social Psychology.* 48: 259–278.

Zeligs, Rose, and Hendrickson, Gordon. 1933. "Racial Attitudes of Two Hundred Sixth Grade Children," *Sociology and Social Research.* 18, 26–36.

PART III

Programming Education for Urban Minorities

Segregated or integrated, schools in Northern central cities and inner ring suburbs are being constrained toward change by a host of pressures. Impoverished, welfare-dependent parents—from the Russian Jews of the 1920's and the Puerto Ricans of the 1950's to the newly arrived Southern Negroes of the 1960's—have always benefited from some features of the neighborhood public school. It is the safest, warmest, cleanest place around for the daytime housing of children. Occasional swarms of rats, breakdowns in the heating system, and over-crowded, over-used facilities have done no more than dilute this fact from time to time. The school has also been viewed by parents as the place where something helpful *might* happen, where a child might improve the quality of his existence.

But until the years of the Depression, the neighborhood school in the slum was only a brief stopover in the cycle of the impoverished household. With some exceptions, school was a brief, detachable interlude that began at age six and ended at age 11 or 14. Seldom did this interlude touch other facets of neighborhood, peer, and adult social life. In the Great Depression, the interlude was irrevocably expanded, but little else changed in the pattern.

Impulses toward penetration of the community by the program of the school gained momentum during the Depression, but by and large, these were dropped during World War II. The schools serving the Northern urban poor were never much affected by the great debates on educational questions that raged so interestingly before 1941. Progressive educationists in New York City repeatedly discussed and studied slum schools, for example, but efforts to revise programs or to relate school to community were sporadic; the programs depended upon a few individual educators who dedicated themselves to these missions with little public response.

Since World War II, the school in the urban and suburban slum has become vulnerable to extramural changes that are transforming thought within universities and teacher training institutions, and stimulating action in federal, state, and local elites by whom resources are allocated. The four articles in this section reflect some of the extramural changes as they have begun to affect public schools.

One of the most urgent involves *rising expectations* among the low-income urban parents themselves. The connections, both mythical and real, between educational attainment and adult economic security have dawned on nearly everyone. As these ties between formal learning and life chances have tightened, the hopes of impoverished mothers and fathers have concentrated upon more and better schooling for their children. The Civil Rights revolution has intensified this new concern. It has also emphasized the fact that opportunities for school learning are not equal from school to school, and that the inequality is racially based. Reliable survey evidence has revealed that the educational hopes of low-income urban parents, and the corresponding occupational aspirations of their children, are high and serious today.

These are not informed or sophisticated aspirations, however. Just as the children do not know what is required educationally in order to become a rocket engineer or a heart surgeon, so the parents, historically detached from the schools, do not know how to work to improve them. Nor are the channels for parental influence which are available (modelled as they are upon middle- and upper-income traditions of polite transaction) worth learning about under the special circumstances confronting depressed neighborhoods. Finally, school staffs have no relevant procedures to draw upon.

Joe Rempson, in his review of what we know to date about "School-Parent Programs in Depressed Urban Neighborhoods," documents the impasse. His analysis suggests the conditions under which efforts to bridge current gaps between low-income urban parents and their public schools are fore-doomed. He also offers positive leads to the kinds of programming that might make future cooperation possible.

Robert Dentler's "Critique of Education Projects in Community Action Programs," reflects the increasing efforts of local and federal agencies to relate anti-poverty programming to education. The fact that the projects his paper examines are devised by auspices *outside* the schools (with a few exceptions) indicates the extent to which the urban school in the slum has been pressed from without toward adaptive change. Some of the programs he assesses have been much improved during the last two years, but it remains true that welfare programs, anti-poverty projects, Title I and III projects funded by federal aid to education, and urban renewal operations still function as fragmented, unintegrated, often contradictory efforts towards urban reconstruction.

We have included the short play "Let's Organize Their Depression," by Elizabeth O'Grady, because it dramatizes the extreme cultural dis-crepancy between the new efforts to help which are flourishing in social welfare circles, and the clientele who are "served." This documentation of an actual program operating within a single-room-occupancy "hotel" in New York City conveys succinctly the boundaries between the worlds of the social worker (qua educator) and the client. In the process, the disabling motives of each are etched.

"An Approach to Primary Education in Urban Slums—A Mental Health Orientation," by Sol Gordon, is expressive of another substantial professional force impinging upon the urban school in the economically depressed neighborhood. Here, the increasing precision and substance of the mental health movement are applied to the question of how the slum school could be reconstructed. Gordon's proposals break the frame of compartmented guidance and counselling as the only current point of contact between psychotherapeutic approaches and the school. In his emphasis upon self-concept and the within-school experiences of the first- or second-grade child, Gordon is calling for changes that exceed all earlier visions of remediation and compensation.

School-Parent Programs in Depressed Urban Neighborhoods

Joe L. Rempson

School-parent programs[1] are an important part of the special effort being made by a few schools in depressed urban neighborhoods to increase the academic achievement of the disadvantaged child.[2] Invariably these schools are those which constitute the small number that are cooperating in either foundation- or school board-sponsored saturation attempts at quality education in depressed neighborhoods.

Hardly, in fact, does one read about a compensatory school endeavor that omits the parent. Some of the schools have even added a new position to the principal's staff, giving it such varied titles as school-community coordinator, school-community agent, school-community counselor, school-community director, community project coordinator, community relations expert, school-home counselor, parent-education counselor, visiting teacher, and home-school visitor. The duties of these persons differ nearly as much as their titles, but their aim is basically the same: to increase school-parent cooperation.

The attempt at such cooperation is not a new development in American public education. As early as the late 1830's, when the public school movement was in its infancy, such notable educators as Henry Barnard and Emma Willard were calling for closer school-parent cooperation (88). And the very existence of the 70-year-old Parent-Teacher Association is testimony to the continued presence of this idea. Nor is the emphasis on school-parent programs for a disadvantaged population original. When disadvantaged (to use the term out of its usual context) mainly meant European immigrants rather than primarily low-income Negroes, school-parent programs were conducted to help hasten their assimilation, too. Principally these programs took the form of day and

[1] In this review, school-parent programs are defined as all of those school-sponsored or co-sponsored activities whose inclusive purpose is to improve home and neighborhood environment or to secure the understanding and cooperation of parents and other citizens. This includes, for example, participating in efforts to improve housing conditions, job training classes, teacher-parent conferences, and the operation of a school-neighborhood council. It also includes such special service activities as those carried out by school social workers.

[2] "Disadvantaged child" here refers to a child of a low-income family, e.g., a family having an annual income of $4,000 or less. This paper is written chiefly with the disadvantaged Negro child in mind.

evening classes in school buildings (137[3]). It is of interest that to get parents to attend these classes, a bulletin of the University of the State of New York, published either in the 1910's or 1920's, urged the use of such present-day techniques as home visits, sending announcements home with pupils, distributing notices through shops and stores, holding Parent-Teacher Association meetings, and having room-mother meetings (129). Philadelphia, among other cities, even employed a device that today is being used nationally because of its presumably intrinsic benefits. It organized day classes for mothers and made it possible for them to attend by setting up kindergartens for their preschool children (129).

An approach used in a few areas, particularly California and Boston, resembles another present-day practice. Both created the position of home teacher, with California, which began the practice in the 1910's, allowing one such teacher for every 500 pupils of a school district (337). The duty of the home teacher was described by the Boston superintendent of schools as:

> *explaining to immigrant mothers the laws and customs of American life, the school attendance requirements for children, the meaning of report cards sent from the school, the existence and location of public baths, libraries, dispensaries, clinics, and many other institutions intended for the comfort and pleasure of their families (137, p. 111).*

He also advocated nation-wide use of home teachers to "persuade attendance [of women immigrants] at classes especially arranged" (137, p. 110). Thus, although such positions as school-community coordinator and parent-education counselor are new to the staffs concerned, they are not new in the history of American public education.

As for public schools generally, however, it was not until around the turn of the century that the interest of the school began to expand beyond the curriculum to the community, and not until after World War I that this changing interest became particularly noticeable (48, 73). Until then, the idea of school-home cooperation had remained largely just that—an idea (59). Three factors operated to change this: the attempt to Americanize the immigrant (11), the need of schools for public financial support (37), and the progressive education movement (32). The need for public financial support appears to have been the most potent of the three. Perhaps for this reason, the change has been partial rather than complete, and cyclical rather than stable (73, 151). For administrators have been most prone to turn to the community

[3] See source number 137 cited at the end of this chapter in the References (pp. 145–55). Other sources are cited similarly throughout this chapter in parentheses.

when they have needed its financial support, and since the extent of this need and the difficulty of getting it have fluctuated, so has the intensity of administrators' interest in school-community relations. Nevertheless, a residual effect, sustained perhaps by the influence of both the attempt to Americanize the immigrant and the progressive education movement has remained, so that today school-parent programs (to use the term loosely) are commonplace, even though they may consist only of such a single event as Open School Night (as is commonly the case in depressed neighborhoods).

Though the usual aim of these programs is to secure the kind of public understanding that can be translated into financial support, a few schools, usually located in rural and slum areas, have also assisted in efforts to improve home and neighborhood life. This they have done through such activities as helping to get new industries to locate in the community, aiding in the improvement of housing conditions, and utilizing the school as a community center (50, 83, 97, 107, 124, 143).

The point is that neither in concept nor in practice is the emphasis on improving the education of a disadvantaged population through school-parent-programs novel.[4]

THE PROBLEM

What makes school-parent programs in depressed urban neighborhoods so paramount today is that the academic achievement of the disadvantaged child is not up to what it could or should be, and the bulk of evidence suggests that this can be attributed largely to his intellectually impoverished home and neighborhood environment (4, 58, 63, 136).

Not all educators, however, subscribe to this formulation. For example, on the basis of the experience and research of Bank Street College in some of the depressed area schools of New York City, John Niemeyer, its president, states as an "unverified" yet "inescapable" hypothesis that:

> the chief cause of the low achievement by children in these schools is the low expectation as to their learning capacity held by the professional staff, and a general unwillingness or inability on the part of the school to make the adaptations of curriculum and school organization necessary if the children in these schools are to learn (106,. pp. 3–4).

[4] On an overall basis, Wayland (142) suggests what this brief commentary implies: that there are closer parallels than have been disclosed between the problems that immigrants experienced and those the disadvantaged of today are undergoing.

"We firmly believe," he goes on to say, "that, regardless of family and neighborhood background, the elementary schools can, if they will, create a program in which the majority of the present non-learners will learn" (106, p. 4). And Kenneth Clark, probably the most outspoken critic of the idea, contends in the HARYOU Report[5] that only the school is responsible for the disadvantaged child's low achievement. The school has low expectations, he says, and the child ends up by fulfilling them. The point is underlined in these words: "effective remedies will come *only* [italics added] from a firm belief and insistence that the pupils *can* [italics in the original] perform" (63, p. 244). In his most recent publication, *Dark Ghetto,* Clark is less emphatic. But his meaning and intent are the same, as is evident from his conclusion:

> *In the light of available evidence the* controlling *[emphasis added] factor which determines the academic performance of pupils and which established the level of educational efficiency and the overall quality of the schools is the competence of the teachers and their attitude of acceptance or rejection of their students (22, p. 47).*

Of course, it is hard to find those who do not place some blame on the school; the difference in perspective arises over how much blame should be placed on it. Too often, however, arguments about this issue seem to spring more from convenience than from the dictates of logic based on facts and observations, and more from a defense of the ego than from a search for a solution. Because of its programmatic implications, the issue needs to be debated, but not in this vortex. In any case, whoever is responsible, in whatever proportion, school-parent programs can help to correct both negative home and school factors.

THE SCHOOL-PARENT PROGRAMS

Goals

Although expressed in myriad ways (56, 103, 121), the aims of school-parent programs include one or more of four objectives: (1) to help parents guide their children's learning development more intelligently; (2) to help parents become better learning models (logically, this goal is part of the first aim, but its importance warrants it being listed separately); (3) to assist parents in improving their home conditions and neighborhood life; and (4) to help teachers gain a better understanding of the disadvantaged child, parent, and neighborhood.

[5] HARYOU is abbreviated for Harlem Youth Opportunities Unlimited, Inc., an anti-poverty organization in the Harlem section of New York City. HARYOU subsequently joined with a companion organization in Harlem, Associated Community Teams, Inc. (ACT), and the result is known as HARYOU-ACT.

Obstacles

To accomplish these four goals, teachers and other school personnel
can visit parents' homes or communicate with them through printed
matter, by telephone, or by radio and television; but contacts limited to
these channels of communication are unlikely to achieve the results
sought. As a rule, parents must also come to the school. There are at
least three reasons for this. First, such a procedure makes it more
practical for the school to have continual face-to-face communication
with parents, the kind of communication that research studies and
experience indicate would be most likely to effect changes in the
parents' behavior and attitudes. Second, it makes possible a more varied
range of school-parent activities, particularly when the school itself, or
a similarly equipped building is used for these activities. And third, it
enables parents to meet in groups and thus reap purported benefits of
group experience.

But the fact is that it is markedly difficult to secure in-school parent
contacts in depressed urban neighborhoods (78, 125, 128). Fusco, who
studied the school-parent programs of 20 depressed urban area schools,
reports that the "parents, as revealed in the interviews, were reluctant
to visit the schools their children attended, did not become involved in
the activities of school-related organizations, and were generally shy
with school personnel and suspicious toward them" (56, p. 59).

The reasons offered for this gulf are numerous. It is held that parents
do not care (78, 85, 126, 133); that they resent the school (99, 106);
that they think that the teacher, whom they perceive as belonging to
a higher social class, looks down on them (56, 80, 99); that they do
not know how to help their children (56, 109); that they do not think
that they can influence their children's school life (79); that they have
had unpleasant experiences with the school (85); that they have no
concern for long-range problems and therefore do not see the need to
go to school unless their children are in trouble (149); and that they
are pessimistic and uncertain about the future (106).

On the other hand, the schools are held responsible for the gulf because teachers fear parents (93); because teachers live outside the
school neighborhood (52); because school authorities are not interested in the welfare of the pupil, some even being antagonistic toward
parents and children (25); because teachers use educational jargon
(106); because the reading level required by communications from
the school is too high (79); because the school does not know what
should be done (105); because the formalized activities of the school
discourage parents (79); because the school has not developed sound

machinery to provide for improved relations (106); and because inadequate staffing precludes having the time for parental contacts (99).

In assessing these reasons, one fact demands preeminent attention: *they all pertain to lower-class parents and to schools in lower-class neighborhoods.* Could it be, then, that the reasons for school-parent estrangement in depressed urban neighborhoods might be explained mainly as a function of social class?

The point of view taken here is that they can be. Research studies show that there is a direct relationship (for any neighborhood) between social class and parent participation in school activities. In perhaps the only investigation addressed exclusively to a study of this relationship,[6] Correll, using data that he secured from 601 families, confirmed his hypotheses that (in his words):

1. *Upper-class parents and middle-class parents of pupils will communicate with the school more frequently proportionately than will parents of the lower social classes.*

2. *The highest proportionate number of parents who failed to honor the parent-teacher conferences scheduled for the parents of all pupils in November 1960, will be found to be the lower social classes.*

3. *The PTA membership will be found to be predominantly made up of upper-class and middle-class parents, with upper-middle-class parents being most active in attendance and service of any of the social classes (32).*

In substance, the findings of at least 11 other directly relevant research studies support these hypotheses (51, 65, 71, 78, 84, 122, 128, 135, 139, 141, 149).

Research studies show, moreover, that there is a relationship between social class and participation in formal voluntary organizations as such—and to parents, the school is a formal voluntary organization. For although persons of low socioeconomic status (SES) participate in indigenous and relatively informal groups (62, 90, 93), research findings consistently reveal that they participate in formal voluntary organizations significantly less than persons of higher SES (5, 9, 46, 54, 62, 86). Foskett (54) reasons that this is because they: lack contact with people who do participate in such organizations; lack the ability to communicate in group situations; have no cultural expectations that would lead them to participate; do not see the relevance of participation to their needs; and lack the time and energy required for participation.

[6] An extensive survey of the literature revealed no other such study.

A comparison of Foskett's reasons explaining the nonparticipation of low SES persons in formal voluntary organizations with the reasons listed above for their nonparticipation in *school* activities makes it clear that the two sets of reasons are basically the same. Although this does not necessarily mean that the underlying operative factors are identical in both situations, the evidence already cited strongly suggests that this indeed is the case.

In sum, then, research evidence conclusively demonstrates that persons of low SES do not commonly participate either in formal voluntary organizations per se or in parent activities sponsored by the school, the school being to parents a formal voluntary organization—and the explanations offered for such nonparticipation are strikingly similar in both instances. The implication of this parallel is inescapable: *to explain the reasons for parent nonparticipation in school activities is at the same time to explain the reasons for their nonparticipation in other formal voluntary organizations, and vice versa.*

This socioeconomic rationale becomes even more credible when one considers that SES has been shown to be significantly related to a wide range of behavior. For example, SES has been found to be associated with the following: self-esteem (76, 150*); emotional and social adjustment (26, 76,* 91*); delinquency (76,* 77, 128); interests (25,* 81,* 89, 111*); values (10,* 36, 69,* 89); child-rearing practices (18,* 68, 74*); academic motivation (76, 118,* 148*); value placed on education by parents (24, 70,* 117, 118*); white attitude toward school integration (61,* 140*); teacher perception of students (1, 37, 44, 148); school offices held by students (1, 69*); student participation in extracurricular activities (1, 25,* 69*); distribution of rewards and penalties to students (1, 128); student promotion (128); student group and track placement (69,* 128, 141, 147); and student attendance (39,* 95,* 128).

More importantly, studies consistently show that school achievement and social class are positively and significantly related (7, 20, 25, 58, 63, 101). To explain school-parent estrangement in depressed urban neighborhoods mainly as a function of social class, then, is to get at the heart not just of parent participation but also of the very problem that parent participation is expected to help solve. This interpretation suggests a crucial question: Does the fact that this estrangement is typically explained by personal, psychological, or school factors, as in most of the explanations enumerated at the beginning of this section, lead the schools to emphasize the wrong approaches? To answer this question, it is necessary to know what schools are doing. This is the concern of the next two sections.

* An asterisk indicates the conclusion is based on statistically significant findings.

APPROACHES TO ACCOMPLISHING GOALS

The schools employ a diversified approach in attempting to accomplish one or more of the four enumerated goals of the school-parent programs. The intent in this section is to indicate the range of this diversity. For the purpose of clarity each goal, with some of the major methods of implementation, is considered separately. It is important to note, however, that the methods used to achieve one goal may be applied simultaneously to achieve other goals as well.

1. *Techniques to help parents guide their children's learning development more intelligently.* Parents are told specific ways that they can assist their children (56, 82, 103, 144), they engage in child study under the direction of the school (16, 56, 96), and they participate in the study of pupil and neighborhood needs (14, 56). Teacher-parent planning for the child is utilized (16, 48, 56), the purposes and program of the school are explained to parents (2, 56, 102), and parents are urged to commit themselves, sometimes in writing, to helping their children (56, 130, 132). Throughout, an effort is made to convince parents of the interest of the school in their children (56, 119, 130).

2. *Techniques to help parents become better learning models.* Basic education is provided, and so are opportunities for cultural enrichment experiences and for personal development (15, 48, 82, 144). Also, opportunities are given for parents to make conspicuous contributions to the school, i.e., to perform meritorious tasks that can be seen by pupils (14, 27, 48, 55, 56, 94, 103, 119).

3. *Techniques to assist parents in improving their home conditions and neighborhood life.* Marketable and job-getting skills are taught (56, 66, 116, 134, 144). Help is given in regard to housekeeping management and human relations problems within the family through short-term courses such as budgeting and cooking, through group counseling, and through personal contact, printed matter, and special field trips (56, 83, 116). Parents are informed as to the community agencies that can help them (15, 56, 60, 102), and in some cases, the school itself renders economic and medical help (87, 96, 102, 127, 138). The aid and cooperation of community agencies are accepted and solicited in various areas, for example, in providing for pupils' recreational, health, and physical needs, and in carrying out extracurricular activities (2, 25, 56, 72, 86, 127, 144, 145, 146, 147). Neighborhood leadership is given and indigenous leadership is developed (56, 72, 85, 127, 144, 145). For instance, one school helped in getting condemned houses razed and in establishing a health clinic. Indigenous leadership has been developed by encouraging the forma-

tion of neighborhood organizations and teaching interested persons how to run them. Finally, the school is used as a center for neighborhood recreational and social activities (45, 56, 85, 96), and, in some cases, notably Flint, Michigan, and New Haven, Connecticut, as a community school (27, 42, 83). Community school here means a school that functions as the center for servicing the educational, cultural, recreational, social, and economic needs of the children, youth, and adults of the neighborhood.

4. *Techniques to help teachers gain a better understanding of the disadvantaged child, parent, and neighborhood.* Teachers interact with parents through home visits and in-school activities (15, 56, 60, 94, 103, 121, 127, 130, 138, 144). Opportunities are provided for teachers to engage in formal study of the disadvantaged through workshops and through in-service courses (56, 93, 121). Within the individual school unit, intrastaff discussion about the disadvantaged is carried on (27, 56, 60, 103, 121), and data about the immediate neighborhood are secured and studied (14, 41, 56). Further, book lists on the disadvantaged are prepared for the staff (121).

GUIDELINES FOR SECURING PARENT CONTACTS

Behind these various approaches is a multiplicity of guidelines, some stated and others implied. The list that follows is an attempt to categorize some of the most important of these (and in the process to convey their diversity).[7]

Administering Contacts

1. Responsibility for administering the school-parent program should be assigned to full-time professional or competent lay personnel (56, 79, 83, 133).+

2. If a school has a large number of disadvantaged students, it should employ either a lay or a professional person to act exclusively as a liaison agent between teacher and parent (79).* (A point to note about this guideline is that it emphasizes *individual* school-parent contacts at the neglect of a comprehensive school-parent program.)

---

[7] The categorization and labeling of these guidelines are subject to question, but the guidelines themselves come from the literature.

+ This symbol signifies that the guideline is both expressly stated and implied in the source(s) cited.

* This symbol signifies that the guideline is expressly stated in the source(s) cited.

3. Where school systems do not want lay personnel to be administrators of school-parent programs, their paid services should be secured in subordinate positions (27).*

4. The person administering the school-parent program should be *specially* trained (83).* (It will be noted that this differs from the first and second guidelines, neither of which calls for special training.)

5. Contacts with parents should be established early in the school year and continued regularly throughout the rest of the year (56).°

6. In like fashion, contacts with parents should be established in the child's preschool years and continued throughout the rest of his school life (16, 27, 56).°

7. Where parental response is unsatisfactory, the aid of other family members should be solicited, and if this does not work, the aid of neighbors should be sought (27, 126).*

8. The school must take the initiative; parents in depressed neighborhoods will seldom do so (56, 112).*

9. Since the school cannot meet the total needs of parents and neighborhood, it should accept and seek the cooperation of private and governmental agencies (2, 104, 144).+

Selecting Methods

1. A variety of methods of contacts should be employed; no one method suffices (55, 56, 126, 132, 133).*

2. Because they are the most effective, methods that involve individual face-to-face teacher-parent contacts should take precedence over all other methods of contact (6, 16, 56, 102).*

3. Because they are better than in-school contacts for learning parents' thoughts and feelings, provisions should be made for home visits (114).*

Notifying Parents

1. A variety of ways of notifying parents should be used to notify them of future activities, e.g., through pupils, by telephone, at neighborhood meetings (55, 56, 103, 121).+

2. Special emphasis should be placed on notifying parents in face-to-face situations (56, 121).+

3. Indigenous groups and parents should be used to help notify other parents (56, 78, 83, 103, 116).+

° This symbol signifies that the guideline is implied, but not expressly stated in the source(s) cited.

Persuading Parents

1. Parents should be used as resource persons and should otherwise be given a chance to make a contribution to the school program (28, 56, 75, 79).+

2. To get parents to come to the school, school personnel must first actually go to the parents rather than notifying them at second hand (79).*

3. Outstanding leaders of the same ethnic group as the particular parents involved should be called upon to serve in appropriate resource capacities (27).*

4. School-parent programs should include activities that provide opportunities for parents to observe their children in the school situations and to see the work they prepare (56, 78).°

5. Special projects should be given precedence over general meetings (130).°

6. An "open door policy" wherein parents are welcomed to visit the school at any time should be practiced and publicized (56, 83).*

7. A theme should be chosen to express the aim(s) of the school-parent program and this theme should be continually used in school-parent communications (104, 130).°

8. The interest of the school in the disadvantaged child, parent, and neighborhood should be made known through both words and deeds; put another way, the school should identify with the neighborhood (56, 83, 100, 104, 106, 120, 121, 130).+ It might do so, for example, by helping parents to get condemned houses razed, assisting them in securing a health clinic, and making the school a center for social and recreational activities.

9. The results of school-parent activities should be shared with parents—for example, at specially arranged school-parent meetings, or through formal written reports (17, 130).°

10. The school should encourage and show appreciation for all parental efforts, even the unsuccessful ones (34).* It might do this by, for example, giving a special dinner for parents or simply writing them a letter of appreciation.

11. The school should be used as a community school (27, 42, 83).*

Conducting Contacts

1. Parents should have the opportunity to help plan and carry out the activities in which the school wants them to participate (56, 83, 104, 121).*

2. Where possible, school-parent activities should be structured so that they are informal and so that they provide for social interaction (6, 56, 78, 103, 109, 112).*

3. In so far as status differences between parents and school personnel manifest themselves in such areas as dress and conversation, school personnel should seek to de-emphasize the difference (79).*

4. Parents should be given a chance to raise their self-concept through success experiences in school-related activities (41, 79).+

Deciding Content

1. The content matter should be kept "light," i.e., simple enough to be understood easily, and yet mature enough to convey respect for parents' intelligence (34, 60).* This is similar to the problem of developing low-vocabulary, high-interest material for the disadvantaged child.

2. Parents should be given specific rather than general information (56, 82, 93, 103, 109, 144).+

3. The interests and needs of parents should be directly solicited and taken into account (6, 56, 104, 114).*

4. A school-parent program should be comprehensive in that it should aim to meet the total educational, cultural, recreational, social, and economic needs of the children, youth, and adults of the neighborhood (27, 42, 83).*

RESULTS

This section turns from the aims, activities, and guidelines of the school-parent programs to their reported results. It should be understood that these reports do not necessarily reflect the potential efficacy of the activities and guidelines per se. They may instead simply mirror the outcomes of these activities and guidelines *as practiced* by the reporting schools. It is within this perspective that the categorical summary which follows should be considered.

1. *Techniques to help parents guide their children's learning development more intelligently* and *to help them become better learning models.* Typical results reported in this area maintain variously that some parents: now plan trips on their own (56); have gained a better understanding of their children (56); have increased their feeling of adequacy and self-esteem, giving up in the process their self-defeating attitudes (56); give moral support to the school (56, 83); have bought

more magazines (133); accept and carry out staff suggestions (114); ask teachers to visit their homes (114); and enroll in adult education classes and even complete high school (83).

2. *Techniques to assist parents in improving their home conditions and neighborhood life.* Some parents are said to have improved the physical appearance of their homes (56); some to have become leaders in school and neighborhood activities (56); and others to have gotten a more realistic view of their problems (90). Several more strictly neighborhood effects claimed by schools are getting traffic lights and signs installed, and getting vacant houses boarded up (56). The Flint, Michigan, school system, which has one of the oldest community-school programs in the country, is reported to have achieved more impressive results in the neighborhood area: among them, elimination of racial tension, increased civic pride, cultural growth, expansion of services, and improved health standards (83). Atypical results (consequences of a concerted anti-poverty effort) are reported by Los Angeles and New Haven, two of the cities that have established pilot projects under the Manpower and Development Training Act (MDTA)[8] of 1962 (30, 114). In the Los Angeles project, as of its last report in 1964, 63 unskilled young adults with a high school education have been trained and 48 of these have jobs; all but four of the remaining 15 have prospects of getting jobs. Of 4,124 applicants in the New Haven project, 1,457 (or 35 per cent) have been placed in on-the-job training situations or have secured regular jobs.

3. *Techniques to help teachers gain a better understanding of the disadvantaged child, parent, and neighborhood.* Reports state in general terms that school-parent contacts are helping to accomplish this goal but give no specifics (56, 85, 114, 147).

What can be said about these results? Such exact figures as the schools provide, as commendable and encouraging as they are in some cases,[9] warrant only the generalization that some schools are attracting some parents to some activities (45, 75, 83, 85, 114, 126, 130). In fact, an estimate based on the literature is that the typical activity draws no more than 20 per cent of the parents.

The large successes claimed for school-parent programs, then, must be called into question, if only on the basis of numbers. And the ques-

---

[8] The MDTA is a federally-financed training program in skills that are in demand. In Los Angeles and in New Haven, the State Employment Service, the State Division of Vocational Education, and the local school board cooperate in implementation of the program, calling upon representatives of labor and management as needed.

[9] Farren School in Chicago, for example, reports almost perfect attendance at teacher-parent conferences for kindergarten through eighth grade (56).

tion of numbers is not insignificant. They represent at least potential power and influence. As any student of history knows, the importance of an event is often judged by the number of people involved or affected. Thus, to evaluate the success of school-parent programs, it is crucial to ask: How many parents plan trips on their own or have a better understanding of their children as a result of contacts with the school? How many houses have been rehabilitated as a result of school-neighborhood cooperation? And how many teachers have improved their teaching because of contacts with or study about parents?

The fact is that the successes reported above rest almost exclusively on evidence based on incidental or subjectively selected comments and observations and on "miraculous episodes" (56, 75, 121, 146, 147). The latter may consist of nothing more than a pupil suddenly getting an "A" for the first time; in doing this he presumably makes the entire program a success! Plans to evaluate school-parent programs using an adequate sample, to say nothing about using appropriate procedures and valid and reliable instruments, are difficult to uncover. Evaluation designs such as those that are part of the Detroit Great Cities Project (40), Mobilization for Youth's School-Community Relations Program (92), and the Richmond, Virginia, Human Development Project (115, 116) are among the few that appear to meet good research criteria. Since school-parent programs are usually part of broader programs, it does make it harder to evaluate them fully, but this does not preclude assessing them to learn certain effects, such as the expressed attitude changes in parents, teachers, and principals, and changes in pupils' perception of their home life.

The ultimate test of school-parent programs, of course, is whether they contribute to the disadvantaged child's school achievement.[10] In this regard, pupil achievement gains have been reported by some schools (16, 56, 83, 105, 126, 130). But these gains have been made under broad programs. It is not possible, therefore, to attribute them to school-parent contacts alone. Nor is it possible to say what part, if any, these contacts had. In fact, there are at least three studies (101, 114, 123) that suggest that such programs exert no influence on pupil achievement.

In sum, as far as can be determined, there is no research evidence disclosing that school-parent programs in depressed urban neighborhoods have had any substantial success in themselves (without other

[10] Since community schools are committed to serving both pupil and community needs, they present an exception to this standard. Their effectiveness must be measured both by pupil achievement and by the quality of community life. This standard applies also to any school that accepts community improvement as a goal in itself.

program changes), in achieving either their immediate objectives or
their ultimate goal. It would be surprising if, individually, the bulk of
the programs has influenced more than 10 per cent of the parents to
improve significantly the intellectual environment they provide for
their children.

DISCUSSION

In view of this analysis, the question posed at the outset becomes
most critical, i.e., inasmuch as school-parent estrangement in depressed
urban neighborhoods can be explained mainly as a function of social
class, does the fact that it is typically explained by personal, psychological, and school factors lead the schools to emphasize the wrong goals?
The position taken here is that while it does not lead to an emphasis
on the wrong goals, it does cause a neglect of other important goals.

A school-parent program that attacks the basic causes of parent non-
cooperation would have to concentrate on the three chief and closely
interrelated factors that determine social class position—namely, education, occupation, and income. Few programs seem to be doing this.[11]
What Fusco (56, p. 63) concludes about the 20 schools that he studied
appears to apply to almost all: "the schools probably . . . [give]
greater priority to activities designed to help parents help their children
take fuller advantage of their schooling opportunities than to any other
practice." Moreover, the schools that are giving attention to parents'
education and occupation and thus indirectly to their income (this
being all that could be expected from the school as regards income)
seem to be doing so in a way not likely to induce significant change.
To teach a parent basic education and to make it possible for him to
get a high school diploma is not enough. Nor is it sufficient just to
teach him some of the vocational and technical skills that the school's
available resources happen to enable it to teach. Where needed, a connection must be established between, on the one hand, the education
and skills with which the school equips a parent and, on the other, the
parent's opportunity to use this *education and skill* in an *occupation*
where he can get an *income* that is above the poverty line. This need
demands that the school work closely not just with welfare and char-

---

[11] Relevant to this point is a study made by the Opinion Research Center at the
University of Chicago in 1963, which showed "that the vast pool of untrained, un-
dereducated, and largely unemployed manpower in this country is not being
touched by adult education," the average adult student having a high school
education or better (84).

itable agencies, as it is doing in many instances, but also with government and industry, as it is doing in only a few instances.

The job-training emphasis that is present in comprehensive anti-poverty programs like those in Los Angeles and in New Haven is worth emulating. The New Haven pre-work basic education program for adults, which was scheduled to have begun April 1965, seems particularly exemplary (30). It calls for long-term remedial education and skill training for educable adults. This training is to be done on an individual basis, and therefore the time spent in the program will vary with individuals. Until there is a focus on social class factors, such as seems to be provided in the Los Angeles and New Haven programs, it is doubtful whether school-parent programs can alter fundamentally the intellectual environment provided by the depressed urban home and neighborhood. Certainly this is the lesson of experience to date.

But this experience does not allow a final judgment. Not enough attention has been given to these programs to be conclusive about what they can reasonably be expected to accomplish.

Regarding school-home relations generally, Pearson (110), in his 1956 study of the research literature in this field, concludes that:

> *Adequate means have not been developed for the appraisal of programs or for evaluating specific activities in an objective manner. Survey studies have been concerned mainly with what was being done, with little effort made to determine the effectiveness of what was being done.*

Three years later, the late Ernest Osborne, a noted authority in school-parent relations, went beyond this in his assertion that there is a "comparative meagerness of experience and thinking in the area of home-school cooperation" (108, p. 47). This situation has not changed (151). It is imperative, then, that a careful assessment be made of what relatively successful programs have really done and how they have done it.

Pertinent to this issue is the fact that at least four studies imply nearly the opposite of what is advanced here: that even in the absence of a concentration on socioeconomic factors, school-parent programs can help to increase the school achievement of the disadvantaged child. Both Schiff (122) and Duncan (47) discovered that children of low SES parents who participated in programs of planned contacts made significantly greater achievement gains in reading and in new mathematics, respectively, than comparably matched children of no- or few-contact parents. Giddings (57) found that although the education and occupational differences between the low SES parents of high-achieving science students as compared with their low-achieving counterparts were minimal, the former were from homes characterized by more living space, by more books and magazines, and by better places to study. Dave (35), in a study that perhaps deserves replication, found the home environment of his 60 elementary school subjects to be substantially more closely related to their academic achievement than the SES of their parents was related to this achievement.

The thinking of several other scholars (in addition to Niemeyer and Clark, already quoted) is in accord with the import of this evidence. On the basis of one research study and data from the 1951 census on educational attainment, Wayland (142), for example, states that factors other than social class variables may be operating to retard the disadvantaged child's educational achievement. He specifically mentions ethnicity, religion, and subculture. In addition to the documentation provided by Wayland, further support for this contention is supplied by the ethnic differences noted among comparable SES groups in, for example, child-rearing practices (38), attitude toward illegitimacy (19), and school achievement (44). And David and Pearl Ausubel even assert that: "The extreme intellectual impoverishment of the Negro home *over and above* its lower social-class status reflects the poor standard of English spoken in the home and the general lack of books, magazines, and stimulating conversation" (4, p. 125).

The validity of these opinions, as well as the reliability of the related studies cited, remain to be established. In the interim, to dismiss these opinions and their supporting evidence is to do so at the pain of some intellectual discomfort.

But on the basis of what has been established, the reviewer cannot help concluding that an approach devoid of emphasis on social class factors holds more hope than promise.[12] Such an approach entails trying to change the behavior of a population without altering significantly the basic contributing circumstances. It assumes that parents' possession of knowledge about what they should do to help improve their children's school achievement will result in commensurate behavior.[13] If this were to come about, hope would have indeed tri-

[12] The problem of getting parents to participate in school-parent programs, for whatever reason, is not likely to vanish automatically by placing the central focus on social class factors, of course (31, 116). But this approach, combining the best from commonly used approaches, would appear to hold the most promise, both in getting parents to participate and in influencing their behavior once their participation is obtained.

[13] It is realized that a change in a person's circumstances may not result in instant behavioral changes either, but the person's receptivity to change is likely to be significantly increased. For this reason alone, it is important to continue the emphasis on helping parents to help their children.

umphed over experience. For this is an eighteenth-century faith in reason per se—without due attention to other relevant considerations—that has long since proved unwarranted. It is true that school-parent programs helped in the assimilation of immigrants (113), but the extent of that help is subject to question. As Berger observes: "Certainly a large number of newcomers at no time during this period [1900–20] came into contact with any formal educational institution—and yet they managed to be 'Americanized'" (11, p. 126). Could it be that they "managed" because of the existence of an open economy (58) which, in offering an opportunity to make a living, at the same time provided and made possible exposure to American traditions? Further, is it not logical to assume that those immigrants who came into contact with some formal educational institution were similarly affected by this open economy, and that in their Americanization the additional element of institutional training only served as a facilitating influence?

The lesson seems to be that to help accomplish with all deliberate speed the central goal of increasing the school achievement of the disadvantaged child, school-parent programs in depressed urban neighborhoods must concentrate not just on the correlates of low SES that retard school achievement, such as parents not reading to their children and not providing a place in the home for them to study, but simultaneously on the very factors that make for low SES: substandard education, subminimal income, and subsistence occupation, or worse, unemployment. This is not said with the expectation that social and economic conditions thereby will be so improved that the low SES category will disappear, but it is stated with the firm belief that if the bottom floor, so to speak, can be raised (say 50 per cent above minimum living standards), an intellectually impoverished home and neighborhood environment and the low pupil academic achievement associated with both would no longer be commanding problems. At this point, school-parent programs in formerly depressed urban neighborhoods would fade away or else would be redesigned either to meet new challenges or to fit the usual historical function of such programs, that is, to secure the kind of public understanding that will result in moral and financial support of the public school.

REFERENCES

1. Abrahamson, Stephen. 1952. "Our Status System and Rewards," *Journal of Educational Sociology*. 25: 441–50.

2. American Association of School Administrators and Research Division. 1963. *School Programs for the Disadvantaged.* Educational Research Service Circular No. 2. Washington, D.C.: Educational Research Service.

3. Atzmon, Ezri. 1958. "The Impact of Education Programs on the Acculturation of Adult Jewish Immigrants in Metropolitan Detroit (1949–1955)." Unpublished dissertation. University of Michigan.

4. Ausubel, David P., and Ausubel, Pearl. 1963. "Ego Development Among Segregated Negro Children," in *Education in Depressed Areas,* ed. A. Harry Passow. New York: Teachers College, Columbia University.

5. Axelrod, Morris. 1956. "Urban Structure and Social Participation," *American Sociological Review.* 21: 13–19.

6. Baltimore City Public Schools. 1963. *An Early School Admissions Project Progress Report, 1962–1963.* Baltimore: Public School System.

7. Barnes, Paul John. 1962. "Community Characteristics Related to Secondary School Achievement." Unpublished dissertation. New York: Teachers College, Columbia University.

8. Barr, John A. 1958. *The Elementary Teacher and Guidance.* New York: Holt, Rinehart and Winston.

9. Bell, Wendel, and Force, Maryanne T. 1956. "Urban Neighborhood Types and Participation in Formal Associations," *American Sociological Review.* 21: 25–34.

10. Bendix, Reinhard, and Lipset, Seymour Martin, eds. 1953. "Differential Class Behavior," in *Class, Status, and Power: A Reader in Social Stratification.* Glencoe, Illinois: Free Fress.

11. Berger, Morris Isaiah. 1956. "The Settlement, the Immigrant and the Public School: A Study of the Influence of the Settlement Movement and the New Migration upon Public Education." Unpublished dissertation. New York: Teachers College, Columbia University.

12. Bloom, Benjamin S. 1964. *Stability and Change in Human Characteristics.* New York: John Wiley.

13. Blyth, Donald J. 1957. "Working with Parents in Disorganized Urban Community Areas," in *Parents and the School.* Twenty-Fourth Yearbook of the Department of Elementary School Principals. Washington, D.C.: National Education Association.

14. Bollenbacher, Joan. 1963. "Cincinnati, Ohio," in *School Programs for the Disadvantaged.*

15. Boswell, Anita Y. 1963. "Some Special Projects of the Chicago Board of Education," in *Programs for the Educationally Disadvantaged.* A Report of a Conference on Teaching Children and Youth Who Are Educationally Disadvantaged, May 21–23, 1962. Washington, D.C.: Government Printing Office.

16. Brazziel, William F. n.d. "An Experiment in the Development of Readiness in a Culturally Disadvantaged Group of First Grade Children." Mimeographed.

17. ————, and Gordon, Margaret. 1963. "Replications of Some Aspects of the Higher Horizons Program in a Southern Junior High School," *The Bulletin of the National Association of Secondary School Principals.* 47: 135–43.

18. Bronfenbrenner, Urie. 1958. "Socialization and Social Class Through Time and Space," in *Readings in Social Psychology,* eds. Eleanor E. Maccoby, Theodore M. Newcomb, and Eugene L. Hartley. New York: Holt, Rinehart and Winston.

19. Cahill, Imogene D. 1956. "Facts and Fallacies about Illegitimacy," *Nursing Forum.* 4: 39–55.

20. Chicago Board of Education. 1964. *The Public Schools of Chicago: A Survey for the Board of Education of the City of Chicago* by Robert J. Havighurst. Chicago: Board of Education.

21. ————. 1963. *Guidelines for the Primary Program of Continuous Development.* City-wide Continuous Development Committee. Chicago: The Board.

22. Clark, Kenneth B. 1965. *Dark Ghetto.* New York: Harper and Row.

23. ————. 1963. "Educational Stimulation of Racially Disadvantaged Children," in *Education in Depressed Areas,* ed. Passow.

24. Cloward, Richard A. and Jones, James A. 1963. "Social Class: Educational Attitudes and Participation," in *Education in Depressed Areas,* ed. Passow.

25. Coleman, Hubert A. 1940. "The Relationship of Socio-Economic Status to the Performance of Junior High School Students," *Journal of Experimental Education.* 9: 61–63.

26. Community Progress, Inc. 1963. "Administration and Budget," *New Haven Youth Development Program.* Part IV. New Haven: Community Progress, Inc.

27. ————. "Programs," *New Haven Youth Development Program.* Part II.

28. ————. "Research," *New Haven Youth Development Program.* Part III.

29. ————. "The Setting," *New Haven Youth Development Pragram.* Part I.

30. ————. 1965. *Community Action Program Review.* New Haven: Community Progress, Inc.

31. Cook County Department of Public Aid. 1962. *A Study to Determine the Literacy Level of Able-Bodied Persons Receiving Public Assistance.* Chicago: The Department.

32. Correll, Nolan E. 1963. "The Effect of Social Class on Parental Contacts with the Public School System." Unpublished dissertation. St. Louis, Missouri: Washington University.

33. Cremin, Lawrence A. 1962. *The Transformation of the School*. New York: Alfred A. Knopf.

34. Daugherty, Louise G. 1963. "Working with Disadvantaged Parents," *NEA Journal*. 52: 18–20.

35. Dave, R. H. 1963. "The Identification and Measurement of Environmental Process Variables that Are Related to Educational Achievement." Unpublished dissertation. Chicago: University of Chicago.

36. Davis, Allison. 1962. "The Culture of the Slum." On file at the Horace Mann-Lincoln Institute of School Experimentation, Urban Education, Teachers College, Columbia University.

37. ———. 1955. *Social-Class Influences upon Learning*. Cambridge: Harvard University Press.

38. ———, and Havighurst, Robert J. 1946. "Social Class and Color Differences in Child-Rearing," *American Sociological Review*. 11: 698–710.

39. Davis, James S. 1953. "Social Class Factors and School Attendance," *The Harvard Educational Review*. 23: 175–185.

40. Detroit Great Cities Project. 1962. "A Plan for Evaluating Major Activities in Great Cities School Improvement Program." Detroit: The Project.

41. ———. 1961. "Working Toward More Effective Education: A Report on the Detroit Cities Project—After One Year." Detroit: The Project.

42. Detroit Public Schools and the Ford Foundation. 1963. *Recommendations for New Eastern High School and Family Center*. A Report prepared by Community Planning for Community Schools in Cooperation with the Department of Planning and Building Studies, School Housing Division. Detroit: The authors.

43. Deutsch, Martin P. 1963. "The Disadvantaged Child and the Learning Process," in *Education in Depressed Areas,* ed. Passow.

44. ———. 1960. *Minority Group and Class Status as Related to Social and Personality Factors in Scholastic Achievement*. The Society for Applied Anthropology Monograph No. 2. Ithaca, New York: New York State School of Industrial and Labor Relations, Cornell University.

45. Disare, Charles F. 1963. "Newburgh, New York," *School Programs for the Disadvantaged.*

46. Dotson, Floyd. 1951. "Patterns of Voluntary Association Among Urban Working-Class Families," *American Sociological Review*. 16: 687–93.

47. Duncan, Roger. 1964. "An Experimental Study of the Effect of Parents' Knowledge on Student Performance in SMSG Mathematics," *The Journal of Educational Research*. 58: 135–37.

48. Dye, Grover C., and Nolte, Margaret C. 1963. "Montgomery County, Maryland," *School Programs for the Disadvantaged.*

49. Elsbree, Willard S., and McNally, Harold J. 1959. "Administering School-Community Relations," in *Elementary School Administration and Supervision.* New York: American Book Company.

50. Everett, Samuel. 1938. *The Community School.* New York: Appleton-Century.

51. Farley, Gene C. 1957. "The Parent-Teacher Association in Selected School Districts of Kentucky." Project Report. Nashville, Tennessee: George Peabody College for Teachers.

52. Finch, William H. 1961. "Bringing Together Family and School," *Chicago Schools Journal.* 43: 84–86.

53. Ford Foundation. 1962. *The Society of the Streets.* A report on the Ford Foundation's Great Cities Program by Walter E. Ashley. New York: The Foundation.

54. Foskett, John M. 1959. "The Influence of Social Participation on Community Programs and Activities," in *Community Structure and Analysis,* ed. Marvin B. Sussman. New York: Thomas Y. Crowell.

55. Furno, Orlando F., and Brunner, Catherine. 1963. "Baltimore, Maryland," *School Programs for the Disadvantaged.*

56. Fusco, Gene C. 1964. *School-Home Partnership in Depressed Urban Areas.* Office of Education Bulletin No. 20. Washington, D.C.: Government Printing Office.

57. Giddings, Morsley G. 1965. "Factors Related to Achievement in Junior High School Science in Disadvantaged Areas of New York City." Unpublished dissertation. New York: Teachers College, Columbia University.

58. Goldberg, Miriam L. 1963. "Factors Affecting Educational Attainment in Depressed Urban Areas," in *Education in Depressed Areas,* ed. Passow.

59. Graham, Grace. 1963. "The School's Job in the Community," in *The Public School in the American Community.* New York: Harper and Row.

60. Great Cities Grey Areas Program. 1961. *One Year of the Great Cities Grey Areas Program in the Hough Community of Cleveland, Ohio, 1960–61.* Cleveland: The Project.

61. Greenfield, Robert Walter. 1959. "Factors Associated with White Parents' Attitudes Toward School Desegregation in a Central Florida Community." Unpublished dissertation. Columbus, Ohio: Ohio State University.

62. Greer, Scott, and Kube, Ella. 1959. "Urbanism and Social Structure," in *Community Structure and Analysis,* ed. Sussman.

63. Harlem Youth Opportunities Unlimited, Inc. 1964. *Youth in the Ghetto: A Study of the Consequences of Powerlessness and a Blueprint for Change.* New York: The authors.

64. Havighurst, Robert J., and Neugarten, Bernice L. 1962. "The School in the Community," *Society and Education.* Boston: Allyn and Bacon.

65. Henderson, Lee G. 1954. "A Study of Certain School-Community Relationships with Special Reference to Working Patterns of School Principals." Unpublished dissertation. Gainesville, Florida: University of Florida.

66. Henly, Benjamin J. 1963. "Washington, D.C.," *School Programs for the Disadvantaged.*

67. Hilliard, Raymond M. 1963. "Chicago's War on Illiteracy Is Paying Off!" *New York Herald Tribune, This Week Magazine.* May 5.

68. Hoffman, Martin L. 1960. "Power Assertion By the Parent and Its Impact on the Child," *Child Development.* 31: 129–43.

69. Hollingshead, August B. 1949. *Elmtown's Youth.* New York: John Wiley.

70. Hyman, Herbert H. 1953. "The Value Systems of Different Classes: A Social-Psychological Contribution to the Analysis of Stratification," in *Class, Status, and Power: A Reader in Social Stratification,* eds. Bendix and Lipset.

71. Kaplan, Abraham A. 1943. *Socio-Economic Circumstances and Adult Participation in Certain Cultural and Educational Activities.* Contributions to Education, No. 889. New York: Teachers College, Columbia University.

72. Kenefick, Thomas A. 1963. "Springfield, Massachusetts," *School Programs for the Disadvantaged.*

73. Knezevich, Stephen J. 1962. "The Community, Its Schools, and the Administration: The Interaction of Forces," in *Administration of Public Education.* New York: Harper and Brothers.

74. Carrol, Melvin L. and Carrol, Eleanor E. 1960. "Social Class and the Allocation of Parental Responsibilities," *Sociometry.* 23: 372–92.

75. Kornhauser, Louis H. 1964. "Improving Language Arts Instruction for Disadvantaged Children and Youth." Third Work Conference on Curriculum and Teaching in Depressed Urban Areas, June 22–July 3. New York: Teachers College, Columbia University.

76. Krugman, Judith I. 1956. "Cultural Deprivation and Child Development," *High Points.* 38: 5–20.

77. Liddle, Gordon P. 1963. "Existing and Projected Research on Reading in Relationship to Juvenile Delinquency," in *Role of the School in Prevention of Juvenile Delinquency,* ed. William R. Carriker. Cooperative Research Monograph Series, No. 10. Washington, D.C.: Government Printing Office.

78. ———. 1963. "Modifying the School Experience of Culturally Handicapped Children in the Primary Grades," in *Programs for the Educationally Disadvantaged.*

79. ———, and Rockwell, Robert E. 1965. "The Role of Parents and Family Life," *The Journal of Negro Education.* 34: 56–62.

80. McNassor, Donald. 1954. "Barriers and Gateways in School-Community Relationships," *The Journal of Educational Sociology.* 28: 1–10.

81. Maas, Jeanette, and Michael, William B. 1964. "The Relationship of Interest Choices to Social Group Membership and to Sex Differences," *California Journal of Educational Research.* 15: 24–33.

82. Manch, Joseph. 1963. "Buffalo, New York," *School Programs for the Disadvantaged.*

83. Manley, Frank J., Reed, Bernard W., and Burns, Robert K. 1961. *The Community School in Action: The Flint Program.* A Joint Project of the Mott Foundation and the University of Chicago. Chicago: Joint Youth Development Committee.

84. Mann, George C. 1963. "The Development of Public School Adult Education," in *Public School Adult Education: A Guide for Administrators,* ed. John H. Thatcher. Revised edition. Washington, D.C.: National Association of Public School Educators.

85. Marburger, Carl A. 1963. "Considerations for Educational Planning," in *Education in Depressed Areas,* ed. Passow.

86. Mather, William C. 1941. "Income and Social Participation," *American Sociological Review.* 6: 380–84.

87. Matthews, Don E. 1963. "Dallas, Texas," *School Programs for the Disadvantaged.*

88. Meyer, Margaret R. 1962. "Parent-Teacher Relationships in the Early Nineteenth Century," *The Journal of Educational Research.* 56: 48–50.

89. Miller, Walter B. 1958. "Lower Class Culture as a Generating Milieu of Gang Delinquency," *The Journal of Social Issues.* 14: 5–19.

90. Minnis, Mhyra S. 1959. "The Pattern of Women's Organizations: Significance, Types, Social Prestige Rank, and Activities," in *Community Structure and Analysis,* ed. Sussman.

91. Mitchell, James V., Jr. 1957. "Identification of Items in the California Test of Personality that Differentiate Between Subjects of High and Low Socio-Economic Status at the Fifth and Seventh Grade Levels," *Journal of Educational Research.* 51: 241–50.

92. Mobilization for Youth, Inc. 1964. "Draft: Research Proposal—School-Community Program: Home Visitation." New York: The authors.

93. ———. 1961. *A Proposal for the Prevention and Control of Delinquency by Expanding Opportunities.* New York: The authors.

94. Mock, Josie. 1963. "Houston, Texas," *School Programs for the Disadvantaged.*

95. Mullin, Margaret M. 1955. "Personal and Situational Factors Associated with Perfect Attendance," *The Personnel and Guidance Journal.* 33: 438–43.

96. Musselman, D. L. 1963. "Fort Wayne, Indiana," *School Programs for the Disadvantaged.*

97. National Education Association. 1945. *Community Living and the Elementary School.* Twenty-fourth Yearbook, Department of Elementary School Principals. Washington, D.C.: The authors.

98. ———. 1955. *The New American School for Adults* by Louis K. Mather. Washington, D.C.: National Education Association.

99. ——— and the American Association of School Administrators. 1962. *Education and the Disadvantaged American.* Washington, D.C.: National Education Association.

100. New Haven Office of the Mayor. 1962. *Opening Opportunities: New Haven's Comprehensive Program for Community Progress.* New Haven: Office of the Mayor.

101. New Rochelle Board of Education. 1962. "Guiding Parents and Motivating Talented Students Who Live in Low-Rent Neighborhoods" by Irving Zweibelson. New Rochelle: Board of Education.

102. ———. "Proposed New Rochelle Project to Guide and Motivate Talented Students Who Live in Poor or 'Deprived' Neighborhoods: Revised 1962–63 Plan." New Rochelle: Board of Education.

103. New York City Board of Education. 1963. *Higher Horizons: Progress Report* by Jacob Landers. New York: Board of Education.

104. ———. *Report of Joint Planning Committee for More Effective Schools to the Superintendent of Schools.* New York: Board of Education.

105. New York State Education Department. 1964. *Project Able: An Appraisal* by Theodore Bienenstok and William C. Sayres. Albany: The University of the State of New York.

106. Niemeyer, John H. 1962. "Home-School Interaction in Relation to Learning in the Elementary School." Working paper presented at the Symposium on School Dropouts held in Washington, D.C., on December 2–4, 1962, under the auspices of the National Education Association's "Project School Dropouts," Daniel Schreiber, Director.

107. Olsen, Edward G. 1949. *School and Community Programs.* New York: Prentice-Hall.

108. Osborne, Ernest. 1959. *The Parent-Teacher Partnership.* New York: Teachers College, Columbia University.

109. Passow, A. Harry. 1963. "Education in Depressed Areas," in *Education in Depressed Areas,* ed. Passow.

110. Pearson, Robert J. 1956. "Public Relations Research Concerned With Public Elementary and Secondary Schools." Unpublished dissertation. Nashville, Tennessee: Peabody College for Teachers.

111. Pierce-Jones, John. 1959. "Vocational Interest Correlates of Socio-

Economic Status in Adolescence," *Educational and Psychological Measurement.* 19: 65–71.

112. Radin, Norma, and Kamii, Constance K. 1965. "The Child-Rearing Attitudes of Disadvantaged Negro Mothers and Some Educational Implications." *Journal of Negro Education.* 34: 138–46.

113. Ravitz, Mel. 1963. "The Role of the School in the Urban Setting," in *Education in Depressed Areas,* ed. Passow.

114. Research Council of the Great Cities Program for School Improvement. 1964. *Promising Practices from the Projects for the Culturally Deprived.* Chicago: The Council.

115. Richmond (Virginia) Board of Education. 1962. *A Proposal to the Ford Foundation for Improving Human Resources Through Education from the School Board of the City of Richmond.* Richmond: The Board.

116. ———. 1964. *Human Development Project Report.* Richmond: The Board.

117. Riessman, Frank. 1962. *The Culturally Deprived Child.* New York: Harper and Row.

118. Rosen, Bernard C. 1956. "The Achievement Syndrome: A Psychocultural Dimension of Social Stratification," *American Sociological Review.* 21: 203–11.

119. St. Louis (Missouri) Board of Education. 1962. *The School and Community Work-Related Education of the St. Louis Public Schools Great Cities Improvement Program: A Ford Foundation Project, Activity and Progress Report, 1961–1962.* St. Louis: The Board.

120. Saltzman, Henry. 1963. "The Community School in the Urban Setting," in *Education in Depressed Areas,* ed. Passow.

121. San Francisco Unified School District. 1962. *San Francisco Unified School District: School Community Improvement Program* by Harold Spears. A Report to the Board of Education. San Francisco: San Francisco Unified School District.

122. Schiff, Herbert Jerome. 1963. "The Effect of Personal Contractural Relationships on Parents' Attitudes Toward and Participation in Local School Affairs." Unpublished dissertation. Evanston, Illinois: Northwestern University.

123. Schoenhard, George H. 1957. "Home Visitation as a Means of Raising the Academic Attainment of High School Students." Unpublished dissertation. Pittsburgh: University of Pittsburgh.

124. "Schools and Community Improvement." 1953. *The School Executive.* Special issue. 72: 19–195.

125. Schussman, Myron. 1958. "Neighborhood Social Characteristics and Elementary Schools in Richmond," *California Journal of Educational Research.* 9: 20–23.

126. Scully, Marion M. 1964. "The Demonstration Guidance Project and the Teaching of English," in *Improving English Skills of Cul-*

turally Different Youth, eds. Arno Jewett *et al.* U.S. Office of Education Bulletin No. 5. Excerpts of speeches given at a Conference, May 31–June 2, 1962. Washington, D.C.: Government Printing Office.

127. Sellars, David. 1963. "Fort Worth, Texas," in *School Programs for the Disadvantaged.*

128. Sexton, Patricia C. 1961. *Education and Income: Inequality of Opportunity in Our Public Schools.* New York: Viking Press.

129. Sharlip, William, and Owens, Albert A. 1925. *Adult Immigration Education.* New York: Macmillan.

130. Shepard, Samuel, Jr. 1963. "A Program to Raise the Standard of School Achievement," *Programs for the Educationally Disadvantaged.*

131. ———. "St. Louis, Missouri," *School Programs for the Disadvantaged.*

132. Sloane, Frank O. 1963. "Dade County, Florida," *School Programs for the Disadvantaged.*

133. Sparks, Paul E. 1963. "Louisville, Kentucky," *School Programs for the Disadvantaged.*

134. Stonecipher, B. L. 1963. "Indianapolis, Indiana." *School Programs for the Disadvantaged.*

135. Stroyan, Homer R. 1956. "A Study of Practices by which Selected Parent-Teacher Groups Contribute to the Elementary School Program." Unpublished dissertation. New York: Teachers College, Columbia University.

136. Taba, Hilda. 1964. "Cultural Deprivation as a Factor in School Learning," *Merrill-Palmer Quarterly of Behavior and Development.* 10: 147–59.

137. Thompson, Frank V. 1920. *Schooling of the Immigrant.* New York: Harper and Brothers.

138. Todd, L. O. 1963. "Meridian, Mississippi," *School Programs for the Disadvantaged.*

139. Tomlinson, Laurence E. 1948. "Parental Participation in Selected Forms of Adult Education in Relation to Population Factors." Unpublished dissertation. Eugene, Oregon: University of Oregon.

140. Tumin, Melvin M. 1964. "Readiness and Resistance to Desegregation: A Social Portrait of the Hard Core," in *Integration vs. Segregation,* ed. Hubert H. Humphrey. New York: Thomas Y. Crowell.

141. Warner, William Lloyd, Havighurst, Robert J., and Loeb, Martin B. 1944. *Who Shall Be Educated? The Challenge of Unequal Opportunities.* New York: Harper and Brothers.

142. Wayland, Sloan R. 1963. "Old Problems, New Faces, and New Standards," in *Education in Depressed Areas,* ed. Passow.

143. ———. 1958. "The School as a Community Center," in *Public Education in America,* eds. George Z. F. Bereday and Luigi Volpicelli. New York: Harper and Brothers.

144. Willett, Henry I. 1963. "Richmond, Virginia," *School Programs for the Disadvantaged.*

145. Wilmington (Delaware) Board of Education. 1960. *An Adventure in Human Relations: A Three-Year Experimental Project on Schools in Changing Neighborhoods* by Muriel Crosby. Progress Report, Section 1, First Year, 1959–60. Wilmington, Delaware: Board of Education.

146. ———. 1962. *An Adventure in Human Relations: A Three-Year Experimental Project on Schools in Changing Neighborhoods.* Progress Report, Section 1, Second Year, 1960–61. Wilmington, Delaware: Board of Education.

147. ———. 1963. *An Adventure in Human Relations: A Three-Year Experimental Project on Schools in Changing Neighborhoods.* Progress Report, Section 1, Third Year, 1961–62. Wilmington, Delaware: Board of Education.

148. Wilson, Alan B. 1963. "Social Stratification and Academic Achievement," in *Education in Depressed Areas,* ed. Passow.

149. Wrightstone, J. Wayne. 1958. "Discovering and Stimulating Culturally Deprived Talented Youth," *Teachers College Record.* 60: 23–27.

150. Wylie, Ruth C. 1963. "Children's Estimate of Their Schoolwork Ability, as a Function of Sex, Race, and Socioeconomic Level," *Journal of Personality.* 31: 203–24.

151. Young, James F. 1964. "An Instrument for Use in Evaluating Programs of School-Community Relations." Unpublished dissertation. New York: Teachers College, Columbia University.

A Critique of Education Projects in Community Action Programs*

Robert A. Dentler

DEFINITIONS

An innovation in education might best be defined as an intentional and somewhat novel change in the policies that control or shape formal teaching and learning. Since the change is by intention, then we assume it is meant to modify the system of instruction and learning for the better. Since it is somewhat novel, then we presume it includes something more distinctive than the introduction of an element that has been tried and tested elsewhere. It involves, that is, more than the introduction of additional resources.

If the innovation applies to policy as well as to practice, the changes might be in physical facilities, sources and amounts of fiscal support, or policies of sorting, combining, and promoting students, as well as in the domains of program, curriculum, or instructional procedures.

Many types of educational innovation may be imagined. I would divide them into four broad categories: innovations in organization, whether of *authority,* or of relations between staff and students, or of staff and administration; innovations in physical environmental arrangements, such as the building of new schools or the renovation of old ones; innovations in technology, including the technology of curriculum and instruction; and, finally, innovations in student or staff *population* size or composition.

I want to make clear at the outset that in my view the institution of urban education encompasses much more than the public schools, with their classroom activities. It includes industrial and commercial training programs, union study groups, parochial and private schools, and entertainments that parade as pleasures but in fact transmit vital formal aspects of modern culture. These entertainments would include the museum, the mass media, the stadium, the concert hall, the fair, and the zoo. Add, too, such total institutions as training schools, prisons, asylums, and nursing homes, where educational programming has a central part in the custodial enterprise.

* Revised version of a paper presented at the Public Policy Institute of Columbia University's School of Social Work, October 1964.

In discussing innovation, there are at least two promising criteria for denoting worthwhile educational change. One is that the change endures and has good consequences for the participants. This criterion is like the congressional standard applied to delinquency control programs. Use of this criterion means, in the educational case, that a classroom stuffed in 1964 with 8 mm films about animal biology will be similarly stuffed, we hope, with updated varieties of film, in 1966 or 1970, when the demonstration, or experiment, or period of innovation has come and gone. It means, too, that some order of measurement or observation will offer *no evidence of a decline* in the learning performance of students and related participants, and hopefully, an increase.

The second criterion deals less with outcomes and more with process. Here one would say that an innovation occurs when some element, usually a group of educators or clients, gets "heated up" and experiments with the educational system. In this case, the innovation might not endure yet could be significant in regard to its effects upon participants, upon imitators, and upon the reconstructionist's esthetic satisfaction over having intensified a variation in the movement of a larger equilibrium.

The purpose of this brief essay is to apply this general concept of educational innovation in reviewing the educational components of community action programs in four Eastern cities. These programs were chosen because they evolved earlier and somewhat more impressively than did programs in other Eastern cities, and thus have set part of the pattern that has since become common.

Note that the aim is *not* to evaluate the programs in operation. Concern is limited, rather, to the programs as planned and proposed in writing. I shall probe the extent to which the *plans* themselves are innovative, for if the plans lack promise, what must we expect from their implementation?

NO INNOVATIONS

The main impression I get from a reading of the educational programs proposed, and in part acted upon, in the community action programs in New Haven, Syracuse, Boston, and New York, is a sense of their *limited scope* and *institutional superficiality*. Indeed, from what is meant in social science by innovation and from the definitions with which I began, I believe we cannot call the work of these action programs in the domain of public education innovations at all! This is not to say that they may not be superb contributions to the public good. It is to assert that if an innovation is deliberate and original change, then these programs are no more innovative than they are means of controlling delinquency. Specifically, the chief objective of the educational program in each of the four communities is improved schooling for children from low-income families living in the less physically attractive parts of the inner city. (I have deliberately not called these children culturally deprived, cognitively deficient, disadvantaged, or simply children from slum school or depressed areas, because I find these distorting and even false terms.) This major goal in every case is to be achieved by *additions* to school program, staff, curricular programs, and related services.

These additions are in no respect novel. The appeal for what the Syracuse group calls the "experience-centered curriculum," for instance, is older than John Dewey. Similarly, most of the programs involve adding such familiar items as better guidance services, materials adapted to the life situation of the low-income urban student, greater resources for teaching reading and for remedial reading work, more lessons for teachers in human relations and urban sociology, and the employment of additional specialists of many kinds. Most of the programs also spend money to buy more time for schooling—for afternoon schools, for summer schools, for weekend study, and for preschool, work-study school, and post-school instruction.

In combination, the total range of (educational) projects seems much like an attempt to *export* the "decent" American suburban public school into the poorer inner-city areas. What is being exported has been tried over and over again in myriads of forms in educational contexts. The attempt is doubtless worthwhile. If we cannot distribute resources equally through ordinary institutional channels—and the evidence is overwhelming that we cannot—then we need a means for piping federal funds into large urban communities to relieve the worst features of the inequality. But since nothing novel or fundamental as to the structure of educational services is being proposed by these programs, why all the fuss about their design and about the difficulties inherent in getting them into operation?

PECULIARITIES OF EDUCATIONAL PROGRAMMING

There are reasons why such educational programs need to be rationalized so self-impressively, but they have nothing to do with novelty.

Basically, it is hard to introduce resources into local community educational practices because the practices *are* local. If a new piece of fire fighting equipment is invented, manufactured, and proven in value as to execution and relative cost, it will find its way by natural social diffusion into all of the pertinent firehouses in the nation. The only problem that might come up in this instance to give us something to fret about would be time. We might want to find ways to speed up the diffusion. Educational resources do not get distributed through the social system in the same more or less inevitable fashion.

A change in economic organization at the federal level—say, in banking procedures or in bond issuances—ordinarily will produce a comparable change in every applicable community in the nation; economic power is so distributed in the private domains in this country that reorganization at the top ramifies to all levels. But among all the agencies of social service and social control, public educational agencies are the least well-integrated organizationally. A national structure of educational policy and practice exists, but it is *shadowier* than even the structures of welfare and of police services. (Social insurance as a welfare system, for example, has become one of our best run and most tightly integrated national organizations. There are other small components of welfare which are also authentically national in their dependence upon common standards, fiscal resources, and definitions of professional personnel.) The U.S. Office of Education remains an *enfeebled* agency, in spite of the significant, if sporadic, growth of federal supports for education.

Under past and present conditions at least, then, power resides in two places in the public national educational system: in state departments of education and with local publics. How do the four programs respond to these conditions? Now, state departments contribute heavily toward the task of equalizing educational opportunity and services across communities within any one state. Thus, if one were seriously interested in upgrading the quality of education in American cities, he would have a quite elaborate set of plans for cooperation with *state* authorities. Such cooperation seems quite absent from the plans for Syracuse, New Haven, Boston, and New York City.

About local publics one might say that if they knew what they wanted educationally and what they were willing to pay for, demonstration projects in education would be irrelevant. Or is this the truth? Is it perhaps rather that local publics do not want or are unwilling to pay for what reconstructionists and selected professionals insist is necessary?

In any case, one finds in the planning of educational projects in the four community development programs under consideration, *no ear-*

marks of citizen participation. Where the word parent comes up in these programs, it comes up as if a parent is a client who is hard to reach; for whom a special project of reaching-out must be devised. Or it comes up as if programs for serving parental interest will build up as the total program takes shape.

REMOTE CONTROL

The hand I see in these educational plans is almost solely the hand of the educational project consultant—that American specialist in transmitting to C what B and A are busy doing, without mentioning that B and A picked up their "experiments" from D and E who got them from other educational project consultants, who have not been inside an elementary school for ten years.

The projects in question may add something to the educational scene in each respective community. This something may even be worthwhile. But it will not at all necessarily change anything fundamental about the educational structure, or process, or goals of the community.

Consider the Boston educational program, or parts of it at least, in detail, as a test of this judgment. Boston offers four principal projects, and four minor ones.

The first main project is concerned with reading. It aims to get pupils to read well by putting two reading consultants into each of three depressed-area primary schools. The reading consultants will not teach. "The bulk of their time will be spent not as teachers of students, but as catalysts who help teachers devise more effective teaching materials and methods." Everything in the Boston reading project depends upon the success of these consultants and their junior-high-level equivalents. Can reading consultants in fact serve as "catalysts who help teachers"? Some teachers in some Boston elementary schools, I would think, must have been doing a fine job of teaching reading before the project ever came along. Others were doing a bad job. Some *pattern* existed by which the better teachers—those who were white, at least—were promoted out to "better" schools in the Boston system or who got themselves jobs in the suburbs.

A test of the reading project would then be the determination of whether some teachers who were doing a bad job before the project are doing a better job thanks to reading consultation from the specialists. The test would have to cover a period of time, of course: Are the improving teachers staying on the job in ghetto schools? However, this project is to be evaluated by giving the students reading achievement tests. As we know, a shift may occur for the student sample without this indicating anything about the educational fates of future students. After all, the catalysts may become principals and the better teachers may move elsewhere.

The Boston reading project also proceeds from the questionable premise that it is reading skills as such that must be worked on. It further introduces a number of consultants into the elementary schools who have the task of teaching teachers how to teach students to read better. Since few teachers now are able to accomplish this with many ghetto school students, even short of explaining *how* they do it, what may we expect of the consultants? If they were successful, moreover, what is the durability of their work likely to be?

Consider another example, this time from the New Haven program. Consider the "Psycho-Education Experiment." Here, a graduate student in psychology, theoretically at the invitation of a teacher, sits in on a class session and observes a particular pupil systematically. The psychologist then consults with the teacher and with other school staff about how to correct the "poor school adjustment" of the child.

The pioneer in this sort of project is Dr. Seymour Sarason, an eminent psychologist. There is no question that the program has value, particularly in preparing clinical and school psychologists for graduation from Yale on the basis of meaningful empirical practice. The other goals of this "experiment" depend, however, upon who takes part. That is, the experiment aims to aid teachers in identifying and handling the special problems of inner-city students. Do we know whether these special problems differ from other special human problems? Who knows? The graduate student? Dr. Sarason? Surely not, under this relationship, the teacher! Of course, this goal will be achieved when the psychologist brings to bear some truly relevant knowledge or understanding, and where he has the skill to transmit his insight to the teacher or other staff. What are the probabilities of effective occurrence here?

In both projects, it comes down to whether we think schools in large cities should have enlarged special staffs. Should depressed-area schools, for example, have the benefit of psychological and remedial reading services? *Of course they should!* What is good for suburban Needham, Massachusetts, is good for ghetto Roxbury! (Or has Needham been chiseling on the introduction of intellectual and human resources into *its* schools, too? Certainly not to the degree common to Roxbury or to parts of inner New Haven, I suspect.) But this cannot be the whole story.

INVESTING IN FAILURE

If the program strategies of some of the educational projects are
unsound because little about them offers promise of improved instruction for students, others make a different type of strategic error. They
represent projects that are unsound because they extend, or invest
monies in, projects that have *failed* educators for decades, projects
which educators no longer have any reason to have faith in.

First, consider the Adult Literacy Program in New Haven. This
"now functions in nine centers—seven schools, a factory, and a voluntary agency community center." The school centers operate two to
three nights a week, and the factory center operates for an hour right
after an eight-hour day, twice a week. As of the winter of 1964, 268
adults were enrolled in the nine centers. Contrast this figure with the
2,609 persons over 25 years of age who were listed in the New Haven
census of 1960 as having completed less than the fifth grade of school.

The progress report states: "Substantial growth is expected in the
scope of this very important program." How will this growth occur?
What is there about the program that differs from hundreds of lagging
adult literacy classes in communities from coast to coast? What incentives have been built into this New Haven project that would give it
greater hope of success than has been achieved in nearly one hundred
years of effort to reach and to teach *adult* illiterates to read, in America? Is the project correlated with employment services? Are new job
possibilities opened up as a student makes progress?

One of the centers is operated for senior citizens. How is this instruction of the aging related to other geriatric services? In any way that
will prove significantly reinforcing for the arduous work of learning
to read in old age?

As a second illustration, take the community-school program in
Syracuse. The goal here is "to expand the role of the school as a
facility in relation to the community. By utilizing the schools for the
entire day and evening, as well as on weekends, a wide variety of programs can be developed which reflect the needs and interests of action
area youth and adults."

Many schools in New York City and in other large cities have aimed
at this goal for years. Moreover, where this effort has been introduced,
educators have found that there are indeed uses for school facilities—
that there is, of course, value in utilizing the school plant on a full day,
full week basis. Educators have also found, however, that opening the
schools will not necessarily attract parents and students who would not

otherwise be attracted! It is a condition in no wise different from keeping the YMCA pool open nights and weekends: the same groups and types of groups use the pool more, but new and different types of users do not come into play.

The Syracuse programmers may properly say, "Wait! We must see first what goes into the community school program." Well, perhaps, but will the success of a given operation depend solely upon the imagination and leadership of the "community-school coordinator" who is employed to administer each "community school" under the authority of the regular principal? We are told that teams will work up programs and that the programs will depend upon the interests of the participants.

Now I favor such a project. Do not mistake my point. Public schools in inner cities should be kept open; a coordinator should supply services and projects in cooperation with neighborhood citizens; and there should be funds for this. That is what the action program in Syracuse is doing.

What it has not proposed to do is to devise a community-school program that has, by virtue of design, leadership, or content, any better chance of reaching households in authentic need than any similar program financed in another section of the same city. This does not make the project worthless. It does mean that in this, as in other instances, Syracuse Action for Youth is but a worthy supplier of minimal social service facilities and personnel that are not now supplied by the board of education. Moreover, what Syracuse Action will be supplying to "community schools" may have no strategic bearing whatever on impoverished families or their children and youth.

OTHER PROBLEMS

Some of the programs are less shopworn than those singled out here for illustration. Syracuse, for example, has a scheme by which high school dropouts may re-enter, and perhaps even graduate from, high school. Elements in this program suggest the application of imagination to the question of how to design an educational service that might be fitted realistically and, therefore, engagingly into the reservations and interests of dropouts. One impressive feature of the re-entry proposal is that re-entry itself is but the last stage of a series of helpful interactions with student clients who have chosen to try to return to school. Insofar as many high school administrators and teachers *reject* such students from school unnecessarily in the first place, or induce withdrawal by providing an antagonistic milieu, this is indeed something that calls for *outside* efforts at change.

Even in the instance of this more novel program, however, two essential strategies may have been neglected. One is a means for attracting into the program the students Syracuse Action for Youth actually wishes to reach. There are some good grass roots qualities to the re-entry program. These may resolve the question of permissive and yet accurate targeting of recruitment, but just how is unclear.

A second neglect may be in the matter of stigma. Students re-enter high school, if they wish to and if they have gone through the prior phases of the program, only with the arrangement of the Neighborhood Help Center, the guidance "team," and the high school principal. With all this fanfare, what the odds may be for returning to school simply as one more student among one's peers is, of course, unknown. But there appear to be no devices for changing the symbolic status of the student from that of a stigmatized dropout or that of a rehabilitated product of the center into that of a high school youth *known only as such*. This neglect, if it is in fact existent, will most likely reinforce problems of attracting the most needy youths into the program in the first place.

NO INCENTIVES FOR THE OLD GUARD

Thus far I have argued that most of the educational programs are old hat, based on questionable assumptions, arranged so as to do little more than is done in some other part of the metropolitan area (and thereby equalizing services a bit by compensation), or so designed as probably to miss their real youth-group targets. This is onerous enough, yet there are perhaps more strategic difficulties involved, and I am determined to put them out for inspection.

Suppose, for example, that we concentrate on projects that work through the public schools in the action areas. Can we agree that the two chief gatekeepers and conductors of policy and practice in these schools are administrators and classroom teachers? Around the administrator is, of course, the structure that extends from the superintendent through his line officers down to the principal. Excluded from either group are the ancillary or special service or technical staff.

In the domain of public school policy and practice, the principal (or his superiors, in some instances) or the classroom teachers have to want change, or it will not occur. Line officials in our public schools and, to a lesser extent, teachers, live in a porous membrane of an institution. They are conditioned, with the usual individual exceptions, to sidestep trouble, social rumbles, and local controversy. Real change and trouble are often synonymous; so principals and teachers—again with important individual exceptions—find ways of preventing change or of slowing its entrance so that it becomes socially imperceptible.

Changes proposed or decided upon *that do not involve them,* but from which they may receive local reaction are changes likely to be subverted, diluted to ineffectiveness, evaded, or slowed down. Moreover, principals and classroom teachers must be involved by reason of sound incentive, not merely by virtue of propaganda or invitation. Local principals and teachers are not socially reactionary, but we cannot expect them to accept responsibility for working well in programs that they did not devise or in programs in which chief control for execution is placed in the hands of ancillary personnel.

In only one of the eight main programs developed by Boston, for instance, is the teacher incorporated in what I would consider a somewhat effective fashion. This is the program for identifying and developing the younger pupil's distinctive talents and aspirations. Here, we learn that "a corps of teachers will be recruited and paid in each demonstration school to plan projects and activities with individuals, with special materials and equipment available for their use." Even the enthusiasm for this is apt to fade as one reads on to learn that this means overtime work in the afterschool period. This type of overtime is available already for most teachers. Therefore, even this program offers limited incentive for attracting able staff. In other Boston proposals, teachers are either not mentioned, are bypassed in favor of guidance counsellors or other special service staff, or are less key participants in professional activity than presumed beneficiaries of additional on-the-job training by consultants.

Incentives, incidentally, may include money but they do not stop there. Any casual observer of New York's Mobilization for Youth efforts within public schools knows that stipends, fees, and honoraria, however appropriate and sizable, will *not* open the gates to change—not unless a principal and some of his teachers find that some of their own goals have been built into the program of change, or see that their ends are closely, even directly, served thereby. And their ends include, as do those of all professionals, their own occupational prestige.

EDUCATING CLIENTS

Ignoring the content of the many programs for the moment, my impression is that very few of them impinge upon one or more of the several obvious components in the *social organization* of educational services for very large urban student populations. These components are the client, the teacher, and the stuff to be taught, all associated over time in an interpersonal process of learning.

Take the clientele, first. Although none of the community action programs in education costs more than a few hundred thousand dollars a year, these dollars are spread across every age and sex group within the action area. If this is sound planning by the thinking of some welfare specialists and community organizers, it is tactical nonsense. The main age group that needs to be aided is, obviously, adolescents. This is generally understood. But there then arises the dilemma of causation—the hypothesis that both educational and behavioral difficulties begin earlier and must be prevented earlier. Thus, many of the programs emphasize the primary grades as heavily as they do the junior high and high school years. The aid that goes to each becomes rather light, however, when all get equal emphasis under limited resources.

This brings one to the deeper question: Who is the main client for educational services in the several action programs? In New Haven, there appears to be no main client. There is merely everyone within the action area, though, of course, different groups are singled out for special service objectives. For the educational programs, the main clientele is generally public school students between kindergarten and high school age who reside within the action areas which house low-income households and a relative excess of ethnic minority groups.

This clientele does not appear to have been consulted directly before the education proposals were developed, except in the case of Mobilization for Youth, where some pertinent survey research was executed. Elsewhere, the allegedly relevant literature about disadvantaged youth has been consulted extensively. From this literature, the programmers have concluded that their clients need new curriculum materials, new types of help in learning to read, extra psychological and vocational and educational guidance, plenty of help from audio-visual technology, and extra time in school or in improved study situations. This is the underlying definition of what clients need. They also need schools that are "less middle class," at the same time they are being provided with more of the options that allow people to become upwardly mobile themselves.

While these programs have value, and while their introduction will indeed give some students a better education than they would otherwise have received, I would ask whether these programs are tailored empirically and authentically to the phenomenological requirements of youths living within the action areas. These youths have high aspirations but they think themselves blocked from achievement by the existing arrangements of their society. These arrangements, so far as they are concerned, include school staff who exhibit status disrespect toward them (unconsciously more often than consciously, though the distinction is of little importance to behavior). School becomes a place where women teachers often suppress boys, and where many teachers expect too little of their students because they themselves are weighed down by a vast bureaucratic establishment within which rewards do *not* go to success in classroom instruction.

Such schools are not so much middle class as they are functionally moribund. They are moribund because they can offer their students very few prospects in the society at large. They are necessarily schools without hope, save for a very few students, parents, and teachers—necessarily, because that is how the macro-social situation is arranged, and there is no reason to expect the little local school in the slum to challenge this arrangement.

Some of these schools have proven that they can break this constraint toward miseducation. And this is, naturally, the hope of the action programmers as well. But the frame has been broken most effectively in those instances where a vigorous principal has revised teaching practices in his school so that they coincide better with the self-defined needs of his students. For example, students in these schools want most of all what students in *all* schools want: what the Japanese call a relation of *mutual respect* between student and teacher. This is more than a vague order of tender loving care. In education, mutual respect means that a teacher's definition of what a student can learn develops out of mutually sensitive exploration of that question, and that once the definition is articulated by the teacher, it comes to be internalized by the student.

The reconstruction of slum schools is a reconstruction of the interpersonal relation between teachers and pupils. The achievement of this depends heavily upon close study of the distinctive attributes and concerns of the students in a *particular* school, since there are class and subcultural differences that must be attended to. Improved technology, additional manpower, and more time, together with additional curriculum resources are worthwhile, but they are not central to acting from one's educational definition of the client and what he needs.

To illustrate this point, I quote the following passage from *Teacher* (1963, pp. 118–119), by Sylvia Ashton-Warner, the experienced pioneer in teaching Maori children in New Zealand.

I burnt most of my infant-room material on Friday. I say that the more material there is for a child, the less pull there is on his own resources. Other children coming to me from other schools are most annoyingly helpless. They want the teacher to do everything for them like a mother. I don't believe in shiny polished blocks. The shine and the colour should be supplied by the child's own imagination. Maybe he will not imagine polish and shine. In which case the polish and colour supplied externally is obviously an imposition. *Which I scream is deadly! Whatever his own imagination* does *supply will be something in character with his own needs. Which is integral, cohesive and organic. I speak of blocks as an example but only symbolically. I mean all the other contraptions. Mrs. S. for example was given the job of preparing mountains of reading cards to supplement the new reading books. Pictures for every word. Pictures illustrating,* believe it or not, *words like "up," "to," "me" . . . over and above the nouns. It's terribly hard to believe that modern teachers can do this and modern inspectors instigate it. Can't a child picture his own nouns when he hears them? Do we have pictures of prepositions and conjunctions? And beyond all this think of the* time *it takes to care for all this stuff. Only infant teachers know the time it takes to keep this stuff in order and in repair. Time that could be used in precious conversation with them. I burnt all the work of my youth. Dozens of cards made of threeply, and handprinted and illustrated. Boxes of them. There will be only the following list in my infant room:*

Chalk	*Books*
Blackboards	*Charts*
Paper	*Paints*
Pencils	*Clay*
Guitar	*Piano*

And when a child wants to read he can pick up a book with his own hands and struggle through it. The removal of effort and the denying to the child of its right to call on its own resources . . .

(I was sad though, seeing it all go up in smoke.)

But teaching is so much simpler and clearer as a result. There's much more time for conversation. Conversation . . . communication. (You should have heard the roaring in the chimney!)

REORGANIZING THE MACRO-STRUCTURE

Changes in the educational and social organization of local public schools cannot be sustained for long without corresponding changes in the social structure of either the city as a whole or, at the very least, in the social structure of the public school system as a whole. The educational economist, Harold Clark, found in his studies in the late 1930's and thereafter that important changes could be introduced rather readily into the nation's very worst rural schools. He showed that these innovations—in the relations between teachers and students, in curriculum, and in goals—had immediate and sometimes stupendous *short-term* effects upon academic achievement among students. The leaps in reading ability and the like *all* disappeared, however, during the decade that Clark allowed to pass before conducting his follow-up research.

The innovations faded out; they could not compete against the massive economic, cultural, and social *constraints* toward rural poverty and despair that were induced by the *regional forces* surrounding each school.

REORGANIZATION THROUGH DESEGREGATION

It is encouraging to discover that each community action program makes some mention of school integration efforts. Each program will obviously make some contribution, however large or small, toward the end of a fundamental reordering of student population distribution. Fundamental changes in ethnic distribution of students in the direction of greater balance per school, per grade, and per class within each school, can prove to be a greater agent of equality of educational opportunity and service than all special programs combined. This would not occur automatically, of course.

Syracuse, Boston, New Haven, and perhaps New York can also make contributions to school integration through their help in preventing *resegregation.* As the history of public schools in the District of Columbia and in Baltimore proves, schools that are racially desegregated in the North without corresponding investments in upgrading quality are likely to become schools that change from all Negro to Negro and white, and then back once again to all Negro—a tragic reversal. Vigorous programs that strengthen school services combat this process by keeping whites in a neighborhood. This is true of low as well as middle-and-high-income neighborhoods, I believe.

Integration is but one form of change in the macro-structure, however. Many of the additions to the services of schools provided by the community action and development programs will die out if and when the outside monies cease to flow in. Programs *may not* have been introduced in such a way as to enhance the political power base of the superintendent or any of his deputies or assistants, for example. If the major additions are made through guidance, infant and pre-school help, remedial programs, and adult education, let us say, none of the primary power bases will be affected. These are the bases that build up over the years within the organization of big-city school systems. The bases stem ordinarily from control over instructional staff, the building program, educational research, and central administration. A power base may be identified by the fact that its holder has some modicum of work-day control over the fates of a substantial cadre of minor officials and teachers within the system; or he controls relations with other city departments, as in the case of power stemming from the building program.

One cannot tell from the project documents just what a superintendent or his deputies and their principals would see themselves as gaining from the introduction of these programs. The programs must, of course, have proven potentially compelling because they carry the promise of money from a new source. But school officials—with some exceptions, and unlike some other city departments—are not after money as graft. They are after resources, including money naturally, that will help them consolidate their positions, since their positions in government are rather like those of politicians who are appointed rather than elected. It may well be that resourceful enhancement of professional educators within the systems has been arranged *informally* in the case of these action programs.

THE ULTIMATE STRATEGY

The ultimate success of the educational proposals depends upon whether federal aid to education comes into being in a way that will sustain the achievements of these efforts in the inner-city schools. While some of the expenditure schedules have been so arranged that in principle the cities are expected to take over the financing of these programs in the long run, I cannot believe that anyone takes this prospect seriously. If this is what is to be counted upon, we may expect that the same schools, or their equivalents elsewhere, will sink slowly to the same levels they were at before the additions were provided.

City services paid for out of municipal and state funds come to be distributed along the characteristic *gradient* of influence. As long as a big city finances the public collection of garbage from its own revenues, for instance, garbage will tend to be better collected in some quarters of town than in others. Public educational services exhibit the same gradient, with some equalization resulting from state aid of course. But if this observation is valid, then low-income children and youth will go on being poorly served until federal intervention and standard-setting become permanent routines. Only the federal establishment is politically in a position, and can afford fiscally, to approach the problem of insuring equality of opportunity for learning in a relatively objective manner.

Again, if this is true, the main business of the educators at work on community action programs is to *educate* the federal administration, the National Education Association, the United Federation of Teachers, and above all, the U.S. Congress, as to the demonstrated value of their services. As this is indeed the most likely concern of the action programmers, it is not hard to understand why the educational programs themselves are not very innovative. Who wants to run big risks with a remote and notoriously fickle set of patrons?

We should, therefore, concentrate, in each city, on fewer and more clearly delineated, manifestly important programs. New Haven appears to be spread so thin at present, for example, that educational programs are lined up waiting to be introduced. Changes, already packaged for use and authorized for expenditure, are backlogged at headquarters. Is this the kind of care to insure results that will truly educate the federal patrons?

A POSTSCRIPT

One conception of a sound strategy—less for educational innovations, which may be a rather specious bit of jargon, and more for the provision of needed personnel and services—should be obvious by now. In case it is not, and in case the reader is so angry over a paper that in his opinion does not seem to direct itself to the myriad problems involved in implementing programs, I shall define the conception. It is a stratagem under which "Everybody Wins, and Youth Is Served."

Urban renewal is sometimes an example of an "Everybody Wins" game (or, more accurately, "Everybody—Except Negroes and Small Merchants")—though not necessarily a game in which there is something for everyone in the way the clientele had in mind or needed most. It is an arrangement under which there are heavy political and dollar *inducements* available for cities whose leaders elect to use them to conserve, rehabilitate, or rebuild neighborhoods.

Educational programs within community action projects could be built to achieve the same kind of inducement. They could also, however, serve to educate low-income urban youths so well that these clients really have options for mobility—geographic and occupational —that they would not have had without the extra services. It is my impression, but certainly not my judgment, that the programs as currently described do not as a whole meet these conditions for success.

REFERENCE

Ashton-Warner, Sylvia. 1963. *Teacher*. New York: Simon and Schuster.

Let's Organize Their Depression*

Elizabeth O'Grady

> Cast—Occupants of an apartment building
> on the Upper West Side of New
> York City
> Landlord
> Welfare Workers
> Group Worker
> Group Coordinator
> Social Service person working in the
> building
>
> Time—The Present

ACT ONE

Scene I

*Basement room, lined at the door with gar-
bage, scattered trash. Walls covered with
filth, upon which cockroaches make aimless
forays. Upturned tables and chairs lie around
the room, covered with a thin cover of
plaster.*

*Enter Mr. ALLEN and Mr. LEWIS. The
latter wears a faded silk waistcoat, a shabby
grey suit, and a Prince Albert collar.*

LEWIS:

(*Grandly*) I can tell you sir, upon delibera-
tion, that this world is indeed very mixed
up, everyone desirous of changing things.
It's the same the world over. What else can
you expect but to find dismembered bodies
around with those young girls goin' and
gettin' themselves all horsed up and walkin'
around like they don't know what they are
doin' or where they are.

ALLEN: (*Nervously*) Yeah, Mr. Lewis, tha's right.

                        *Cop walking by on the sidewalk can be
                        heard from a distance:* "You dumb bastards,
                        go somewhere else if you want to carve your
                        initials on each other."

LEWIS: (*Vaguely, with a faraway look*) And us in-
                        telligent folks think something must be done
                        to keep this neighborhood respectable.

                        Cop's voice fading away . . . "All of you
                        in this neighborhood, just the same way,
                        drinking, murdering know-nothings."

LEWIS: (*Reflecting*) They won't be comin' anyway,
                        not today. This is check day. They'll be out
                        gettin' their stuff, all those folks in the
                        buildin' will. (*Eyes light up at the sugges-
                        tion. He starts to go out.*)

                        *Enter Mrs. WATERS, enormous Southern
                        colored woman, dressed in bright purple
                        dress and black wig.*

MRS. WATERS: (*Sharply*) Oh, no, you don't, not you, too,
                        Mr. Lewis. Someone's goin' to come to the
                        meeting, them others won't. And Martha,
                        I said to her, "Don't get on the bottle. Come
                        down, have some cake and coffee in our
                        new club."

                        *Two Negro men pass by on the street out-
                        side. One pulls out a bottle, takes a long
                        swig and stumbles past. Catching sight of the
                        Welfare Worker approaching, he stows the
                        bottle, straightens up, and heads quickly
                        inside the building.*

LEWIS: (*Goes to the corner and pulls out a bag,
                        takes out a* New York Times *with a grand
                        flourish*) Just brought some reading stuff

for the folks, for when they come down to the coffee hour. (*Brings out some ripped, wrinkled, brown curtains*) These are for our club room.

MRS. WATERS: (*With distaste*) Where did you get them awful things?

LEWIS: Oh, the welfare people gave them to me. (*Adds lazily*) You know this day is almost over. Let's have the coffee hour another time. Mr. Group Worker is the one who wanted to have it anyway. So let him run it. I think those social service people need a club more than we do, because they're all hepped up about it. Who needs—(*Catching sight of the Group Worker approaching on the sidewalk outside the window, he assumes a fixed smile. Leans out the window. Ingratiatingly*) Good afternoon Mr. Group Worker, how are you this afternoon? We were saying that we were anxious to get the coffee hour goin'. Come on down.

(*Enter GROUP WORKER*)

GROUP WORKER: Hello everyone. I'm fine, but (*Surveys the room*) are you going to have the party with the place like this?

MRS. WATERS: (*Casually*) We'll clean it up now *if* you like.

(*Air of busy activity fills the room as the tenants assume an attitude of work*)

GROUP WORKER: (*Curiously*) I thought you would be having the coffee hour when I arrived. It's getting late now. What happened?

MRS. WATERS: (*Aimlessly*) Oh, we was goin' to get around to it. (*Changes the subject quickly*) Look out the window, see that bitch, the one with the pink coat, having a man live with her and collecting welfare checks. And he beats her till she nearly dead. She taking care of him real good, too. I told Martha to watch her drinkin' (*She speaks faster and faster until the rhythm of the speech is the only meaningful element*) and she went and fell off the fire escape, brokeher collarbone, lucky she didn'tbreak her neck, and Mr. Welfare Worker, he comearoundandheknow they are uptheredrinkintheywon't everbecomindownheretotheclubbecausetheywon'tbe outalldaybuttogetanotherbottleandGeorgehe sayhewon'teverbeattheclubbecausesomeone saidhewassellingwineinthehallsandhesayit ain'ttrueMargretwon'tbecomineithershesay therearetoomanybossesaroundhere.

GROUP WORKER: (*Carefully*) What do you mean, too many bosses?

MRS. WATERS: Margaret been here thirty-nine years. She was knowing and in to everything with the other landlord. Mr. Landlord comes in and turns her off. If she ever talked to me, I never knowed it.

GROUP WORKER: (*Innocently*) Doesn't she get along with *you*, Mrs. Waters?

MRS. WATERS: (*Quickly*) She don't get along with nobody!

GROUP WORKER: How many people do you think will come down to your first club hour?

MRS. WATERS: Some come down to get out of the cold, to get something to eat.

LEWIS: Them people might be occupied elsewhere today. (*Winks*)

ALLEN: (*Seriously*) I don't know . . .

Scene II

Small office in the apartment house where the social service people confer. Gathered for this purpose are all the officials.

COORDINATOR:

(Formally) We've been through this before. I guess you know what it's all about. *(Looking toward GROUP WORKER)* I have to have news of your activities at the club. I'm submitting a report to the committee next week and they expect some action on this thing.

GROUP WORKER:

(Seriously) Things are going along at a slow pace, but that's what I expected. I hesitate to adopt a directive attitude as far as these people are concerned. I want to watch them, see their frustrations and the ways they deal with their problems. I want to get to know them on their own terms and this takes a great deal of time.

COORDINATOR:

But the committee—

WELFARE WORKER:

Do you want to know something about this building and the people in it? I've been on this block for years and I know these people. The place is a haven for the dregs of mankind, your drunks, prostitutes, nuts, addicts and believe it or not, this place is a lot "cleaner" now than it was. That's because the landlord has been trying to get rid of undesirables. I knew this place when there was a 14-foot barbwire fence on the roof to keep the addicts from communicating between buildings.

COORDINATOR:

(Loudly) I talked with the head of—

WELFARE WORKER:

(Interrupts) Not so long a time ago you could get anything you wanted in here, and it would cost you anywhere from a nickel

to a quarter and the male prostitutes would
be lined up in the hall.

COORDINATOR: (*Sharply*) What has gone on down there
so far?

GROUP WORKER: (*Evenly*) I've gotten to know a few of the
people. Only a few as yet, who have come
down to the club. Some of them have invited me to their rooms and we've tested
each other out a bit.

COORDINATOR: (*Impatiently*) Do you realize the activities
that could be promoted here? You could—

GROUP WORKER: (*With a forced calm*) You mean things that
look good for the committee's reports? You
seem to have all the conclusions from a
project that we've just begun. The prede-
termined conclusion seems to be that group
activities are desirable to these people. The
motivation has to come from them if these
functions are to be successful . . . if they
will belong to the tenants and not to us, if
the club will be carried on after we have
gone, because they think it's important, not
because we tell them so. This club idea will
come very slowly. Only two or three people
even trust me to the point where they are no
longer saying what they think I want to
hear. The rest have built little worlds inside
their rooms and that's the reality with which
they live each day. Perhaps group work
would be unsuccessful in this building. Perhaps in six months that will be the most
valid conclusion I can make. I'm here to
see what really goes.

COORDINATOR: (*Angrily*) Really goes!?

GROUP WORKER: (*Cynically*) Do you know what we do? We
come in here, unasked, with all our ideals,
unsought, and judge these people by a moral

code to which we do not even adhere ourselves. And we think we can provide leaven-
ing by which all the people will be raised.
And then we leave . . . and that's the
easiest part of all.

Scene III

*Played in stage foreground. Stage is in dark-
ness. Spot of light off center to stage left.
Silently and singly each player moves into
the spot, offers a mechanical recitation of
his piece, and exits into the darkness.*

PAGE:

No heat in my room. I put my heavy coat
on and stay under the blanket all day to
keep warm. They shipped me over here
and I don't get my check for two weeks
. . . There are so many other things, too.

DIAZ:

You want coffee? See I got money, see how
much. Money, that's easy . . .

COP:

You think you'll have a club here? You're
crazy! These bums will rob you blind. Get
out, you can't help them. This isn't your
kind of neighborhood, so what're you doin'
here anyway?

LESTER:

I've seen you around here before, and I
don't like it. You try coming back again
and I'm goin' to get my boys together and
we'll take care of you.

LEWIS:

And then I spent time in the institution.
But you see, I was in there for other
reasons. Oh, not like the others. Do you
know, the smartest people in the world are
in those places. They can tell you anything.

ALLEN:

And they come in through that window last
night and stole the things out of the club.
They want stuff to pawn. Listen have you
ever been to Mars? Me and Mr. Lewis are
goin'.

EDWARDS: Can I talk with you, private? So they took me off welfare. They say I spend all my money on the gambling. I need to get that fixed up.

KING: I know these people like a book. Sometimes I like to be very quiet and just observe. I'm classified blind you know. Where was I? Oh about the James Bond flick. The machinations in it were superlative.

MRS. COMPSON: Listen, I'm telling you, honey, I'm only 63 years old and I want a man. Maybe I get him over there.

MRS. WATERS: And Mr. Welfare Worker, he lookin' at me and at my dress and I know what he's thinkin'. And he says, as sweet as pie, where did you get that nice dress Maud? And I say to him, for your information, I bought this dress five years ago. I told the other welfare man I needed a Sunday dress for church and he give me the money. They want us all to look like bums, on welfare. Then they be happy.

GARRETT: I hear you've been spreading rumors that I drink. I guess you can see everything from your office as the folks come and go. You here to spy on us?

CRAIG: Listen, you don't know the rules of the game. I don't want to beat you at it. I'll show you how to win . . . do it anyway you can.

PETERS: I'm an old man you know. My mother was a Southern slave. When she was freed, they sent her out West to homestead. She got mixed up with a white feller out there and that's how I came to be. The ending to all of this isn't very far away.

MRS. WARREN:	Hey, hey, just what you mean! I'll punch your face in if you look at me like that. I'm just feeling the stuff. The words mean the same, but they sound funny.
EMILY:	At the hospital, they took my baby and I have been looking and asking them . . . ten years ago at the hospital and I ask them for my baby and they don't give him to me. You see what they give me (*Points to idiot son in corner*) You see that boy, but I want my baby. Where is he?
ANDREW:	There's a place in here somewhere for God, but I can't fit him in.

ACT TWO

Scene I
Hall of the apartment house. To stage right, stairs lead up to a small darkened room, which is seen as a walled silhouette. As the characters ascend the stairs, they become moving, silhouetted forms.

Enter GROUP WORKER

GROUP WORKER:	(*Puzzled*) What's going on here, officers?
FIRST COP:	(*Carelessly*) We're going to take Martha in.
SECOND COP:	She has been pretty much out of it for a long time. I could see this coming.
WELFARE WORKER:	(*Defensively*) I had to call them in on this. Martha has fallen downstairs a number of times, left the gas on in her room, nurses that bottle day and night and doesn't even know who or where she is anymore. We need you as a witness.
FIRST COP:	The wagon is outside, let's go and get her.

(*Enter ORDERLY—a big, burly Negro*)

ORDERLY: (*Loudly*) Is this the place? Where is she?

                        *Occupants coming in and out of the build-
                        ing assume the same frightened pose, look-
                        ing from one of the authority figures to
                        another, lastly and lingeringly at GROUP
                        WORKER.*

WELFARE WORKER: (*Quickly*) It's unavoidable. I don't want to
                        break up that hearts and roses routine with
                        you and the tenants by bringing you into
                        this, but we need a witness to legally com-
                        mit her.

FIRST COP: Hey, what's the stall?

                        *Procession winds its way up into the dark-
                        ness. Sound of sharp knocking can be heard.*

WELFARE WORKER: Martha, c'mon and open the door.

                        *Sound of frenetic scrambling—then absolute
                        stillness. Finally the door opens a little.*

MARTHA: (*Shrilly*) What do you folks want? I'm busy
                        right now. You'll have to come back an-
                        other time.

                        (*Starts to close door.*)

SECOND COP: (*Entering the room*) We want you to come
                        with us for a little while.

MARTHA: (*Frantically*) What do you mean? I paid for
                        this room. The rent is all paid for, and
                        you're not going to give it to anyone else.

WELFARE WORKER: Just for overnight you're going down with
                        these people to have a little checkup. Then
                        you can come back.

(*Figure can be seen backing away from the door*)

MARTHA: (*Angrily*) Well, I can't go *now*. I have other things to do. Besides I'm not even dressed to go anywhere. (*Pleadingly*) I don't even have my stockings on.

FIRST COP: (*Brusquely*) We can't leave this room. You'll have to try and get changed this way.

(*Figure is seen retreating to a corner, awkwardly posturing to retain its dignity. Sounds of clothes being pulled on. Light falls on stage left where a small group has gathered.*)

LEWIS: Say, what's going on upstairs? Did you see all those cops at the door?

MRS. WATERS: I heard 'em say they come to get Martha and take her away.

MRS. COMPSON: She been here a long time, 'bout ten years, ever since her husband died.

LEWIS: She's a fine woman. Did you know that she used to be some kind of legal secretary, a real nice-looking woman when she first came here. Started the drinkin', then she quit her job.

MRS. LINCOLN: She belongs here in this building. We want her here. Whose rules say she got to go?

(*Stage left darkens*)

WELFARE WORKER: Ready, Martha? (*MARTHA turns to GROUP WORKER*)

MARTHA: I need a cigarette.

GROUP WORKER: Here.

MARTHA: Thank you, honey. (*Suddenly terrified at the realization of what is happening*) All the folks seeing me coming out of here will think I've been arrested.

                       Exit all but GROUP WORKER. Spotlight falls upon the room and his eye catches sight of a picture on the dresser—picture of a young couple, hand in hand. The sound of gently mocking laughter fills the room as the curtain closes.

Scene II   *Basement room, two weeks later. Room is cleaner than in Act One. Several pictures of sunshine and springtime hang on the wall, curtains are up, same untouched* New York Times *lies on the table. A partition to stage left suggests another room, the social service office. Voices from the office are dimly present in the background. The tables in the club are spaced apart in large checkerboard formation, at diagonals to one another. At each table there are a couple of people manipulating their smaller boards. Strings from the ceiling are attached to the players' arms, making them look like puppets. Most of the time they are unaware of the strings' presence, but as the strings occasionally force an involuntary movement, they seem to be momentarily conscious that something is controlling them. The manipulation proceeds on these levels throughout the scene.*

CRAIG: (*Studying the board intensely*) Hurry up Paul. Move it!

COORDINATOR: (*From the office*) Our goal for this project is to straighten these people out. Do you really think they can make the right decisions themselves?

EDWARDS: O.K. I moved. I moved him backwards. He's safe there, you can't touch him.

CRAIG: (*Intensely*) I will get you sooner or later. I can wait.

VOICE: (*From the office*) But these people don't even trust us. If we come pushing into their lives, they'll move farther away from us than ever.

KING: Do you know that was a stupid move. Oops, put that back, you can't change it now.

ROBINSON: I'm still deciding if I wanted to make that move. Suppose you've already done it and then you change your mind?

KING: Then you stick by it, for it's done.

VOICE: (*From the office*) It's a case of poor planning on life's part, not theirs. Even if they knew what could be had from life, what would many of them do about it? Then again, maybe they know something about it that we don't.

COORDINATOR: Your slant is all wrong. They see us in a power position, so we're in a good position to influence them. I know what makes these people tick.

GROUP WORKER: Just how well do you know them?

WALLACE: (*Fiercely*) One, two, three jumps on one move and I got a king too. You thought he'd be protected. No more king. He was easy to knock off!

(*Enter Mr. LINCOLN*)

LINCOLN: (*Loudly*) Can I get in on a game?

CRAIG: You're lookin' happy. How did it go today?

LINCOLN: (*Spiritedly*) They didn't need no one right now. But I'm afraid that Mrs. Lincoln will be lookin' up some more ads for me to check out. Lordy, it ain't hardly worth it, no, man.

KING: (*Intensely*) There is a strategy to this, you know. There are two types of players. To the corners, keep safe, move carefully, back yourself up. The other, head right into the middle, where everything is going on, take a chance, lose one, then take what you can from your opponent. The first way is really a case of delaying the inevitable. The other alternative is to get it over with. You're never sure which one you'll do.

COORDINATOR: (*Confidentially*) We know what rehabilitation measures will be successful here. We give them a club and this place will begin to develop a social tone.

KING: (*Pensively*) You're never sure . . .

GROUP WORKER: (*Tonelessly*) Just like that, huh?

KING: (*Savagely*) Aha, one, two jumps. Didn't you *see* that? You thought I would move your way. Guess I fooled you, stupid!

                    (*The lights dim gradually until all is complete darkness. The curtain falls.*)

END

Primary Education in Urban Slums:
A Mental Health Orientation*

Sol Gordon

For the most part, educators and the general public tend to think that the best way to improve the educative process is to offer new courses of study. As society's need for greater numbers of highly trained people has increased, the rearrangement of textbooks and course outlines has multiplied, often without meaningful evaluation of the underlying problems created by a rapidly changing social order. Curriculum change is certainly a worthwhile endeavor, but I would argue that it is successful only when teachers understand the nature of the reasons for the change and when the school itself is operating at a "profit." By "profit" I mean the academic "surplus" that accrues when large numbers of children in a school appear to be learning, when a favorable teacher-student ratio is operative, when academic expectancy is high, and when both teachers and administrators appear genuinely receptive to new ideas. On the other hand, when the school is operating at a "loss," curriculum innovation does not have a significant impact unless it is grounded in a sound examination of the "here-and-now" problems particular to a given situation.

The discussion in this paper falls into two parts. The first examines some of the critical issues faced by schools in depressed areas, and the second presents the rationale for a primary school program designed to meet these problems. This rationale takes its starting point from the hypothesis that school failure in urban slum neighborhoods need not necessarily be a function of the perceptual or cognitive style of a particular subculture and, further, that at very early ages such "style of life" factors do not crucially affect the development of academic orientations and skills.

Until now, attempts to solve the problems of educating the urban slum child have centered on remediation. A more pertinent approach, however, is to examine the impact of the early school experience upon the educational performance of the child. One must examine the school, the child's perception of his role in the school, and (equally important) the teacher's perception of the child.

* The author gratefully acknowledges the assistance given him by Martin Berlin.

189

Admittedly, the total problem is greater than the sum of the parts I am about to describe. Given the state of our present knowledge, however, any attempt to improve the educative process in urban slums will hinge upon the discovery of answers to the specific issues I will outline. My hope is that such answers will be used as a starting point for clearer and more comprehensive solutions.

THE URBAN SLUM CHILD AND HIS TEACHERS

At the outset, let us discard the notion that schools in poor neighborhoods are caught in an environmental trap from which they cannot escape, and examine the academic problems of the urban slum child without preconceptions.

In the report *Schools for the 60's*, the National Education Association (1963, p. 10) noted:

> *An important fact which is not always recognized by educators is that every child has an inner push to become a more complete self, to learn what can become meaningful to him. The art of teaching lies in stimulating this force and in keeping it alive, free and developing. To do so, it is essential to understand the learner, to know what he is working on, what he is against, what his basic assets are.*

Yet, if one examines the academic achievement of many of our urban slum children, it is just this "inner push" that appears to be missing. In kindergarten, these children appear as receptive as middle-class children. But by the time they reach the fifth grade, a great many have become sullen and angry, and are impervious to education.

Martin Deutsch (1963) suggests that the slum child, from the moment he enters school, is so poorly prepared to produce what it demands that failures of this sort are almost inevitable. Examining the environmental and psychological factors upon which intellectual growth is predicated, Deutsch suggests that stimulus deprivation, the experience of poverty, and inadequate training in auditory and visual discrimination are responsible for the slum child's handicaps. Yet Deutsch also makes the point that in the first grade one sees only a very small difference among individual socioeconomic or racial groups on measures of their intellectual, linguistic, and conceptual abilities. The implications of this comment are worth further exploration.

As Deutsch makes clear, children from disadvantaged areas are likely to be deprived of many of the experiences that facilitate learning. Equally important, however, is the fact that the educational system has failed to develop a climate for learning which is geared to the needs of such children. James Baldwin (1963, p. 60), in "A Talk to Teachers," has written that "any Negro who is born in this country and undergoes the American educational system runs the risk of becoming schizophrenic." I think it fair to suggest that Mr. Baldwin's statement is applicable to all children who are educated in urban slum schools, where they readily discover that equality and freedom of choice are not part of their heritage. As Baldwin points out, children are not yet aware that it is dangerous "to look too deeply at anything," and thus they look at everything, and very early draw their own conclusions. It is not surprising that as a result they depreciate themselves and exhibit "acting out" behavior.

To what extent does the school contribute to the child's negative feelings? For one thing, when teachers think of their students as being indifferent and disadvantaged, they have a tendency to conclude that little can be done to educate the children unless changes are effected in their family or environment. The position of the Educational Policies Commission of the NEA, in its publication *Education and the Disadvantaged American* (1962), supports such a view (emphasis added).

The special educational problems of disadvantaged children generally have their roots in infancy and early childhood. They continue to be reinforced in the home after the child begins schooling.

Yet a child's attitude of indifference is not necessarily the result of an economically impoverished home. Brookover and Gottlieb (1963), reviewing recent studies of the relationship between social class and school achievement, have concluded that the commonly held belief that social classes differ in the value they attach to education is questionable. The lower classes may be less sophisticated in communicating their values to the educational bureaucracy and in defining their level of aspiration; however, minority-group pressure for equal educational opportunities indicates that these groups do place a high premium on education. Even more noteworthy in this respect is the observation by Deutsch that the slum child comes to school with a relatively neutral attitude about education.

The real danger in misperceiving the abilities and desires of a child is that it leads to an attitude which treats him as different, and when this happens, the child in fact tends to become "different." Children who are treated in school as if they were ineducable tend to see themselves in this way and almost invariably become ineducable. Similarly, children who are placed in inferior groups suffer a sense of humiliation—a feeling that influences their attitude toward school and the entire learning process. In simple terms, they come to dislike themselves, and tend to function in a self-defeating, self-destructive manner. Either they become consumed with self-hate, which can take the form of depressed, apathetic behavior, or they come to project their self-hatred onto society, in the form of delinquent behavior.

If we are to help make it possible for every child to reach the optimum development of which he is capable, we must discover ways to show him that he is a worthwhile human being, that he has a place in society, that he is needed and not surplus. We may develop the most advanced curriculum innovations, we may construct the most modern school buildings, but we still fail to educate if we do not succeed in giving youngsters the "chest-filling" pride that is essential to the learning process.

The teacher is responsible for achieving the kind of classroom that supports feelings of personal adequacy in children. Through his relationship with the child, the teacher can contribute toward the development of those positive feelings toward self and others that make learning possible. Davidson and Lang (1960) found that the more positive the child's perception of his teacher's feelings, the higher his achievement. Combs and Snygg (1959) and George H. Mead (1934) have hypothesized that the child learns what he perceives he is able to learn, and that such self-perception is acquired through interacting with "significant others" who hold expectations of the child as a learner. Evidence by Staines (1956) suggests that teachers, through their role as "significant others," can enhance the self-image of their students by creating an atmosphere of greater psychological security. In the urban slum school, a dynamic teacher can have a dramatic impact upon the learner, both by providing the child with a reason for learning and as a focal point for positive identification.

In the middle-class suburban school, the teacher-student relationship develops, for the most part, in a "natural" way. In urban slum schools, morale. What are some of the obstacles which the urban slum teacher turnover, and suffer from a general climate of frustration and low morale. What are some of the obstacles which the urban slum teacher faces?

Too often teachers are handicapped in their efforts by a lack of direction from school administrators. As Niemeyer (1963, p. 65) has stated, "the *full weight* of the school system should be aimed *directly*, and not just indirectly, at helping the teacher teach." Too often the direction teachers receive is ambiguous, unrealistic, and self-defeating.

Also, though teachers generally pride themselves upon their objectivity and lack of prejudice, they are often influenced by subtle motivational forces, difficult for them to perceive. The work of Videbeck (1960), Brookover (1962), and Wylie (1961), analyzing the teacher-learner "transaction," has developed the view that the teacher, like the learner, brings much more to the teaching-learning process than a knowledge and skill in presenting subject matter. The teacher brings to the situation, as well, a certain awareness (or lack of it) that the process is basically a delicate human transaction requiring skill and sensitivity in human relations, and an awareness (or lack of it) of his own needs and motivations and of their effects upon the learning process. As Bradford (1961, p. 8) writes:

> *To what extent do his [the teacher's] needs to control people, to maintain dependency upon himself, or to seek love and affection, distort and disturb his helper function and the learning transaction? To what extent does his fear of hostility develop repression in the learner so that healthy conflict as a basis of learning is lacking? . . . Knowing one's own motivations and their possible consequences for others better enables one to keep motivations under direction and control.*

The teacher also brings an ability—or lack of ability—to accept the learner as a person. Such acceptance connotes the ability to respect and listen, and to separate the individual, as such, from the disagreeable aspects of his behavior. Bradford concludes (p. 9):

> *The teacher is a second part of the teacher-learning transaction. His emotional, motivational, perceptual, and attitudinal systems, and his awareness of them and their consequences for learning and change are important forces in the effective teaching-learning.*

Jersild (1955, p. 3) elaborates upon this theme in his excellent book, *When Teachers Face Themselves,* when he raises the question: "What does this effort to help students mean in a distinctly intimate, personal way in the teacher's own life?" The question is especially pertinent in regard to teachers in urban slum schools. What, indeed, are the personal meanings to the teacher when Johnny comes into the classroom and says, "I ain't got no pencil"? If the teacher feels that "ain't" is used by ignorant, stupid people, and translates that feeling to Johnny, Johnny is apt to recall that his own parents and relatives use the term. Or what if Johnny is caught fighting and is informed that only the "scum of the earth" allow themselves to be caught up in physical violence? Such responses, as Hodgkinson (1962) points out, serve only to place the students in an untenable position, with the school's values contradicting his accustomed way of life.

The values of the modern school are contained in the dicta of hard work, delayed reward and gratification, cleanliness, obedience, and intellectual achievement. The urban slum child is often unable to equate his personal ambitions with these values. If teachers are to utilize the school experience as a form of social investment, they must recognize that the school's values are *goals, rather than prerequisites of learning.*

The aim of the school in urban slum neighborhoods should be to move beyond the myth that low-income children need a special remedial setting in order to learn, and to commit itself to the concept that the school can promote the greatest possible individual growth within the existing classroom structure. Under responsible leadership and through dynamic teaching, the school can—and should—make headway with a child, even if his home and neighborhood are reinforcing "inappropriate" attitudes and habits.

THE MALADJUSTED CHILD

But even given the best staff, it nonetheless remains true that every classroom in a slum school contains a high percentage of physically and emotionally handicapped children who are not learning.

It has been argued by some educators that the school is not the proper setting for programs designed to rehabilitate the maladjusted child. I am convinced otherwise—that the most hopeful opportunity for success in this area is within the framework of the elementary school.[1]

Current estimates of the total number of maladjusted children being seen in mental health clinics, both private and public, range from five to ten per cent of all children diagnosed as maladjusted (1960). Colleagues and I have detailed elsewhere (Gordon, Berkowitz, and Cacace; 1964) the failure of social agencies to meet the mental health needs of an ever growing number of disturbed children from working-class fam-

---

[1] Of course, as Bower (1963) has pointed out, "Neurotic processes in individuals can and do result in culturally defined successful behavior, just as one can be a blatant failure without benefit of personality defect or neurosis." There are many socially and emotionally disturbed children—anxiety ridden, compulsive, or phobic children, for example—who do learn. But especially in the setting of a poor neighborhood, the disturbed child who is not learning has a problem of great magnitude. Further, as the school focuses on the needs of the latter, it hopefully would provide the best mental health climate for the former as well.

ilies. All too often, the intake policies of such agencies are geared to meet the needs of maladjusted children from intact, middle-class, white families (Gordon, 1965). Schools, welfare agencies, and courts which have the greatest involvement with disturbed children from lower-class backgrounds are all becoming increasingly aware that they cannot rely on the "best social agencies" for any significant help.

Personal experience in a South Philadelphia district, which had a school population of some 20,000 children, most of whom came from Negro and Italian working-class families, has revealed the following: that the number of children of latency age needing special help ranges from five per cent in stable neighborhoods to 25 per cent in depressed areas. Moreover, only a handful of elementary school children in any one year are ever successfully referred to, or accepted by, social agencies for treatment. At the elementary school level, especially in the predominantly Negro schools, it is usually the case that not a single emotionally disturbed child is in treatment at any clinic or social agency. Yet, in one elementary school, which is located in a relatively stable, working-class neighborhood (approximately 70 per cent Italian, 20 per cent Negro, and ten per cent Jewish and others), 18.6 per cent of the pupils were identified by the faculty as emotionally disturbed (Gordon, Berkowitz, and Cacace; 1964). It is impossible to calculate in terms of dollars the loss of classroom time and the gradual erosion of teacher morale created by a problem of such magnitude.[2]

Very often, by viewing treatment strategies for emotional and social maladjustment as psychological and medical matters, we have neglected educational methods that may well be more effective. But whatever the method of rehabilitation, it should be applied in proportions commensurate to the nature of the problem. For instance, it is ludicrous to apply national educational norms in regard to children in urban slum areas. Slogans such as "one counselor for every 600 pupils," or "one mental health team for every 20,000 pupils," or "one teacher for every 30 pupils," make sense in stable middle-class neighborhoods, but when applied to urban slum neighborhoods, they have the effect of depriving up to one-third of the children of their opportunity to learn.

A chief defect of recent programs for educating emotionally handicapped children has been to realize a greatly expanded diagnostic service without a corresponding expansion of special services. This discrepancy served to compound the frustration of school officials, who now

[2] It should be noted, however, that the plight of the urban slum school is unique only in detail and degree. Suburban "middle class" schools also have their problem children. The important difference is that the avenues open to urban slum schools for "remediation" are practically nonexistent (Gordon, 1964).

had to contend with "that many more" *fully diagnosed* pupils whom they did not know where to refer or how to manage.

On the other hand, too many school administrators fail to realize that remedial education, special classes for emotionally disturbed and brain injured children, group counseling, creative dramatics, and re-classification and transfer opportunities within the school are also valid programs if properly handled. As Redl and Wattenberg (1959, p. 206) note:

> *Success in any area of living can act as an emotional tonic. Damage done to a child in his home or neighborhood may be partially repaired by satisfactory school experiences. Since school is built around learning activities, the mastery of new skills and knowledge is the focus of such pleasant experiences. Their importance as such should not be undervalued.*

Special classes should be regarded as opportunities for the child to achieve success and satisfaction, often for the first time.

It may be useful at this point to confront more explicitly the concept of emotional and social maladjustment as it pertains to the school setting.[3] A very useful concept for educational centers is the one developed by Bower and Lambert (Bower, 1963; Bower and Lambert, 1961). They define the emotionally handicapped child as an individual who, to a significant extent and over a period of time, has had a moderate to marked reduction in behavioral freedom. In the classroom, this loss of freedom results in a noticeable susceptibility to one or more of these five patterns of behavior:

1. An inability to learn which cannot be adequately explained by intellectual, sensory, neurological, or general health factors.
2. An inability to build or maintain satisfactory interpersonal relationships with peers and teachers.
3. Inappropriate or immature types of behavior or feelings under otherwise normal conditions.
4. A general pervasive mood of unhappiness or depression.
5. A tendency to develop physical symptoms, such as speech difficulties, or other pains or fears.

Bower (1960) emphasizes the importance of not equating certain types of nonconformity with emotional disturbance. What distinguishes transient manifestations of disturbance—that is, isolated incidents that

[3] In this paper I use the terms "emotionally disturbed," "emotionally handicapped," and "emotionally maladjusted" interchangeably.

are suggestive of disturbance (such as grief reactions)—from serious chronic disturbances, is precisely the relatively brief duration of the former. Further, the behavior of the "well-adjusted" child is adaptive, i.e., it can be altered by the child through success and failure, reward and punishment, or persuasion. In the emotionally disturbed child, the motivating forces behind the behavior are predominantly on an unconscious level.

Basically, Bower's approach is descriptive and avoids the complications inherent in diagnostic categorizations (see for example, Eisenberg [1960]). Difficulties arise, however, when we consider the problem of defining the socially deprived and the delinquent child.

There is a growing tendency to consider delinquency as a "normal" response to a particular cultural milieu (Cohen and Short, 1958; Kobrin, 1962; Miller, 1958). Moore (1958), in a handbook issued by the National Education Association to "help teachers cope with the problems of delinquency," makes a distinction between cultural and emotional delinquency. He defines the cultural delinquent as the otherwise normal youth who is antisocial primarily as a matter of "going along with the gang." In contrast, the emotional delinquent is the bully, the sadist, or the violent child motivated by inner urges.

While there is no question that culture, caste, class, prejudice, and poverty are factors in delinquency, I find myself, for the most part, unimpressed with the arguments of the cultural determinists. How, for example, given the view of the cultural determinists, can we explain the fact that even in the worst slums the majority of the children are neither delinquent nor disturbed (if such a dichotomy can be made)? A visit to schools in the most disadvantaged areas indicates that many children are learning and are reasonably well-adjusted. My own experience (Gordon, 1962) during the last ten years with more than two hundred chronic delinquents—in both group and individual psychotherapy—supports the views of Kaufman (Kaufman, Makkay, and Zehack, 1959), Reiner (Reiner and Kaufman, 1959) and Burks (Burks and Harrison, 1962), all of whom see delinquency primarily as a response to rejection by the mother (and as a means of coping with the resultant depression). In almost all cases of delinquency with which I have been acquainted, the father either was not present in the home, was an alcoholic, or was ineffectual.[4]

---

[4] While I am relatively pessimistic about what can be done for chronic delinquents by the time they reach their teens, I am very optimistic about what can be done within the setting of the school for *younger* predelinquent children—given the existence of certain special programs. As a rule, if the delinquent child is seen as "unsocialized" rather than emotionally disturbed, and if the parents are known to be uncooperative, the educator tends to refer the child to a disciplinary

In summary, the majority of low-income children are *not* emotionally disturbed. It is the responsibility of the school to plan programs for the children who are "damaged" and require rehabilitation. Involved here is the concept of "secondary prevention": a series of measures based on early recognition and prompt treatment of a disturbance, in order to modify it. At the same time, the school must focus seriously on the learning disturbances that children exhibit in kindergarten and first grade, and devise educational measures aimed at "primary prevention."[5]

THE "ACADEMIC SCHOOL"—AN APPROACH TO PRIMARY EDUCATION

Many approaches to the solution of educating the urban slum child have resolved themselves into the creation of special programs. Representative is the work of Frank Riessman (1963). In his effort to design better educational opportunities for disadvantaged children, Riessman has advanced a program of curriculum innovation based on the "mental style of low-income people" (p. 11). He maintains that when the urban slum child begins school, he is:

1. Oriented to the physical and visual rather than the aural.
2. Content-centered rather than form-centered.
3. Externally oriented rather than introspective.
4. Problem-centered rather than abstract-centered.
5. Inductive rather than deductive.
6. Spatial rather than temporal.
7. Slow, careful, patient, persevering (in areas of importance), rather than quick, clever, facile.
8. Prefers games and action rather than tests.
9. Has an expressive rather than instrumental orientation.
10. Follows a pattern of one-track thinking and unorthodox learning rather than "other-directed" flexibility.
11. Uses words in relation to action rather than being word-bound (inventive word power and "hip" language).

---

school. In recent years there has been a significant increase in the number of elementary school children who have been referred to such schools. Frequently the effect of these referrals is to reinforce a criminal career. Yet I do not know what else can be done, in school settings where no special programs exist, to protect the large majority of students who want to learn.

[5] Bower (1963) develops brilliantly a conceptual framework for the primary prevention of mental and emotional disorders.

On the basis of these attributes, Reissman has advanced 11 specific suggestions for curriculum innovation.[6] Curiously, many of the suggestions mirror programs developed for maladjusted, brain-injured, and retarded children. I have already discussed the pitfalls of viewing a total school population in terms of a minority that has been diagnosed as maladjusted. My own observations have led me to believe that the learning disabilities seen in urban slum schools can be found (though at lesser degrees of intensity) in all schools. It follows from this, I believe, that special programs are justified in the urban slum only to the extent that such programs are applicable to *all* schools regardless of social class and geographic location. A similar point of view is expressed by a New York City teacher (Johnson, 1963, p. 16), who writes:

> *Stop building special programs to make the child more entrenched in the prestige vacuum by accepting his plight and weaving curriculum and projects around him. End the waste of taxpayers' money by considering him educable as any other child. If he doesn't learn to read, he's either in need of a very thorough medical examination or he has not been properly taught.*

In short, programs and curricula for urban slum schools should be such that they will be viewed with favor in the most advanced and advantaged suburban white schools. These programs and curricula should ignore entirely the fact that the pupils for whom they are specifically designed are members of an economically disadvantaged group or a minority that suffers the experience of discrimination, but should assume, instead, that urban slum children are as capable of learning as "middle-class" children, if only provided with the proper opportunities.

---

[6] These suggestions are: (1) to adapt the Montessori methods, which have a strong sensory-motor orientation; (2) to segregate the sexes in the early grades, since the disadvantaged boy is more antagonistic to school than is the disadvantaged girl, and his work is generally poorer; (3) to develop a program of teacher sponsors where every child sees a teacher other than his own for a half hour per week—"just to talk," acquire school know-how, have a friend, etc.; (4) to develop a program where role-playing is the central method of instruction; (5) to develop a program of school (and class) competition through the use of spelling bees, special projects, contests, etc.; (6) to plan for a special summer session program, possibly for individuals having special educational problems; (7) to develop reading materials that utilize "hip" language to be used essentially as a transitional technique to provide motivation and stimulation; (8) to provide low-income youngsters with paper textbooks which they would own and be encouraged to mark up and use "physically"; (9) to experiment with the new British phonetic Augmented Roman Alphabet; (10) to develop films appropriate for teaching low-income groups and for preparing teachers to do so; (11) to train guidance workers and teachers in special methods of "learning analysis" so that they will be able to utilize the learning styles of low-income youngsters.

An "academic school" approach to primary education in urban slum areas is an approach grounded on the assumption that the school, during the primary grades, can enrich the experiential background of the child, and provide him with the tools and attitudes necessary for later academic success. It is an approach that relies on creative teaching rather than on curriculum innovation, on early prevention rather than remediation. It proceeds on the basis of the thesis that a child's emotional life cannot be considered apart from his cognitive and perceptual field—that is, that his ability to learn is closely related to his self-perception and to his understanding of his role in the learning process.[7] In addition to developing programs specifically for children, an "academic school" approach would seek to involve parents and to improve their influences in the educational development of children. It would also seek more effective relationships between health and service agencies and the schools.[8]

It is no longer practical to wait for children to reach "readiness periods" for learning. It is essential to give the child experiences that *make* him ready to learn. I believe the academic school is an approach that will reclaim potential problem children before they reach the stage of remediation. I further believe that the experience of successfully meeting academic challenges in the primary grades will provide these children with a firm foundation for later school success.[9]

The school has enormously expanded its function as American society has become more complicated and more demanding. Today it is generally agreed that education should aim at developing the students' abilities to write and speak clearly, to deal competently with numbers and figures, to think critically, to appreciate personal and cultural differences, and to enjoy the worlds of art and music. At the same time, the

[7] Perhaps most damaging to the child's self-perception have been IQ tests, the results of which also affect the teacher's attitude toward the child. The evidence is now overwhelming that high intellectual potential exists in a large percentage of individuals from lower status groups and that such potential need only be "minded" by an approach to learning that tailors fundamental knowledge to the interests and capacities of the child (Grossack, 1963; Clark, 1963). Research findings have also indicated that IQ tests are "culture bound," and that they should be used with the greatest care and only by professionals who understand their function.
[8] However, even if parental and community support should prove inadequate, the school as such should and can meet its educative responsibilities.
[9] I am now in the process of developing a program for a model school grounded on the approach described here. The program also seeks to encourage integration in the anticipation that a school of this nature will be attractive to children of all races. Such an approach is related to New York City's "saturation plan." (Cf. *The New York Times,* Educational Supplement, 1964.) I might mention that the program I am developing utilizes virtually none of the proposals advanced by Reissman.

school is expected to function as a "social conditioner," that is, to prepare the young for entrance into the existing social order.

When we consider the urban slum, it is clear that the school has defaulted in both these functions. We discover youngsters who are living apart from and outside of the mainstream of American "middle-class life." These youngsters are not prepared to enter the existing social order as useful citizens, and, in reality, seldom do.

We have failed to come to grips with this problem largely because of our tendency to blame our educational failures on flaws in the social environment of the children. But, as I have already noted, an extensive body of evidence and theory suggests that children, despite genetic and environmental predisposition, are more educable than has been traditionally supposed. In the first grades, slum children are as bright and eager to learn as any other. It is the *school* environment that determines whether or not they will.[10] Studies indicate that even intelligence is subject to development within the school. Lagemann (1964, p. 4), paraphrasing Hunt (1961), writes that "the practice so widespread in American schools of using a child's IQ score to rate him more or less permanently as mentally inferior or superior to other children his age . . . [is] invalid. A child's score on an IQ test merely indicates in a very tentative way the intellectual progress he has made so far in solving certain kinds of problems. His future intellectual potential depends on the learning experiences still in store for him." Hunt, Bloom (1964), and others have reviewed many techniques that have been successful in fostering the development of advanced intellectual abilities in young children. These techniques might also be employed to encourage the intellectual development of the disadvantaged.

Reviews and studies of this sort also serve to highlight the importance of the early school years in the development of human capabilities. The mental processes which become established exert a determinate effect upon the mental growth and educational development of the individual. Bloom even suggests that the stage of development bypassed in one period cannot be fully recovered in another. The early school years are especially important for those urban slum children who at the present time find neither success nor fulfillment in school. As John Niemeyer (1963, p. 64), president of the Bank Street College, has observed, by the time such children "get to the third grade, their attitudes toward the task of the school world, and their attitudes about themselves as participants in that world are pretty firmly fixed. From that point on, for the most part, we face the problem of remediation."

[10] Admittedly, not all "poor" groups manifest the same problems. The problems of Negroes, for example, are as much a product of prejudice as of poverty, and as such must be given special attention.

REFERENCES

Baldwin, James. 1963. "A Talk to Teachers," *Saturday Review*. December 21.

Bloom, B. S. 1964. *Stability and Change in Human Characteristics*. New York: John Wiley.

Bower, E. M. 1963. "Primary Prevention of Mental and Emotional Disorders," *American Journal of Orthopsychiatry,* 33:832–847.

Bower, E. M., and Lambert, M. H. 1961. *A Process for In-School Screening of Children with Emotional Handicaps—Manual for School Administrators and Teachers*. Princeton: Educational Testing Service.

Bradford, L. P., editor. 1961. *Human Forces in Teaching and Learning*. Washington, D.C.: National Training Laboratories.

Brookover, W. B. 1962. *The Relationship of Self-Image to Achievement in Junior High School Students*. Final Report of Cooperative Research Project No. 845. East Lansing, Michigan: Office of Research and Publications, Michigan State University.

Brookover, W. B., and Gottlieb, David. 1963. "Social Class and Education." In *Readings in the Social Psychology of Education,* ed. W. W. Charter, Jr., and N. L. Gage. Boston: Allyn and Bacon, Inc.

Burks, H. L., and Harrison, S. T. 1962. "Aggressive Behavior as a Means of Avoiding Depression," *American Journal of Orthopsychiatry*. 32:416–422.

Clark, Kenneth B. 1963. "Educational Stimulation of Racially Disadvantaged Children," in *Education in Depressed Areas,* ed. A. Harry Passow. New York: Teachers College, Columbia University.

Cohen, A. K., and Short, J. F. 1958. "Research in Delinquent Subcultures," *The Journal of Social Issues*. 14:20–37.

Combs, A. W., and Snygg, D. 1959. *Individual Behavior*. Revised Edition. New York: Harper and Brothers.

Davidson, H. H., and Lang, G. 1960. "Children's Perceptions of Their Teachers' Feelings Toward Them Related to Self-Perception, School Achievement, and Behavior," *Journal of Experimental Education*. 29: 107–118.

Deutsch, Martin. 1963. "The Disadvantaged Child and the Learning Process," in *Education in Depressed Areas,* ed. Passow. Teachers College, Columbia University.

Eisenberg, L. 1960. "Emotionally Disturbed Children and Youth," in *Children and Youth in the 1960's*. Golden Anniversary White House Conference on Child and Youth.

Gordon, S. 1962. "Combined Group and Individual Psychotherapy With Adolescent Delinquents," *Corrective Psychiatry and Journal of Social Therapy*. 814.

Gordon, S. 1964. "The Cost of Not Educating the Maladjusted Child in the Public Schools," *N.J.E.A. Bulletin*. March.

Gordon, S. 1965. "Are We Seeing the Right Patients," *American Journal of Orthopsychiatry*. 35:131–137.

Gordon, S., Berkowitz, M., and Cacace, C. 1964. "Discovering and Meeting Health Needs of Emotionally Disturbed Children of Normal Intelligence Whose Parents Are Inadequate," *Mental Hygiene*. 48:581–586.

Grossak, M. M. 1963. *Mental Health and Segregation*. New York: Springer Publishing Company.

Hodgkinson, H. L. 1962. *Education in Social and Cultural Perspectives*. Englewood Cliffs, New Jersey: Prentice-Hall, Inc.

Hunt, J. McV. 1961. *Intelligence and Experience*. New York: The Ronald Press Co.

Jersild, A. T. 1955. *When Teachers Face Themselves*. New York: Teachers College, Columbia University.

Johnson, E. C. 1963. "The Child in the Prestige Vacuum," *Integrated Education*. 1:13–16.

Kaufman, I., Makkay, E., and Zehack, J. 1959. "The Impact of Adolescence on Girls with Delinquent Character Formation," *American Journal of Orthopsychiatry*. 29:130–143.

Kobrin, S. 1962. "The Impact of Cultural Factors in Selected Problems of Adolescent Development in Middle and Lower Classes," *American Journal of Orthopsychiatry*. 32:387–390.

Lagemann, J. K. 1964. "A New Way for Children to Learn," *Redbook*. CXXII:4.

Mead, G. H. 1934. *Mind, Self and Society*. Chicago: University of Chicago Press.

Miller, W. B. 1958. "Lower Class Cultures as a Generating Milieu of Some Delinquency," *The Journal of Social Issues*. 14:5–19.

Moore, B. M. 1958. *Juvenile Delinquency—Research, Theory and Comment*. Washington, D.C.: National Education Association.

National Education Association. 1962. *Education and the Disadvantaged American*. Washington, D.C.: The authors.

National Education Association. 1963. *Schools for the 60's*. A Report of the Project on Instructions. New York: McGraw-Hill.

The New York Times. 1964. Educational Supplement. January 16.

Niemeyer, J. H. 1963. "School Integration: The School's Responsibility," in *Integrating the Urban School,* eds. G. J. Klopf and I. A. Laster. New York: Teachers College, Columbia University.

Redl, F., and Wattenberg, W. 1959. *Mental Hygiene in Teaching*. New York: Harcourt, Brace and World, Inc.

Reiner, B. S., and Kaufman, J. 1959. *Character Disorders in Parents of Delinquents*. New York: Family Service of America.

Riessman, F. 1963. "Cultural Styles of the Disadvantaged," *Integrated Education*. 1:9–15.

Staines, J. W. 1956. "Self-Picture as a Factor in the Classroom," *British Journal of Education Psychology*. 28:97–111.

Videbeck, R. 1960. "Self-Conception and the Reaction of Others," *Sociometry*. 23:351–359.

Wylie, R. C. 1961. *The Self-Concept*. Lincoln: University of Nebraska Press.

PART IV

Negro Children and Youth in Northern Big Cities

A major problem today in planning educational services for children and youth is an uncertainty about their individual needs. One can plan in a vacuum, one can plan from stereotypes, or one can plan from specific and definitive information. Earlier sections of this book dealt with broad aspects of education: the urban context, intergroup relations, educational programs, and how we learn about these areas. We turn now to the individual child who—often with embarrassment at the inadequacy of the terms—is variously called economically disadvantaged, culturally deprived, urban poor, or educationally disadvantaged. The point is, no phrase or slogan can subsume millions of children who live in big cities. In this collection, we have focused on the child who is handicapped for *one* obvious reason, his skin color. We are not proud of this emphasis. But once we face the reality of racial prejudice, hoping to remove stereotypes and our own biases, we can seek understanding of the actual abilities of black children, how they learn under different conditions, their attitudes towards minority status, what their school and their world look like, and how they are raised at home.

The varied papers in this section address themselves to uncovering stereotypes and myths by trying to understand children and by describing previously uncharted situations in which they are involved. The first paper, by Bernard Mackler and Morsley Giddings, confronts the stereotype of cultural deprivation. Humans cannot live in a social vacuum; therefore, each child *must* live in a culture. As a term, "cultural deprivation" simply conveys the alienation and prejudice of professionals towards Negroes, who are defined as inferior because they do not live in the dominant culture. The irony of the term lies in its accurate reflection of the white man's bias toward Negroes—in its coinage, usage, and, worse, its initial national acceptance.

The studies by Harold Greenberg and David W. Johnson uncover more of the stereotype. Greenberg found that for Negro adolescents, reading skill and social attitudes are not significantly related. He concludes that the widely assumed importance of reading for learning about the environment should be reevaluated. Youths can be well-informed about racial problems whatever their reading level. Moreover, Greenberg's youths shared middle-class occupational aspirations.

Johnson has addressed himself to understanding what happens to youngsters who attend a Freedom School. He asked questions about changes in self- and racial attitudes before and after attending a school whose aim was to enhance the child's self-acceptance of being Negro. One of his major findings is that participation in this program gave the children an increasing conviction that Negroes and whites were equal.

The educational implications of these two studies are worth noting. Greenberg's work asks about the importance of reading for knowing about social problems, thereby implying that the educator must reevaluate the importance of reading in the school curriculum. Johnson modestly raises the central issue that Negro children's self-concept can be increased over a short period of time, if personal worth is initially acknowledged and consistently and honestly reiterated.

Thelma Catalano extends Johnson's ideas on self-enhancement, worth, and respect. In her paper, she describes how understanding and misunderstanding occur between teacher and child. Catalano examines the importance of trust in knowing oneself and another—here the teacher and child—and how this can lead to personal growth in both individuals through fruitful (though often painful) encounters. The respect developed for one another increases the youngster's understanding of himself, his school, teacher, and authority figures. With these new perceptions and insights, the teacher can then reach and teach the youngsters in a more profound way.

Nelia Reynolds, in her paper "The Influence of Emotional Disturbance and Social Class on Sensitivity to Vocal Expression," shows how research can be used to understand children. She compares poor Negro children with more affluent white children to see if emotional disturbance and social background influence a child's sensitivity. The results of her study indicate that children from middle-income homes are significantly more attuned to vocal expressions of emotion than are children from lower-income families. This finding occurs regardless of the I.Q. of a given child. The data reveal that the degree of emotional health seems less important in gauging the vocal expression of emotion than family income and race. Although the data appear conclusive, Reynolds cautiously and honestly raises the issue of reliability: the white testers who recorded the data and worked with the Negro children could have created the unexpected results. We see here that the question of trust and mutual redefinition discussed in Catalano's paper has implications not only for classrooms, but for all interpersonal involvement, including the brief research encounter between white and Negro which occurred in Reynolds' inquiry. What we study may be affected by what we are as well as what we do.

Imogene Cahill, in her study "Child Rearing Practices in Lower Socioeconomic Ethnic Groups," examined the rearing of Puerto Rican as well as Negro children. With the present emphasis on preschool programs and Head Start programs, we need to understand the very young child, his home, and the way he has been raised. Parents transmit a culture to their offspring through their values, customs, affect, learning, and behavior. The fit between home and school is often misunderstood by schoolmen, partly out of ignorance, partly out of fear, partly from both. Cahill's detailed inquiry concludes that there is a good fit between child-rearing practices and the child's life across all three groups, but there is an inappropriateness for school existence. If this is so, one must question a school program that does not attend to such discrepancies. Cahill concludes her study with a question. If the child's peer group looks contemptuously at education while his parents long for his educational attainment but show little day-to-day interest in learning, what are the prospects for the youngster persistently pursuing educational goals?

Cahill's paper describes the poor fit of middle-class life with lower-class behavior. What happens to children who cannot fit in the school situation for more special reasons? How does the big-city school system provide services that compensate for children's behavioral or emotional handicaps? Bernard Mackler, in his paper "A Report on the '600' Schools: Dilemmas, Problems, and Solutions," describes the schools for emotionally disturbed children in New York City. The special-service schools serve over 5,000 youngsters and are ethnically segregated. The Negro and Puerto Rican youngsters receive inferior education and services while white children attend clinics or are given better treatment in segregated white schools. The schools for the "disturbed" mirror the way services are distributed for the remaining "healthy" children.

Cultural Deprivation: A Study in Mythology*

Bernard Mackler and Morsley G. Giddings

The education of children from disadvantaged areas, although not a new problem in the United States, has recently become a matter of national concern. Differences between the educational attainment of children from white-collar families and children from blue-collar families continue to widen. Ausubel (1964), Hunt (1964), and Deutsch (1964) maintain that children from disadvantaged areas are inadequately prepared for an academic environment and need preschool enrichment programs if they are to do well in it.

Some educators have argued that it is difficult to teach these children because their parents are not interested in education and therefore do not provide their offspring with favorable educational attitudes. Other arguments have focused on the school's inability to motivate the youngsters. At present, the term "cultural deprivation" is used to account for the academic failure among these pupils. Frank Riessman (1962, p. 3) describes cultural deprivation as "those aspects of middle-class culture —such as education, books, formal language—from which these [disadvantaged] groups have not benefited."[1] Generalizations such as this one are too broad and far too premature in the light of the data from which they are extrapolated. In this particular instance, moreover, the generalization is misleading and inconclusive. In the past, parents in disadvantaged areas rejected the schools and all they had to offer because of their own poor experiences there and because they had no hope that education was really for them or their children. Today, however, partly because of the civil rights movement, many parents of disadvantaged children believe and see a hope that the schools can be an instrument for both the realization of their own aspirations and the yearnings they have for their children. The report prepared by

* This paper is a revised version of an article that appeared in *Teachers College Record,* April 1965. Preparation of the original paper was facilitated by a grant, 200-4-102, from the Welfare Administration, U.S. Department of Health, Education and Welfare. The authors appreciate the suggestions and criticisms of Thelma Catalano and Herbert J. Gans.
1 Many educators and social scientists would like to avoid the term "cultural deprivation" and apologize for its use by indicating its inaccuracy. Yet the term continues to be used. Riessman himself provides an excellent example of such an attitude. After noting the inherent contradictions in the term, he nonetheless accepts it "because it is . . . in current usage."

HARYOU (Harlem Youth Opportunities Unlimited, Inc., 1964) and studies by Cloward and Jones (1963), Durkin (1961), Lewis (1963), and Cagle and Deutscher (1964) have all indicated that the parents of disadvantaged children are "interested in education" and want their children to receive a good education. The civil rights movement also attests to this fact.

Riessman refers to the anti-intellectualism of the disadvantaged. To an extent, he is correct. Hofstadter (1963) points out that anti-intellectualism is pervasive in present-day America. But why should the disadvantaged be singled out as a prime example of anti-intellectual propensities when the majority of us is anti-egghead?

If the youngsters from disadvantaged areas are to be helped, if they are to be offered equality of educational opportunity, we must discard the tags, labels, misunderstandings, and myths which have blocked the paths to progress in the past, are doing so at the present time, and if not changed, will continue to do so in the future. The child from a minority group, particularly the Negro child, is already heir to the characteristics of caste status. As a member of a minority group, he carries the scars of every type of discrimination and of legal and forced segregation. He also has available to him only limited channels of mobility. Far too often, tags such as "cultural deprivation" have served as alibis for the country's failure to provide an adequate educational program for disadvantaged children.[2] Every American Negro child is the victim of the history of his race in the United States.

A closer consideration of the individual meaning of the words "deprived" and "culture" will help shed some light upon the contradiction they embody when used together. Sociologically, the word culture is much broader in meaning than in its popular usage. Butts (1955, p. 1) defines it as:

> *the whole way of life that is created, learned, held in common, and passed on from one generation to another by the members of a particular society. Culture is the sum total of ways of behaving that a group of people builds up and expects its members to acquire, share and live by. It includes the entire range of social institutions; the organized patterns of behavior; the customs and expectations, the tools and technology; the bodies of knowledge, thought and belief; the cherished ideals, values and sanctions; the forms of creative expression; and the language and modes of communication.*

[2] In all fairness to Riessman, it should be said that he is certainly sympathetic to the Negro minority group and to its ambitions. Yet he fails to realize that by using a term like "cultural deprivation," he continues to maintain the inferior status of the Negro in a more subtle and confused manner.

The Thorndike and Barnhart Dictionary defines deprivation as:

> *act of depriving; state of being deprived, and deprived as: take away*
> *from by force; keep from having or doing. Synonyms are: dispossess;*
> *divest; debar.*

Thus, when these two words are used together, they suggest, very incorrectly, that a culture can of itself be deprived, or that a culture can somehow deprive its members of the goods, skills, and behaviors that are necessary for survival and adjustment.[3]

One of the most important aspects of our present scientific-technological society is the rapid changes taking place in it. These changes occur at a faster pace than has ever before been experienced. The changes, however, are not all taking place at the same rate. The material changes, by and large, come about more rapidly and are accepted more readily than the changes in institutions. The changes in ideologies underlying institutional and material change come about most slowly of all. And this resistance to ideological change—the unwillingness, for instance, to accept a minority group member as an equal, behavior which by nature is deeply personal—appears in educational thought, in its persistent but confused utilization of "cultural deprivation" as a central term.

On the surface, the professional person is saying that the minority group member is his equal, but he does not *behave* this way. The Negro is looked down upon. The white professional is guilty on this score every time he says he has *the* answer, *the* culture, and the black man is "deprived" of it. The caretakers, the persons who are publicly responsible for the well-being of others, have reared their heads again, and in the role of those who always know what is best. On the basis of their subjective values, they have decreed that the white man has the correct culture. Anything else is inferior, inadequate, and deprived.

Until the white professional gives up his seat of omnipotence and looks at Negroes as fellow human beings, we shall not have true equality. As in psychotherapy or any comparable interpersonal relationship, when one person continues to define, restrict, or diagnose the other, there is little risk-taking on his part, little chance of both persons learning and sharing with each other. And this appears to be the case when one continually uses a term such as "cultural deprivation," which dehumanizes both the defined Negro and the white definer. It objectifies

[3] An author of this paper, Mackler, once presented findings to a group of parents that children in Harlem were being kept at home and that after-school peer relationships were kept at a minimum for fear of injury in the streets. One of the members of the audience maintained that this was cultural deprivation. If we have not agreed upon the definition of culture, then cultural deprivation becomes simply whatever we choose to so label.

both as if there were no possibility for change and growth. It also continues the authoritarian tone of the nineteenth-century white abolitionist, looking down his nose while giving a genuine, but arrogant, helping hand to the Negro.

The literature in this area appears to assume that deprivation leads to one universal reaction. But is this a sound interpretation? The research by Hebb (1949) and his associates at McGill (Bexton, Heron, and Scott, 1954), as by others conducting sensory deprivation studies, reveals that the stimulus of sensory isolation evokes a *range* of individual differences. Some subjects, although only a few, can adapt in a constructive way. Others show a variety of susceptibilities to deprivation. In short, there is a continuum of individual reaction patterns, ranging from adaptive to severely crippling and maladaptive.

A parallel situation seems evident in regard to so-called "cultural deprivation." Given equally severe, incapacitating external forces, all children do not fail. Individuals can and do succeed academically, economically, socially, and personally. Certainly, there is a preponderance of failure; still, any theory of deprivation—material, cultural, or sensory—must be broad enough to conceptualize more than one type of reaction. To maintain unequivocally that deprivation leads to a depressed reaction does not allow for individual responses which, at times, can surmount the most depriving of situations, even concentration camps (Frankl, 1963). A theory must allow for a more complex interplay of social forces and individual motivations, and for an understanding of how these factors influence both success and failure. An adequate theory of deprivation must eventually explain why certain pupils succeed and others do not, given the same social background. And we are still awaiting that theoretical formulation.

Meanwhile, we must recognize that in the United States, the shadow of slavery is still largely with us. Tags or labels such as "cultural deprivation" do not help to banish the myth of Negro inferiority. Especially in the field of civil rights, such labels only complicate the existing problems, social and otherwise. They serve to promote strife and hatred and to perpetuate the myth that disadvantaged children are of inherently inferior ability compared to children from more privileged sectors of the community.

In short, those persons whose behavior and beliefs do not conform to the dominant American culture patterns are by no means without a culture. This central fact has implications of high importance for education. So long as our perceptions of the country's race relations problem are stated in terms of the absence of culture rather than of the presence of a different subculture, we will continue to misinterpret our difficulties and their basic dimensions.

PORTRAIT OF ACHIEVEMENT

Visits to homes in disadvantaged areas indicate that the label of
"cultural deprivation" is singularly unfortunate. By a variety of criteria,
many such homes are comparable to those in more privileged areas.
Not all children coming from these homes remain illiterate. They desire
success in school, and they sometimes achieve it, quite notably. A review of the literature shows that very little is really known about the
attainment of academic success among disadvantaged youngsters,
except that it occurs with far more than chance frequency.

What follows is a sketch of the "disadvantaged" high achiever in
science in a junior high school (Giddings, 1965). The portrait is descriptive rather than explanatory, for the research on which it is based
made no attempt to examine why the students became successful. Nonetheless, the sketch is offered in the hope that until more definitive
methods of identification are available, it will help teachers, supervisors,
and administrators to identify children from less privileged neighborhoods who show potential in science. More important, it may aid
teachers in their *expectation* of success and in providing a class milieu
that contributes to learning rather than defeats it.

The "disadvantaged" high achiever in science tends to come from a
family characterized generally as working-class, in which one or both
parents are gainfully employed as chambermaids, practical nurses, jani-
tors, porters, or cab drivers. Unemployment is familiar. Usually one or
both parents are migrants to the city, in many instances coming from
the rural South. In more than half of the families, the father is missing
from the immediate family. Born and reared in the metropolitan area,
the pupil has lived and attended elementary and junior high school in
one and the same neighborhood and has usually played in the street.

His parents or guardians are interested in the educational enterprise
and tell him continually that they are interested. They inquire about his
studies and help to budget his study time. They allow him to visit the
local library regularly. He generally receives a free lunch at the school.
Assuming that information on lunch applications is a valid evidence of
need, one can describe the youngsters as being from low socioeconomic
circumstances. There are usually many persons living in the home, and
there typically is no place in it which is conducive to study. The overcrowding in many instances is produced not only by the pupil's own
large family, but also by persons who rent space in the already jammed
apartment.

Generally well-adjusted in school, the achiever in science enjoys a higher self-estimate and higher aspirational levels than many of his peers. He also expresses himself orally and in written assignments much more articulately than they usually do.

The high achiever in science, at least in junior high school, shows a general interest in science. He makes contributions to science fairs and science contests. Sometimes he is interested in electronics. He may fly model aeroplanes as a hobby, or he may show an interest in raising fish in an aquarium. As a rule, he indicates his choice of a scientific or science-related career by the time he is ready to leave junior high school, usually at about age 14. In high school, he gravitates toward academic programs, and is interested and participates in the competitive examinations for the specialized high schools of art and science.

Undoubtedly, disadvantaged pupils across the United States represent a pool of hidden talent. This group offers a great potential for our technological society, which faces serious shortage of trained scientific and technical ability at all levels. If high achievers in science, coming from disadvantaged backgrounds, can be adequately described and identified, they can play important social roles while healthily meeting their own strong needs for self-realization.

This example of success in science is only one instance of the inadequacies of the notion of "cultural deprivation." Similar examples of success can be found in the other academic areas. The point is that certain children from disadvantaged areas can do well in school. What is lacking is a means for the schools to help more of these youngsters rid themselves of hopelessness and dedicate themselves to the possibility of altering their circumstances. Teachers need to look freshly at these children and their parents. Parents, although desirous of a better education for their children, often are in need of professional guidelines and directions if their attitudes are to be converted into constructive behavior. Here again, the responsibility of the educator is to furnish new modes of teaching that incorporate parents and the community into school life and that guide parents toward self-betterment and improved family life.

To start on this road, we must purge ourselves of the concept of "cultural deprivation" and all its derogatory implications. If a concept is needed, then we must seek a more accurate, authentic, and honest term. If we conclude that no term is needed, perhaps that will be all the better.

REFERENCES

Ausubel, David P. 1964. "How Reversible Are the Cognitive and Motivational Effects of Cultural Deprivation? Implications for Teaching the Culturally Deprived Child," *Urban Education.* 1: 16–39.

Bexton, W. H., Heron, W., and Scott, T. H. 1954. "Effects of Decreased Variation in the Sensory Environment," *Canadian Journal of Psychology.* 8: 70–76.

Butts, R. F. 1955. *A Cultural History of Western Education.* New York: McGraw-Hill.

Cagle, L. T., and Deutscher, I. 1964. "Social Mobility and Low-income Fatherless Families." Paper read before the Society for the Study of Social Problems. Montreal, September.

Cloward, R. A., and Jones, J. A. 1963. "Social Class: Educational Attitudes and Participation," in *Education in Depressed Areas,* ed. A. Harry Passow. New York: Teachers College, Columbia University.

Deutsch, M. 1964. "Facilitating Development in the Pre-school Child: Social and Psychological Perspectives," *Merrill-Palmer Quarterly.* 10: 249–264.

Durkin, Dolores. 1961. "Children Who Learn to Read Prior to First Grade: A Second Year Report." Paper read before the American Educational Research Association. Chicago, February.

Frankl, V. E. 1963. *Man's Search for Meaning.* New York: Washington Square Press.

Giddings, Morsley G. 1965. "Factors Related to Achievement in Junior High School Science in Disadvantaged Areas of New York City." Unpublished dissertation. New York: Teachers College, Columbia University.

Harlem Youth Opportunities Unlimited, Inc. 1964. *Youth in the Ghetto: A Study of the Consequences of Powerlessness and a Blueprint for Change.* New York: HARYOU.

Hebb, D. O. 1949. *The Organization of Behavior.* New York: John Wiley.

Hofstadter, R. 1963. *Anti-intellectualism in American Life.* New York: Alfred A. Knopf.

Hunt, J. McV. 1964. "The Psychological Basis for Using Pre-School Enrichment as an Antidote for Cultural Deprivation," *Merrill-Palmer Quarterly.* 10: 209–248.

Lewis, H. 1963. "Culture, Class, and the Behavior of Low Income Families." Paper presented at a Conference on Lower Class Culture. New York, June.

Riessman, Frank. 1962. *The Culturally Deprived Child.* New York: Harper and Row.

Negro Adolescents, Minority Status, and Literacy

Harold Greenberg

DOES READING REALLY MATTER?

The belief that literacy is important to the attitudes and behavior of citizens in a democratic society is one of the underlying assumptions of American education. The assumption is not just a matter of popular opinion, but is based on long historical tradition. Since the very inception of the common school, reading has occupied the attention of educators. As H. R. Huse has noted (1933, p. 21):

> When our public schools were founded, the problem of democratic education seemed simple. Illiteracy alone, and in a technical sense, appeared as the great sullen oppressor of men's minds. It seemed that if the common man could be endowed with a key to the mysterious symbols that open up a treasure of knowledge, a democratic utopia would be at hand.

More recently, in a statement of purpose on behalf of the National Commission on Literacy, Ambrose Caliver (1957, pp. 13–14) wrote:

> Illiteracy among adults still blots our record. The problem has always been serious, but with today's scientific and technological advances it becomes even more so. If we are to keep up our advances, if we are to maintain our democracy, we must have a literate society. . . . The kind of decisions we most need today require our citizens to understand many issues. Since they can gain understanding only if they are literate, we must do what we can to make them so.

In this nation of immigrants, education, particularly literacy, has traditionally been viewed as a fundamental necessity for responsible citizenship. In regard to disadvantaged minority groups, literacy has long been assumed to be the most important single skill that school could impart as the child prepared to face the realities of life and the labor market.

These assumptions about the relationship between reading skills, on

215

the one hand, and social attitudes and behavior, on the other, continue to have wide acceptance today. The activities of many social agencies proceed on the basis of their validity. In Chicago, welfare recipients are required to attend literacy classes (Brooks, 1962). In New York City's racial slums, many remedial reading programs have been undertaken, under both school and social agency auspices. Street club workers teach the ABC's in tenement hallways, and great publicity has accompanied the broadcast of "Operation Alphabet" over New York's educational television channel (National Association of Public School Educators, 1962).

WHAT READING DOES TO PEOPLE

Most students of written communication are convinced of its superiority over speech in transmitting ideas from one generation to another, and across social and physical barriers (Winger, 1955). Interestingly, Hoijer reports that many scientists date the beginning of true civilization from the invention of writing (Hoijer, 1960).

Waples, Berelson, and Bradshaw (1940) have identified the following possible effects of reading upon the individual:

1. The instrumental effect (i.e., fuller knowledge of a practical problem and greater competence to deal with it);
2. The prestige effect (i.e., relief of inferiority feelings by reading material which increases self-approval);
3. The reinforcement effect (i.e., reinforcement of an attitude or conversion to another attitude regarding a controversial issue);
4. The aesthetic effect (i.e., obtaining an aesthetic experience from works of literary art);
5. The respite effect (i.e., finding relief from tensions by reading whatever offers distraction).

They also maintain that reading can facilitate self-expression, insofar as a written work sometimes states the feelings and views of a reader more clearly than he himself can state them.

Most authorities on the significance of reading have continued to emphasize its importance even with the advent of the electronic mass media, arguing that reading serves to *check* the media, the media do not *replace* reading (Gray and Rogers, 1956). Regardless of these assertions, there is still a dearth of research on the specific issues of whether the possession of this highly prized skill actually is an asset to attitude formation, and of how it reflects attitudes. Reading specialists have generally concerned themselves with the etiology of reading failure, rather than the sociological concomitants of literacy (Gray, 1960).

However, there are some who have questioned the general assumptions regarding reading. Recently, Philip Jackson called attention to the great differences between reading skill as taught in schools and the ways in which reading is applied in daily life (Jackson, 1964). William Gray (1952, p. 971) has made a related point: "the fact that one acquires information through reading is no guarantee that beliefs, attitudes and behavior will *ipso facto,* be modified."

READING AND CLASS DIFFERENCES

Of the little empirical research that has been done in this area, some indicates that there are differences in the social attitudes and adjustments of good and poor readers (Mingoia, 1962; Norman and Daley, 1959; Tabarlet, 1958). One researcher even reports success in modifying the antisocial attitudes and behavior of delinquents through remedial reading (Roman, 1957).

In more specific class terms, many researchers who have examined the academic failure of lower-class children have raised questions about the importance attached to reading in the total school curriculum. One researcher, Allison Davis (1948), has questioned whether reading really helped the young lower-class child to solve basic mental problems. Davis has argued that reading fails to develop problem solving skills among these children for two reasons: first, it limits the type of problem analyzed largely to issues that are purely verbal; and second, problems of this sort are rarely felt by the pupil to have relevance to his life out of school.

Others have noted that several aspects of slum life—for example, the sparsity of manipulatable objects (which affects visual perception), the presence of a nonverbal orientation and of lower auditory discrimination (which affect the memory and produce a lower level of attentiveness)—are the very antitheses of the characteristics that are believed to contribute to mastery of reading skill (Deutsch, 1963). Relevant here is the fact that among Central Harlem eighth graders, 75.3 per cent are reported to be below their grade level in word knowledge (Harlem Youth Opportunities Unlimited, Inc., 1964).

Paul Goodman, addressing himself to the question of lower-class illiteracy, argues as follows (1964, p. 47):

> *There is a widespread anxiety about teaching reading. And indeed reading deficiency is an accumulating disadvantage that results in painful inferiority, truancy, and dropout. Reading is crucial—by the*

*standards of the school and because of the kinds of success that
schooling leads to. Yet there is something phony here. What does
reading mean today? . . . In the decision-making of our society,
serious literacy is of no practical importance whatever. It is as powerless as it is rare. Anyway, those who achieve it do not do so by the
route of "Run, Spot, Run" to Silas Marner.*

Goodman's remarks serve as a useful point of departure for the
present research, which is concerned with the relationship between
literacy and the problems facing urban Negro youth.

The major question this study considers is: Does the level of reading
skill among urban Negro adolescents correlate with their attitudes
toward minority status? This particular cluster of attitudes was selected
because of the urgency of the current civil rights situation. Given the
general assumption regarding the value of literacy in a democracy, one
would expect superior reading skill to be correlated with more positive
attitudes toward minority status and civil rights action. To be of importance in practical terms, such an effect would have to be more significant than the effects correlated with other factors to which the subjects
of this study are exposed, such as class or Southern parentage. Such a
positive correlation would support those who hope to upgrade Negro
adolescent slum dwellers through the improvement of their reading
skill.

However, it is quite possible to suppose that, given the conditions
under which these youths live, good reading skill leads them neither to
improved reading habits nor to an increased knowledge of, or a greater
interest in, their own status. Literacy may not reflect *any* important
attitudinal differences, and bear no relation to the individual's attitudes
toward minority status, the Negro's demand for equality, or to his own
place in the Negro community. If this hypothesis were found to be
true, it would indicate that the effort invested in remedial reading programs could not, in itself at least, be a fruitful source of aiding Negro
adolescents. It would also suggest that what is needed is a broader
attack on the social disorganization that characterizes slum life.

YOUTH IN THE NEGRO REVOLT

The bulk of the literature on the Negro demand for equality has
focused on the opinions, attitudes, and actions of adults. Although
grade schools have played a pivotal role in the attack on segregation,
the students have not generally been true participants in the struggle.

Where do Negro adolescents fit into this picture? We know that during adolescence young people are deeply involved in a series of personal developmental processes. At this stage of their growth, they re-evaluate adult models and, typically, develop personal standards which increasingly are based on individual experiences (Jersild, 1957; Josselyn, 1959). Further, we have reason to believe that adolescent values are relatively autonomous from those of adult society (Coleman, 1962; Smith, 1962). Thus, at first glance, one might expect Negro youngsters to have concerns quite unlike those of their elders (whatever the nature of such differences), and to remain aloof from the adult's struggle for rights.

Further analysis, however, leads to the very opposite conclusion. Kingsley Davis calls attention to the rejection of adult "working ideals" by adolescents in general. Such ideals tend to be seen as simple expediency and lip service (Davis, Kingsley; 1940). By adding to this general portrait the concept of "marginality" as used by Lewin (1948)—who applied it to both minority group status and the status of adolescents in the adult world—the following parallel suggests itself: as adolescents demand that their elders live up to their ideals, so Negro adolescents are likely to demand that Americans live up to their democratic ideals.

We may thus expect Negro adolescents to be keenly identified with the civil rights movement, to be less restrained than adults in their demands, and to be more vehement in their expectation of immediate rectification of wrongs. Fishman and Solomon (1960), using a more psychoanalytic approach, apparently arrived at a similar conclusion with regard to older Negro adolescents in the South. Whether their results hold true for adolescents in New York is not clear. Nevertheless, their discussion suggests that more literate, better schooled youths tend to be more actively involved in the civil rights effort than students who are relatively unsuccessful in school.

RESEARCH DESIGN

The organizing hypothesis for this study is as follows:

Urban Negro youths who are skilled readers will differ from less skilled readers on measures testing knowledge of current events, understanding of race relations, views of civil rights, attitudes toward involvement in political activity, and aspirations towards jobs.

The specific working hypotheses were as follows:

1. More skilled readers will reflect higher mean scores than the less skilled readers on measures of: general knowledge of current events,

general knowledge of racial current events, understanding of race relations and prejudice, use of established political channels, confidence in the effectiveness of the civil rights struggle, optimism about prospects for the solution of social problems in general, and job aspirations.

2. Less skilled readers will reflect higher mean scores than the skilled readers on measures of: extreme high or extreme low group solidarity; concern for concrete or material improvements for Negroes; and anomie.

To test these hypotheses, 77 15-year-old Negro boys residing in Harlem were interviewed regarding their attitudes and backgrounds, and their exposure to such sources of influence as peers, church, and various forms of mass communication. Of those interviewed, 58 were grouped as *high, middle,* and *low* readers on the basis of the Reading Section of the Wide Range Achievement Test (Jastak and Bijou, 1946).

TABLE 1

READING LEVEL OF STUDENTS

Reading Level	Number
High (9th grade and up)	16
Middle (6th-8th grade)	25
Low (below 6th grade)	17
TOTAL	58

These groups were arranged so as to be statistically comparable on a series of controlled variables, which included: age, sex, length of Harlem residence, school registration, community center membership, level of "life chances" (measured by a scale including parent's occupation and education, stability of home, and number of siblings [Dentler and Monroe, 1961]), intelligence (measured by the Peabody Picture Vocabulary Test [Dunn, 1959]), and distribution of Southern- and non-Southern-born parents. The means of the three groups were not found to differ significantly on any of these variables. After the tabulation of the interview data, the variance of the differences among the means of the three groups on each of 44 attitudinal indicators was analyzed to determine the dimensions on which they differed significantly.[1]

[1] The most important sources in the construction of the interview schedule were: Asheim, 1960; Coleman, 1962; Gray and Rogers, 1956; Hyman, 1962; Lenski, 1963; Roberts and Rokeach, 1956; Schramm and White, 1960; Silvey, 1944; Singer and Stefflre, 1956; and Weiss, 1964.

THE SOCIAL CORRELATES OF LITERACY LEVELS

Since attitudes toward both reading and social problems are subject to community and peer group influences, the means of the three reading groups on peer group friendships, center attendance, and church affiliation were compared, but no significant differences appeared in any of these areas. As regards exposure to mass media, however, Table 2 reveals that there were significant differences on two out of nine items —specifically, on the number of magazines read and on the content of the magazines.

TABLE 2

ANALYSIS OF VARIANCE OF MEANS ON EXPOSURE
TO COMMUNICATIONS MEDIA

| Variable | Means of the Reading Levels | | | S.S. | M.S.S. | F | p |
	High	Middle	Low				
Radio Hours	2.156	2.080	1.779	1.368	.684	.239	n.s.
Radio Content[a]	2.250	2.200	2.117	.149	.074	.035	n.s.
TV Hours	1.891	2.140	1.823	1.184	.592	.141	n.s.
TV Content[a]	1.625	1.680	1.705	.056	.028	.015	n.s.
No. of Books Read[c]	1.500	1.600	1.411	.365	.182	.125	n.s.
No. of Magazines Read[b]	1.750	4.120	1.411	93.018	46.509	7.190	.01
Magazine Content[d]	2.250	3.320	1.252	40.022	20.011	4.433	.05
No. of Newspapers Read[b]	2.250	2.480	2.117	1.409	.704	.300	n.s.
Newspaper Content[d]	3.062	3.880	3.529	6.531	3.265	2.572	n.s.

[a]*The radio and television programs reported by the subjects were scored on the basis of a weighting scale devised by Silvey (1944).*
[b]*Newspapers and magazines reported by the subjects were scored on the basis of a weighting scale devised by Gray and Rogers (1956).*
[c]*Books reported by subjects were weighted in accordance with the book's civic or racial significance.*
[d]*Newspaper and magazine content was scored on the basis of a weighting scale devised by Asheim (1960).*

Further, on a measure of General News Information, the group means were found to differ significantly at the .01 level. Examination showed the significant difference to be between the *high* and *middle* readers, on the one hand, and the *low* readers, on the other (see Table 3).

Table 3 also shows that on Racial News Information, differences were significant at the .05 level. Further study established that the scores of the *middle* and *low* readers differed significantly. The mean score of the *high* readers did not differ significantly from either of the other two means. Thus, while the significant differences on General News Information roughly follow the expected pattern—the scores on Racial News Information do not clearly reflect such a correlation.

TABLE 3

ANALYSIS OF VARIANCE OF MEANS ON NEWS INFORMATION SCALES
AND OF ACTION-APATHY

| | Means of the Reading Levels | | | | | | |
Variable	High	Middle	Low	S.S.	M.S.S.	F	p
	News Information Scales						
General News Information	1.375	.840	.352	8.611	4.305	7.186	.01
Racial News Information	1.312	1.640	.941	4.964	2.482	3.581	.05
	Action-Apathy						
Action-Apathy	5.000	4.080	6.882	79.999	39.999	3.609	.05

No significant differences were found on measures of group solidarity, understanding of race relations, or concern for concrete or material improvements for Negroes.

In regard to Action-Apathy (Table 3), which reflects the individual's readiness to use established political channels, the three groups' means differed at the .05 level. Further analysis showed that *low* readers were most apathetic and *middle* readers least apathetic; *high* readers were medial and not significantly different from either extreme. Even the scores of the *low* group, however, do not indicate marked apathy.

On the remaining measures—dealing with job aspirations, optimism about social problems, belief in the potency of individuals and groups in influencing the course of social events, and other various positions related to civil rights strategy—no further significant differences were reflected.

SUMMARY AND CONCLUSION

The findings thus reveal that of 44 indicators tested, significant differences among the means of the three groups occur only on five. Even on these, moreover, the more skilled readers did not consistently score higher than the less skilled readers. In light of such findings, the organizing hypothesis of the study must, as a general rule, be rejected. While all subjects reported more reading than was expected, the assumption that for Negro adolescents there exists a significant relationship between reading skill and social attitudes is cast into serious doubt. This assumption (along with the belief that increased reading ability is an aid in finding employment) is one of the underlying rationales for the continued centrality of reading in the curriculum. The findings strongly suggest that the assumption be re-evaluated with regard to urban Negro youth.

In general, while the attitudes of all 58 subjects, whatever their reading group, reveal considerable sophistication about racial problems, the individuals themselves show only a limited degree of personal involvement in the civil rights movement. All shared middle-class occupational aspirations, and contrary to expectation, did not reflect the social disorganization of slum life in their scores on the anomie or apathy scale.

REFERENCES

Asheim, Lester. 1960. "Portrait of the Book Reader," in *Mass Communications,* ed. Wilber Schramm. Urbana: University of Illinois Press.

Brooks, Deton J. 1962. *A Study to Determine the Literacy Level of Able-Bodied Persons Receiving Public Assistance.* Chicago: Cook County Department of Public Aid.

Caliver, Ambrose. 1957. "For a More Literate Nation," *School Life,* 40: 13–14.

Coleman, James S. 1962. *The Adolescent Society.* Glencoe, Illinois: Free Press.

Davis, Allison. 1948. *Social Class Influences on Learning.* Cambridge: Harvard University Press.

Davis, Kingsley. 1940. "Sociology of Parent-Youth Conflict," *American Sociological Review.* 5:523–535.

Dentler, Robert A., and Monroe, Lawrence J. 1961. "The Family and Early Adolescent Conformity and Deviance," *Marriage and Family Living,* 23:241–247.

Deutsch, Martin. 1963. "The Disadvantaged Child and the Learning Process," in *Education in Depressed Areas,* ed. A. Harry Passow. New York: Teachers College, Columbia University.

Dunn, L. M. 1959. *Peabody Picture Vocabulary Test.* Minneapolis: American Guidance Service.

Fishman, Jacob, and Solomon, Frederic. 1960. "Psychological Observations on the Student Sit-in Movement," *Proceedings of Third International Congress of Psychiatry*. Toronto: University of Toronto Press.

Goodman, Paul. 1964. "The Universal Trap," in *The School Dropout*, ed. Daniel Schreiber. Washington, D.C.: National Education Association.

Gray, William. 1952. "Sociology of Reading," in *Encyclopedia of Educational Research*, ed. Walter S. Monroe. New York: Macmillan Co.

————. 1960. "Sociology of Reading," in *Encyclopedia of Education*, eds. Chester Harris and Marie Liba. New York: Macmillan Co.

————, and Rogers, Bernice. 1956. *Maturity in Reading*. Chicago: University of Chicago Press.

Harlem Youth Opportunities Unlimited, Inc. 1964. *Youth in the Ghetto*. New York: HARYOU.

Hoijer, Harry. 1960. "Language and Writing," in *Man, Culture and Society*, ed. Harry Shapiro. New York: Oxford University Press.

Huse, H. R. 1933. *The Illiteracy of the Literate*. New York: Appleton-Century Co.

Hyman, Herbert, *et al.* 1962. *Applications of Methods of Evaluation*. Vol. VII. Berkeley: University of California Press.

Jackson, Philip. 1964. "The Solitary Art," *The University of Chicago Magazine*. 58:12–15.

Jastak, Joseph, and Bijou, Sidney. 1946. *Wide Range Achievement Test*. Wilmington, Del.: C. L. Story Co.

Jersild, Arthur T. 1957. *The Psychology of Adolescence*. New York: Macmillan Co.

Josselyn, Irene. 1959. *The Adolescent and His World*. New York: Family Service Association of America.

Lenski, Gerhard. 1963. *The Religious Factor*. Garden City, New York: Doubleday and Co.

Lewin, Kurt. 1948. "Bringing Up the Jewish Child," in *Resolving Social Conflicts*, ed. Gertrud Lewin. New York: Harper and Brothers.

Mingoia, E. 1962. "Possible Causes of Underachievement in Reading," *Elementary English*. 39:220–223.

National Association of Public School Educators. 1962. *Operation Alphabet*. TV Home Study Book. Washington, D.C.: The authors.

Norman, R. D., and Daley, M. F. 1959. "Comparative Personality Adjustment of Superior Readers," *Journal of Educational Psychology*. 50:31–36.

Roberts, Alan, and Rokeach, Milton. 1956. "Anomie, Authoritarianism and Prejudice: A Replication," *American Journal of Sociology*. 61:355–358.

Roman, Melvin. 1957. *Reaching Delinquents Through Reading*. Springfield, Ill.: Chas. C. Thomas.

Schramm, Wilbur, and White, David. 1960. "Age, Education and Economic Status as Factors in Newspaper Reading," in *Mass Communications,* ed. Schramm.

Silvey, Robert. 1944. "Radio Audience Research in Great Britain," in *Radio Research 1942–3,* eds. P. Lazarsfeld and F. Stanton. New York: Duell, Sloan and Pearce.

Singer, S. L., and Stefflre, M. 1956. "A Note on Racial Differences in Job Values and Desires," *Journal of Social Psychology.* 43: 335.

Smith, Ernest. 1962. *American Youth Culture.* Glencoe, Illinois: Free Press.

Tabarlet, B. E. 1958. "Poor Readers and Mental Health," *Elementary English.* 35:523–525.

Waples, D., Berelson, B., and Bradshaw, F. 1940. *What Reading Does to People.* Chicago: University of Chicago Press.

Weiss, Carol H. 1964. *Attitude Changes in the Domestic Peace Corps.* New York: ACT, Inc.

Winger, Howard. 1955. "Historical Perspectives on the Role of the Book in Society," *Library Quarterly.* 25:295–305.

The Effects of a Freedom School
on Its Students*

David W. Johnson

THE PROBLEM

Much of the literature on Negro children states that they have negative
racial and self-attitudes (Ausubel and Ausubel, 1963; Bernard, 1958;
Clark and Clark, 1958; Deutsch, 1963; Jefferson, 1957; Kardiner and
Ovesey, 1951; Myrdal, 1944). The actual extent and depth of such
attitudes has not as yet been fully established. Research has shown that
they can affect a Negro's view of society (Bernard, 1958; Clark, 1955;
Harris, 1963 a and b), his maturation processes (Ausubel and Ausubel,
1963; Carlson, 1963; Engel, 1959), his motivations and aspirations
(Carlson, 1963; Clark, 1955; Jefferson, 1957), and his academic and
vocational performance (Harvey, 1953; Katz and Braly, 1958; Katz
and Benjamin, 1960; Katz and Cohen, 1962; Katz and Greenbaum,
1963; Klineberg, 1963; Woodward, 1957).

Generally, there are two broad approaches toward changing such
negative self-appraisals. The first is to change the way in which society
views and treats the Negro. Under this approach come legislation, civil
rights pressure, the creation of new job opportunities, and the elimination of prejudice. The second approach is to institute special programs
which attempt to broaden the educational and vocational opportunities
of Negro youth. Under this approach come programs like Higher
Horizons, HARYOU-ACT, Mobilization for Youth, and so forth.

It is important to note, however, that many of these programs have
made no *direct* attempt to change underlying negative self- and racial
attitudes. One of the few that has is the program that aims at teaching

* The investigator wishes to express his appreciation to Isaiah Robinson, Chair-
man of the Harlem Parents Committee, and Robert Washington, Director of the
Freedom School, for their cooperation in conducting this study; also to the
children in the Freedom School, the Freedom School staff, and the members of
the Harlem Parents Committee for making this study possible.

The investigator is deeply indebted to Dr. Robert Dentler, director of the
Center for Urban Education, for his unfailing encouragement and indispensable
help, and for his financial support of the study.

Grateful acknowledgement is also extended to Morton Deutsch and Dr. Mat-
thew Miles for their valuable assistance.

Negro history. Such efforts are based on the hypothesis that through a positive presentation of Negro history and culture the distorted and disparaging view which many Negroes hold about themselves will be ameliorated.

It is the purpose of this study to determine the effects on Negro children, ages nine to 13, of participation in such a program.

THE FREEDOM SCHOOL

One of the first long term programs in the country to teach Negro history was initiated in New York City during the academic school year of 1963–64, by the Harlem Parents Committee, a civil rights organization concerned primarily with the education of Negro children living in the slum areas of the city. This program was called "Freedom School." It was founded, to quote from a publication of the committee, for two basic purposes:

1. To teach our children to reclaim and proudly identify with their history and culture;
2. To teach all people that the heritage and culture of the American Negro is not a barren one.

The Freedom School was first planned during the summer of 1963, in anticipation of a boycott of New York City schools that fall. Some sort of school was needed for the children during the boycott in order to avoid possible action against them for truancy, and the occasion seemed an ideal opportunity to teach them about Negro history and current civil rights activities. Though the boycott was cancelled after negotiations with the Board of Education, it was decided that the Freedom School was a worthwhile project in and of itself. The parents committee, as part of an overall program to improve the education of Negro children in New York City, therefore planned and organized the school to meet during the school year.

Four goals were set for the school:

1. To dispel negative self-images in Negro children;
2. To change the image of Negroes in the minds of whites;
3. To give Negro children knowledge of a culture with which they could identify in a positive way;
4. To teach Negro children a pride in their ancestors.

The school met for two hours every Saturday morning from November 1963 to June 1964. It consisted of three groups: adults, teenagers, and children from seven to 13.

As a voluntary civic undertaking, the Freedom School had not set curriculum or program. Though there was some coordination and exchange of ideas at meetings held after the weekly school sessions, each teacher was left to develop his course for himself. Subject matter varied a great deal from class to class, with some teachers emphasizing current civil rights, some emphasizing African history, and some emphasizing American Negro history. Africa received the main emphasis: most of the arts and crafts activities centered on African art and culture, an African language was taught for part of the year, and a record on the African heritage of the Negro was published by the Freedom School. Involvement in civil rights activities was also an integral part of the program.

The teachers were mostly public school teachers with an interest in civil rights or Negro history or both. Both white and Negro teachers participated. All volunteered their time. Turnover varied, but every class changed teachers at least once during the year.

METHODS OF STUDY, SAMPLE, AND HYPOTHESES

Design

To measure the change in the children's self- and racial attitudes during their participation in the Freedom School, two interviews were given, four months apart. The first interview was administered two months after the Freedom School had opened. The parents committee, in conflict with the Board of Education, was slightly suspicious of an outsider from an educational institution, and so it took several weeks to gain access to the program and set up the study.[1] The first interview was given to 36 children between the ages of eight and 13 (30 Negroes and six whites) randomly selected from the classrooms. This group constituted approximately half of the children attending the Freedom School at the time.

The second interview was given to 41 children (39 Negroes and two whites) at the end of the school's first year. This group constituted a majority of the children in the school at the time. Of the 39 Negro children, ten had received the first interview, 12 others had attended the Freedom School for the entire year, and the rest had begun attending the school some time after the first interview.

Three Negro girls interviewed the Negro children, and the white investigator interviewed the white children. The interviewers had no

---

[1] Because of the suspicions of the school, it was not possible to attend classes (and teachers' meetings) on a regular basis. As a result, this study cannot directly relate the content of the school's program or the actual classroom experience to changes in the students' attitudes.

previous experience, but were carefully selected for their intelligence and dependability. The investigator carefully discussed the interview with them, and each had administered the interview to several children before the study began.

The design of the study included two main controls. The first was the group of 12 children who had been enrolled in the school from the start but who had received only the second interview. The use of such a group controlled for the effect of the first interview on the second.

The second control was provided by the set of statistical norms given for Cattell's Child Personality Questionnaire. These norms allowed a comparison between the children in the Freedom School and the "average" American (white) child. The race of the Freedom School students, connected as it is with experiences of discrimination, was in all probability the only significant difference between the two groups of children. It was assumed, therefore, that any variance from the norms would be a result of accumulated discriminatory experiences (Kardiner and Ovesey, 1951).

Subjects

The subjects of the study were the ten children who received both interviews and the 12 children who, serving as a control group, received only the second interview. There was very little difference between the panel and the control group. The control group had a higher percentage of girls, was slightly younger, had a higher percentage from intact homes, and its members had slightly more other children living in their homes. The differences are slight.

Hypotheses

1. *Attitudes toward the self will become more favorable as a result of participation in the Freedom School;* and 2. *Attitudes toward Negroes will become more favorable as a result of participation in the Freedom School.* By teaching a pride in being a Negro and by giving the child a knowledge of the positive aspects of his Negro heritage to counterbalance the negative stereotypes projected by society, the Freedom School would provide a basis for (1) rejecting society's evaluation and (2) gaining a belief in his own personal worth and value. This process would be supplemented by increased knowledge about outstanding Negroes whom the child could respect, identify with, and use as models. Self-attitudes and attitudes toward Negroes, therefore, would be likely to become more favorable as a result of participation in the school.

3. *Attitudes toward whites will become less favorable as a result of participation in the Freedom School.* An increased knowledge of Negro history and a corresponding identification with Negro culture should lessen a Negro's acceptance of the privileged status of whites in American society. Further, a clearer understanding of how the Negro attained his present position in American society should have an unfavorable effect upon the child's attitude toward whites. For these reasons it was hypothesized that the attitudes toward whites would become less favorable as a result of participation in Freedom School.

4. *Attitudes toward the civil rights movement will become more favorable as a result of participation in the Freedom School.* A sounder knowledge of the civil rights movement, its history and leaders (historical and contemporary), and exposure to teachers and staff deeply committed to the movement should result in a more action-oriented and committed involvement.

Instruments

Four instruments were used to gather data: (1) the child personality questionnaire, (2) an attitude questionnaire, (3) a picture interview, and (4) a qualitative questionnaire.

1. *The Child Personality Questionnaire.*[2] This questionnaire, devised by Cattell to be used with children from eight to 12, provides the most complete, valid, and reliable personality information in the shortest possible time. Of the 14 factors included in the CPQ, the five most relevant to the child's basic self-attitudes were used for this study. These factors were: Factor C—dissatisfied emotional instability vs. ego strength (emotional, immature, unstable vs. mature, calm); G—lack of rigid internal standards vs. superego strength (casual, undependable vs. conscientious, persistent); O—confident adequacy vs. guilt proneness (confident vs. insecure); Q_3—poor self-sentiment formation vs. high strength of self-sentiment (uncontrolled, lax vs. controlled, showing will power); and Q_4—low ergic tension vs. high ergic tension (relaxed composure vs. tense, excitable).

2. *The Attitude Questionnaire.* This questionnaire was specially developed for the present study as none used in previous research was found to be applicable. It consists of a total of 36 questions, worded either positively or negatively, on five scales: equality of Negroes and whites (five questions); favorableness toward Negroes (eight questions dealing with four of the most common stereotypes of Negroes, as found in Myrdal [1944], Katz and Braley [1958], and Harris [1963]); felt solidarity with Negroes (five questions); attitudes toward whites (nine

---

2 Cattell's designations will be used throughout the paper.

questions based primarily on Harris [1963]); and attitudes toward civil rights (nine questions dealing with action-apathy, optimism-pessimism, identification with the civil rights movement, commitment to the movement, and the perceived goals of the movement).

The child could respond to each question in one of three ways: false, no opinion, and true. Responses were scored by summated ratings. If the question was stated positively, the response of "false" was given the score of 1, "no opinion" was scored 2, and "true" was scored 3. This was reversed when the item was stated negatively.

No pretesting of the instrument was conducted (due to the pressure of time). The questions were worded as simply and straightforwardly as possible. Words which the children might have trouble with were called to the interviewers' attention and a standard procedure for their explanation was established.

The primary purposes of this instrument were: (a) to obtain a measure of the children's racial attitudes and attitudes toward civil rights activities, (b) to measure the children's self-attitudes connected with their racial membership, and (c) to measure any changes in these attitudes resulting from participation in the Freedom School.

3. *Picture Interview.* A separate picture interview was also administered with the second regular interview. In the picture interview the children were presented with five photographs and asked to rate each on a semantic differential consisting of nine pairs of evaluative words. To avoid the possibility of a "response set," the pairs of words were randomly reserved, half with the "good" word first, half with the "bad" word first. The child was asked to respond to the main figure in each of the pictures randomly handed to him, in terms of a seven point scale. The purpose of the interview was to present the children with specific stimuli from common and familiar situations, and on the basis of a child's reactions measure his racial, civil rights, and self-attitudes.

4. *Qualitative Questionnaire.* The purpose of the questionnaire was: (a) to obtain the necessary background information on the children, (b) to determine how and why the children attend the Freedom School, (c) to determine how the children perceived the school, (d) to examine the role they saw themselves playing in the school and the civil rights movement, and (d) to obtain other miscellaneous information for exploratory purposes.

RESULTS

1. *Attitudes toward the self will become more favorable as a result of participation in the Freedom School.* This hypothesis was tested pri-

marily by Cattell's Child Personality Questionnaire. However, two other measures were also used: Scale 2 of the attitude questionnaire (favorableness towards Negroes), which provides a measure of general attitudes toward racial membership; and Question 5 of the qualitative questionnaire, which provides information on whether the children felt that their self-attitudes had changed due to their participation in the Freedom School. Further information was also obtained from the picture interview. (Since this interview was given only at the termination of the Freedom School, it does not provide a measure of change and, therefore, cannot *test* the hypothesis. However, it provides relevant data as to the nature of the children's self-attitudes after their participation in the school.)

From the data in Table 1, it is clear that the panel, as a whole, did not change significantly during its participation in the school in Factor C (ego strength), Factor O (confidence), Factor Q_3 (strength of self-sentiment), and Factor Q_4 (tension level); and that it decreased significantly ($p < .05$) in Factor G (superego strength).

The table also shows that, when the data are considered in terms of boys and girls, there were some changes. On Factor G (superego strength) the boys did not change significantly while the girls de-

TABLE 1

CHILD PERSONALITY QUESTIONNAIRE: CHANGES TOWARD SELF
AFTER FOUR MONTHS IN FREEDOM SCHOOL
(N of BOYS = 4; N of GIRLS = 6)

Factor	$\bar{X}_1$	$S.D._1$	$\bar{X}_2$	$S.D._2$	Probability of No Difference[a]
C (Ego Strength)	2.90	9.88	3.10	1.08	
Male	3.00	0.82	3.25	1.26	
Female	2.83	0.98	3.00	1.41	
G (Super Ego)	3.40	1.08	3.00	0.82	.05
Male	3.25	1.71	2.75	0.96	
Female	3.50	0.55	3.17	0.75	.10
O (Insecure)	1.70	0.95	1.20	1.03	
Male	2.25	0.50	0.25	0.50	.01
Female	1.33	1.03	1.83	0.75	.05
Q_3 (Self-Sentiment)	3.80	0.79	3.80	1.13	
Male	3.50	1.00	3.25	0.96	
Female	4.00	0.63	4.17	1.17	
Q_4 (Tension)	1.50	1.08	1.10	0.99	
Male	2.25	0.50	1.75	1.26	
Female	1.00	1.10	0.67	0.52	

[a] *T Test of mean of a population of differences between two measures for each individual.*

creased significantly (p < .10). On Factor O (confidence), the boys gained significantly (p < .01) while the girls decreased significantly (p < .05). In other words, the boys at the beginning of their participation in the Freedom School were less confident than the girls and at the end of their participation were more confident.

TABLE 2

COMPARISON OF MEANS OF FREEDOM SCHOOL
STUDENTS WITH CPQ NORMS

Factor	$\overline{X}_1$	$\overline{X}_2$	Standard Mean	Control Group
Form A[a] — Boys				
(Panel = 2; Control Group = 2)				
C	3.5	2.5	3.10	3.5
G	2.5	2.5	2.65	2.5
O	2.0	0.5	2.26	1.5
Q_3	4.0	3.0	3.31	4.5
Q_4	2.5	12.5	2.15	2.0
Form A[a] — Girls				
(Panel = 3; Control Group = 4)				
C	3.33	4.00	3.10	2.75
G	3.33	3.00	2.65	2.50
O	1.33	2.00	2.26	2.50
Q_3	4.33	5.00	3.64	3.75
Q_4	1.00	0.67	1.94	1.50
Form B[a] — Boys				
(Panel = 2[b])				
C	2.5	4.0	2.56	
G	4.0	3.0	3.11	
O	2.5	0	2.01	
Q_3	3.0	3.5	2.96	
Q_4	2.0	1.0	1.63	
Form B[a] — Girls				
(Panel = 3; Control Group = 6)				
C	2.33	2.00	2.56	2.67
G	3.67	3.33	3.11	2.17
O	1.33	1.67	2.01	1.83
Q_3	3.67	3.33	3.24	3.67
Q_4	1.00	0.67	1.33	1.00

[a] *Forms A and B are different arrangements of the same material.*
[b] *As noted, the form is distributed randomly, and there were no boys.*

Finally, the girls were more relaxed than the boys (Factor Q_4). On the basis of Cattell's findings, this difference can be considered normal.

From Table 2 it is seen that the children in the panel, when compared with the statistical norms given for the CPQ, generally are: (1) slightly above average in ego strength (Factor C), (2) above average in superego strength (Factor G), (3) very confident for children of their age (Factor 0), (4) above average in the strength of their self-sentiment (Factor Q_3), and (5) slightly below average in their tension level (Factor Q_4). In short, the children in the panel perceived themselves to be (1) mature and calm, (2) conscientious and persistent, (3) confident, (4) controlled and showing will power, and (5) of relaxed composure. This was true both before and after participation in the Freedom School.

From Table 2, it is also seen that the control group is: (1) above average in ego strength (Factor C), with the boys being slightly higher than the girls; (2) slightly below average in superego strength (Factor G), with no difference between the boys and the girls; (3) slightly more confident than the average child of their age (Factor O), with the boys being slightly more confident than the girls; (4) well above average in strength of self-sentiment (Factor Q_3), with the boys higher than the girls; and (5) below average in tension level (Factor Q_4), with the girls more relaxed and composed than the boys.

The findings for the control group, while differing in some respects from those for the panel, confirm the basic results—that the children attending the Freedom School, when tested at the school's termination, had positive self-attitudes as found by the CPQ.[3]

Data from the attitude questionnaire in regard to attitude changes in the panel between the two interviews are shown in Table 3, and indicate that the boys changed significantly in a positive direction ($p < .05$) in favorableness toward Negroes (Scale 2), while the girls did not. The girls, however, were still slightly more favorable. In other words, the boys were less favorable than the girls in their attitudes toward Negroes when they entered the Freedom School and almost as favorable afterward.

From the qualitative questionnaire (Table 4), it also can be seen that at the time of the second interview, nine of the ten children in

[3] Due to the small number of children in the panel and the control group it is difficult to tell whether there was any effect of the first interview on the second in regard to the CPQ. The handbook for the CPQ states: "One can safely readminister the full test, without risk of recall, after two or three weeks." It is assumed, therefore, that the first interview had no effect upon the second. Though there were variations between the panel and the control group, these were small and insignificant.

TABLE 3

ATTITUDE QUESTIONNAIRE: CHANGES AFTER
FOUR MONTHS IN FREEDOM SCHOOL
(Boys = 4; Girls = 6)

Scale		X_1	$S.D._1$	X_2	$S.D._2$	Probability of No Difference[a]
1	*(Equality)*	11.80	1.99	12.80	2.04	.025
	Male	11.50	2.65	12.25	2.22	.05
	Female	12.00	1.67	13.17	2.04	.10
2	*(Negroes)*	20.10	1.98	20.40	1.84	
	Male	19.25	2.50	20.25	1.71	.05
	Female	20.67	1.51	20.50	2.97	
3	*(Solidarity)*[b]	12.10	1.98	11.70	1.70	
	Male	11.75	2.36	12.50	1.29	
	Female	12.33	1.86	11.17	1.84	
4	*(Whites)*	18.40	2.37	18.20	3.19	
	Male	17.50	0.58	17.75	2.06	
	Female	19.00	2.97	18.50	3.94	
5	*(Civil Rights)*	24.50	1.84	25.40	1.43	
	Male	24.50	1.30	26.00	0.82	.05
	Female	24.50	2.26	25.00	1.67	

[a]*T test of mean of a population of differences between two measures for each individual.*
[b]*Difference between male X_1 and female X_2 is significant (p. 10).*

the panel felt that their feelings toward themselves had changed because of participation in the Freedom School. Nine out of the 12 members of the control group also believed such a change had taken place. Although most of the children did not specify the direction of this change, every explanation made in the course of the interview was positive.

Two pictures were used to obtain another measure of self-attitudes at

TABLE 4

FELT CHANGES DUE TO PARTICIPATION IN
FREEDOM SCHOOL—SECOND INTERVIEW

	Panel		Control Group	
	Yes	No	Yes	No
Self	9	1	9	3
Negroes	2	8	7	5
Whites	5	5	8	4
Civil Rights	4	6	5	7

the end of the school year—a picture of a Negro boy playing and a picture of a Negro boy sitting alone in a park with his head in his hands. Both the boys and the girls of the panel rated the first picture favorably—indicating positive self-attitudes. With the second picture, the ratings diverged. The boys rated it favorably, the girls negatively. This difference was highly significant ($p < .005$). The boys' rating indicates favorable self-attitudes. The ratings of the girls, however, suggest two possibilities—unfavorable attitudes toward either themselves or the Negro male.

The picture interview does not measure change and therefore cannot test the first hypothesis. However, it does show that the self-attitudes of the children in the panel were primarily positive at the termination of the Freedom School, and this supports the other findings.

In summary, the CPQ indicates that the boys became more confident during their participation in the Freedom School, and that the girls became less so and decreased in superego strength. The attitude questionnaire indicates that the boys became more favorable toward Negroes (Scale 2); no such change occurred in the girls. The qualitative questionnaire indicates that both the boys and girls felt that their self-attitudes had changed during their participation in the Freedom School—and the change appears to be in a positive direction.

On the basis of these findings, Hypothesis 1 is accepted for the boys and rejected for the girls.

2. *Attitudes toward Negroes will become more favorable as a result of participation in the Freedom School.* Both the attitude and qualitative questionnaire were used to measure change in this area, along with information derived from the picture interview.

From Table 3 it is seen that there was no significant change in the panel as a whole in favorableness towards Negroes (Scale 2). As already noted, the boys became significantly more favorable in their attitudes ($p > .05$), while the girls did not change (though they were slightly more favorable in their attitudes toward Negroes than the boys even at the time of the second interview).

In regard to felt solidarity with Negroes (Scale 3), the panel as a whole did not change significantly. This is also true for boys and girls separately (sign-test significant [$p > .11$]). However, the difference between the boys' and the girls' means at the termination was significant ($p > .10$), indicating that at the termination of the school the boys felt more solidarity with Negroes than the girls.

In regard to equality of Negroes and whites (Scale 1), the panel changed significantly toward the attitude that Negroes and whites are equal ($p > .025$). This was true for both boys ($p > .05$) and girls ($p > .10$) separately. In other words, one of the major results of participation in the Freedom School was an increasing conviction that Negroes and whites are equal.

From the qualitative questionnaire (Table 4), it is seen that at the time of the second interview only two of the children in the panel felt that their attitudes toward Negroes had changed. In the control group, seven of the 12 felt that the Freedom School had changed their attitudes about Negroes. From the responses and the other evidence dealing with Hypothesis 2, it can be supposed that the children meant the change was in a positive direction.

A rather indistinct picture of the face of a Negro man was used to obtain further information about the children's attitudes. The panel rated this picture neutrally (see Table 5). There was, however, a significant difference ($p > .05$) between the ratings of the boys and the girls, with the boys rating the picture favorably and the girls unfavorably. As with the picture of the lonely Negro boy, the boys' responses indicated favorable attitudes, while the girls' responses indicated either a generally unfavorable attitude or an unfavorable attitude toward the Negro male. Since this measure is not a measure of change, it cannot test the hypothesis. It simply adds supporting information and a reality check on the other data.

In short, the boys in the panel became more convinced that Negroes and whites were equal (Scale 1), became more favorable in their attitudes toward Negroes (Scale 2), did not change in felt solidarity with Negroes (Scale 2), and did not feel that participation in the school had changed the way they felt about Negroes (Question 5 of the qualitative questionnaire). On the basis of this evidence, Hypothesis 2 is accepted for the boys.

The girls in the panel became more convinced that Negroes and whites were equal (Scale 1), did not change in favorableness towards Negroes (Scale 2), and did not feel that the Freedom School had changed the way they felt about Negroes. On the basis of this evidence, Hypothesis 2 is rejected for the girls.

3. *Attitudes toward whites will become less favorable as a result of participation in the Freedom School.*

The attitude questionnaire and the general questionnaire were used to measure change in this area.

From Table 3, it is seen that the panel as a whole did not change significantly in attitudes toward whites (Scale 4). There were large changes in individual children but these changes were in different directions. On Scale 1 (equality of Negroes and whites), the panel changed significantly in a positive direction ($p > .025$). This was true for boys ($p > .05$) and girls ($p > .10$) separately.

From Table 4, it is seen that at the time of the second interview five of the ten children in the panel felt that their attitudes toward whites had changed due to their participation in the school. (Four of these children were girls.) In the control group, eight of the 12 children said that the school had changed their feelings about whites. For either group, the direction of the changes is not known.

From Table 5, it is seen that both the boys and the girls rated very favorably the picture of a white teacher standing by a table that seated four Negro children and one white child. Although the panel was only asked to rate the teacher, it seems reasonable to suppose that the rating tapped attitudes toward two separate types of experiences common to most of the children, the experience of having a white teacher and the experience of being in an integrated classroom. Moreover, since these children were actively engaged in a struggle to integrate the New York City school system, a picture of an integrated classroom would signify the attainment of a major goal to them. This measure does not test the hypothesis, but adds only supportive information.

In summary, the panel changed significantly ($p < .025$) in a positive direction on Scale 1 (equality of Negroes and whites), did not change significantly in attitudes toward whites (Scale 4), and five of the ten children felt that participation in the Freedom School had changed the way they felt about whites. Hypothesis 3 was therefore rejected.

4. *Attitudes toward civil rights will become more favorable as a result of participation in the Freedom School.* From Table 3, it is seen that there was no significant change in the panel as a whole in its attitudes toward civil rights (Scale 5). The boys, however, changed significantly ($p < .05$) in a positive direction and were more favorable toward civil rights than the girls. The girls did not change significantly.

At the time of the second interview (Table 4), four children in the panel felt that their attitudes toward civil rights had changed due to their participation in the Freedom School. Five of the 12 children in the control group stated that they felt their attitudes toward civil rights had changed as a result of their participation in the Freedom School. In addition, both the boys and the girls rated a picture of a Negro civil rights worker very favorably (Table 5). This does not test the hypothesis, but adds supporting information. Hypothesis 4, then, was supported only for the boys.

On the attitude questionnaire, the control group differs very little from the panel (Table 6). The only significant difference is in Scale 5

TABLE 5

PICTURE RATINGS[a]

Picture	$\bar{X}$	S.D.
Boy Playing	23.00	4.39
Male	20.75	3.78
Female	24.80	7.26
Boy Head in Hands[b]	40.22	13.60
Male	27.75	9.74
Female	50.20	4.61
Negro Man[c]	32.89	10.50
Male	26.00	8.13
Female	38.40	9.37
White Teacher	14.11	3.82
Male	13.50	4.58
Female	14.60	2.88
Civil Rights Worker	17.61	4.20
Male	20.00	3.37
Female	18.40	5.81

[a]*The lower the score, the more favorable the response. Range is 9 to 63.*
[b]*Probability of difference between male and female means: ($p < .005$)*
— t test of difference between group means.
[c]*Probability of difference between male and female means: ($p < .05$)*
— t test of difference between group means.

(attitudes toward civil rights), where the control group is significantly lower ($p > .05$) than the panel. (This difference could be due to the predominance of girls in the control group, as the girls were found to score lower than the boys on this scale.) Table 6 indicates that the first interview had no effect upon the second, with the possible exception of the responses on Scale 5.

TABLE 6

ATTITUDE QUESTIONNAIRE: COMPARISON
OF GROUP MEANS
(Panel = 10; Control = 12)

Scale	Panel X_2	Control Group	Probability of No Difference[a]
1	12.8	12.9	
2	20.4	19.6	
3	11.7	11.6	
4	18.2	17.1	
5	25.4	23.8	.05

[a]*T test of difference between group means.*

DISCUSSION

Self- and Racial Attitudes

The basic purpose of this study was to examine the effects on Negro children of participation in a Freedom School and to see whether the teaching of Negro history is an effective way of improving negative self- and racial attitudes. It was not known in advance of the study what types of children would be at the school, but it was assumed that to varying extents, they would have such attitudes. Much of the design of the study was premised on this assumption.

As it turned out, the assumption was false. The sample population did not have negative self- and racial attitudes at the time of the first interview, at least as measured by the instruments in the study, and it seems obvious that they did not have such attitudes a few months earlier, when the school began. In many ways, the students in the sample were, statistically speaking, an unusual group of Negro children. Most came from intact middle-class homes. Their parents were involved in the civil rights movement, and many of the children had civil rights experience. The majority of the parents belonged to the Harlem Parents Committee, the sponsoring organization of the Freedom School. Several, if not all, of the children had been taught in the home much of what was taught in the Freedom School.

Theoretically, there are many possible explanations of why the children did not have negative self- and racial attitudes: (1) the quality and stability of their home life; (2) the personal characteristics of the children, their personality, temperament, and physical traits; (3) the social class of their families; (4) the self- and racial attitudes of their families and peers; (5) the involvement of their families and peers in the civil rights movement; (6) the knowledge of and identification with Negro history and culture in the family and the peer group; (7) the changing status of the Negro in American society. It is possible, too, that the instruments did not measure what they were designed to measure. Finally, it may be that the literature on the self- and racial attitudes of Negro children is faulty.

Assuming the reliability of the instruments in the study, it follows from the findings here that the literature on the self- and racial attitudes of Negro children needs some re-evaluation. The present study suggests that, at the least, finer lines of differentiation should be drawn between Negro children from different backgrounds and environments.

Racial Attitudes of Negro Girls

The negative ratings of the girls in the panel of the pictures of the Negro man and the Negro boy with his head in his hands requires further analysis. One explanation of this finding is that the girls have negative attitudes toward all Negroes. However, other information on their attitudes (not to mention common sense) does not support this interpretation.

Another possible explanation is that the girls have negative attitudes toward the Negro male. The literature provides some support for this thesis. Kardiner and Ovesey (1951) stated that the Negro female tends to regard the male as being irresponsible and exploitative. They note that there is a great deal of protest against his failure as a provider and protector. Ausubel and Ausubel (1963) maintain that in the segregated Negro community the children live in a matriarchal family atmosphere where girls are openly preferred by mothers and grandmothers, and where the male sex role is generally depreciated. Both these arguments, however, are very difficult to match against the homes of the girls in the present study. For the most part, these are intact homes where the father is a white-collar worker. Such a situation is likely to provide the girls with a positive male figure. Moreover, the fact that the civil rights movement is dominated by males (at least on a national level) and that the girls are involved in civil rights should further strengthen a positive conception of the Negro male.

Another alternative is that the girls were expressing negative feelings about the Negro male obtained from their peer groups and the general community in which they live. Some support for this explanation is found in the fact that the girls who were not in the panel and who were given the picture interview also rated the two pictures negatively, and that a few boys not in the panel also rated the pictures negatively.

In any case, there is nothing definite in the data to indicate what underlies the response of the girls. When the study was designed, the wide sex differences in regard to the pictures were unanticipated. The fact that the girls responded positively to the picture of the Negro boy playing further complicates the problem.

Effect of Participation in the School

From the findings of this study, it is apparent that the girls had more favorable self- and racial attitudes than the boys at the beginning of their participation in the Freedom School and that the boys were much more affected by participation than the girls. The reasons for these differences are not clear.

The greater effect on the boys could be due to a self-selection factor. Boys tended to come only a few times and then drop out, and therefore those who did stay with the program may be the ones who found it relevant to their interests and needs.

There is no definitive explanation for these sex differences in the data. It is apparent, however, that the differences are very real and should be studied thoroughly in future research.

Effectiveness of the School

The findings of the study show that participation in the Freedom School affected the self- and racial attitudes of the boys who attended regularly and that it had a less clear effect on the girls. The small number of children in the panel, however, makes it difficult to evaluate in any complete way the effectiveness of the school and its program, and the main question of whether such programs as this will have widespread effectiveness in enhancing the self- and racial attitudes of Negro children remains, to some extent at least, unanswered.

In this regard, it is relevant to note some of the data collected about children who were not in the panel or the control group. Many of these children did feel that participation in the school produced large changes in their feelings about themselves. The following responses are examples: "Freedom School made me realize that I'm smart enough to learn about my background." "I know that I'm as good as anyone else." "I want to be treated equal."

When asked about changes in their feelings toward Negroes, the children tended to respond as follows: "They are as equal as whites." "I now know that everyone is equal." "When I was younger I thought whites were better than Negroes, but since I've been attending Freedom School I've learned that there is no superior race." "Wanted to be white, but now I don't." "I found out that whites are not better than Negroes and that all men are the same."

When asked about changes in their feelings toward whites, the children responded: "I don't trust them because some of them don't keep their word about helping Negroes." "They are against Negroes." "Sometimes they make the Negroes get in trouble." "I think they are unfair." "Freedom School taught you to understand them." "I was scared at first that whites might harm me. Was afraid to sleep at night. By learning about civil rights I'm not as afraid anymore."

Many of the leaders in the civil rights movement state that the Negro will not be accepted fully in American society until the white majority also learns a less distorted account of Negro history. There was some evidence from the white children who attended the Freedom School that a positive account of Negro history and the civil rights movement did affect their feelings about Negroes in a meaningful way. The following responses are examples: "In some things I could be wrong. About people—I was thinking the wrong things about them." "I learned that Negroes are just as good as whites—thought they weren't before." "I used to think that whites were a lot better than Negroes, but now I know they are not." "Never knew how much whites segregated Negroes—never knew how bad the situation was." "The whites are silly."

REFERENCES

Ausubel, David P., and Ausubel, Pearl. 1963. "Ego Development Among Segregated Negro Children," in *Education in Depressed Areas,* ed. A. Harry Passow. New York: Teachers College, Columbia University.

Baldwin, James. 1963. *The Fire Next Time.* New York: Dial Press.

Bernard, Viola W. 1958. "School Desegregation: Some Psychiatric Implications," *Psychiatry.* 21: 149–158.

Carlson, Rae. 1963. "Identification and Personality Structure in Preadolescents," *Journal of Abnormal and Social Psychology.* 67: 566–573.

Clark, Kenneth B. 1955. *Prejudice and Your Child.* Boston: Beacon Press.

Clark, Kenneth B., and Clark, Mamie P. 1958. "Racial Identification and Preference in Negro Children," in *Readings in Social Psychology,* ed. Eleanor E. Maccoby *et al.* New York: Holt, Rinehart and Winston.

Deutsch, Martin P. 1963. "The Disadvantaged Child and the Learning Process," in *Education in Depressed Areas,* ed. Passow.

Engel, Mary. 1959. "The Stability of the Self-concept in Adolescence," *Journal of Abnormal and Social Psychology.* 58: 211–215.

Festinger, Leon. 1957. *Theory of Cognitive Dissonance.* Row Peterson.

Harris, Louis. 1963. "The Negro in America," *Newsweek.* July 29, 15–36.

———. 1963. "What the White Man Thinks of the Negro Revolt," *Newsweek.* October 21, 44–57.

Harvey, O. J. 1953. "An Experimental Approach to the Study of Status Relations in Informal Groups," *American Sociological Review.* 18: 357–367.

Jefferson, Ruth B. 1957. "Some Obstacles to Racial Integration," *Journal of Education.* 26: 145–154.

Kardiner, Abram, and Ovesey, Lionel. 1951. *The Mark of Oppression.* New York: The World Publishing Company.

Katz, Daniel, and Braly, Kenneth W. 1958. "Verbal Stereotypes and Racial Prejudice," in *Readings in Social Psychology,* ed. Maccoby.

Katz, I., and Benjamin, L. 1960. "Effects of White Authoritarianism in Biracial Work Groups," *Journal of Abnormal and Social Psychology.* 61: 448–456.

Katz, I., and Cohen, M. 1962. "The Effects of Training Negroes Upon Cooperative Problem Solving in Biracial Teams," *Journal of Abnormal and Social Psychology.* 64: 319–325.

Katz, I., and Greenbaum, Charles. 1963. "Effects of Anxiety, Threat, and Racial Environment on Task Performance of Negro College Students," *Journal of Abnormal and Social Psychology.* 66: 562–568.

Klineberg, Otto. 1963. "Negro-White Differences in Intelligence Test Performance," *American Psychologist.* 18: 198–203.

Myrdal, Gunnar, 1944. *An American Dilemma.* New York: Harper & Brothers.

Nordholt, J. W. Scholte. 1960. *The People that Walk in Darkness: A History of the Negro People in America.* New York: Ballantine Books.

Whyte, W. F. 1943. *Street Corner Society: The Social Structure of an Italian Slum.* Chicago: University of Chicago Press.

Woodward, C. Vann. 1957. *The Strange Career of Jim Crow.* New York: Oxford University Press.

The Process of Mutual Redefinition—Counseling and Teaching Children from Urban Slums

Thelma P. Catalano

Why was I born?
Why-'m I livin'?
'N . . .
Who am I?
When all God's chillun' got shoes.

Pathways enabling human beings to open themselves to each other also deepen the levels of communication between them. Where there is genuine communication, there appears, as well, the capacity for people to learn from one another. Indeed, it is this process of mutual learning that helps to lighten many of the burdens and to create some of the joys of our simply human condition.

Of all the problems that beset slum schools, none seems so apparent as the failure in communication between staff and children. Their mutual inability to open themselves to each other, to communicate genuinely, has reduced learning to the lowest common denominator for all concerned. A situation has been created in these schools in which neither staff nor children is engaged in a process of growth and learning. Instead, both spend their energies in a psychological crossfire —sustained hostility, sullenness, or apathy on the part of the children, and chronic frustration on the part of the staff.

Children from impoverished homes in slum neighborhoods often come from very large families living in cramped quarters. Many are not living with their own parents. They know that the relative or adult they live with cares, but the "how" of the interest may be focused primarily on subsistence needs. Often the adult's most reliable concern is simply, "Do right . . . Don't get into no trouble." The means for self-expression and communication used by these children often seem crude and genuinely repulsive to adults outside their immediate sub-culture. The pleasures in their lives are not so much rare as uncertain and undependable. The children appear to have little incentive to delay gratification. Most of them have grown up knowing that police and other authorities are more often prosecutors than protectors. The accepted attitudes among them toward adults, law, rules, and authority

245

of all kinds, are fear, mistrust, and hatred. School, teachers, and "guidance" are all seen as part of the authority system, an inevitable fate to be submitted to, endured, at best outwitted. Their "in" language may well be one form of self-protection against this system.

School personnel, on the other hand, long accepting the school's standards of language, manners, beliefs, and values, assume that these children should respect adults, and accept and appreciate the teacher's authority and "rightness." Though they may recognize, at times, that official school standards are inappropriate, still they feel uncomfortable, even threatened, when confronted with crude language, overt hostility, and sullen defiance of their legitimate authority. Most of these personnel have grown up in a world in which the legitimate authority system enforced the "proper" manners, morals, and behavior, protected the "good" and punished the "wrong," and thereby assured their own security. They genuinely believe that the purpose of school should be learning. But they assume the prior necessity of "the proper school atmosphere." When this is violated, their first impulse is to re-establish it. Consequently, their main efforts in school are to maintain discipline and uphold the legitimate authority system of the school.

The cultural differences between staff and children in slum schools make the processes of opening up, communication, and learning extremely difficult, if not at times impossible. Nor can schools properly be viewed as totally responsible for all the learning, or the lack of it, in the lives of the youngsters. The children are affected, and profoundly affected, by the slum culture in which they were born and in which they live. Still, what we often forget, is that the school itself is part of the environment that influences and shapes the child: *student behavior reflects what occurs in school as well as out of school.* In sum, I believe the source of problems lies outside the schools; hence, the schools cannot solve the problems. But it does not follow that therefore the school can do nothing.

HUMAN RELATIONSHIPS, COMMUNICATION, AND LEARNING

One major responsibility of slum schools concerns the interpersonal relationships established between adult and child. It is in the context of these relationships that learning does or does not occur. We must begin to recognize, and accept, the human relationship as the significant process basic to communication and learning.

The ordinary pattern of adult-student relationships in slum schools is often a lifeless compromise between the adults, holding firm to their own life-orientation patterns, and the children, sullen and resentful, holding firm to theirs. Both, it seems, devote their primary attention and major energy to this endless tug-of-war.

Initial contacts in counseling or teaching these youngsters are filled with hostility. The children view members of the school staff primarily as representatives of the authority system, the external world which they dislike, fear, and close themselves off from. Consequently, the children respond immediately with their usual school-role behavior: hostility, apathy, and sullenness. What is more, a close look at both sides of the interaction reveals that often the adult responds to the child with as much hostility and defensiveness as the child had displayed toward him. It is quite common for an adult to feel threatened in the face of such hostility. Anyone's natural response to threat is to reciprocate with hostility in self-defense. The personal interaction, then, becomes nothing more than a battleground for mutually defensive needs.

Very little is known about the psychology of how any two people communicate and learn from each other in the course of human relationships. Even less is known about the psychology of communication between those from dissimilar backgrounds who almost literally speak different languages. However, I shall make some tentative assumptions about the nature of human relationships, communication, and the learning process.

No two people apprehend the same reality in exactly the same terms. Thus, for genuine communication to occur between them, there must be an exchange of meanings. Apprehending a new point of view, a new perspective on reality, or reaching an understanding of someone else's different understanding, implies learning something new. Learning something new implies a change in one's previous set of cognitions. It is literally impossible, then, for anyone to communicate genuinely with another human being without undergoing some form of change. Genuine communication, therefore, implies change. Further, since all the cognitions of an individual are more or less closely related to one another, a change in one has implications, ultimately, for all the others. By far the most significant cognitions, for most of us, are those that define ourselves, our identity. Genuine learning, then, can be understood as implying a change, however minute, in our own identity. The change in understanding required for genuine communication between two human beings can be seen, then, as a change in identity for each of them. Put another way, genuine communication and learning imply, for an individual, the ability to alter his own sense of identity. Thus, when genuine communication and learning are in process, *both* parties are undergoing change; both are altering their identities. When there is no communication, there is no learning, no change, and an individual retains his old sense of identity, or keeps "self" intact.

What can we know of the inner experiences of children who grow up in slum neighborhoods? How can we account for their frequent outbursts of hostility and aggression toward adults and school in general? What is the connection between what is going on inside these children and their behavior? Why do they express themselves in ways supposedly compatible with their own needs, yet so totally incompatible with the needs and expectations of supervising adults?

Such behavior might be understood as the children's way of attempting to deny, negate, or dissociate themselves from the direct experience of anxiety. Their feelings and attitudes about their own identity, home environment, culture, and school life are such that the anxiety of facing any of these realities might well represent extremely threatening —for some, even terrifying—experiences.

We can assume that many experiences—feelings of insecurity, of not being understood, of being "unworthy" or "incompetent"—are potential sources of anxiety. All children have a good many such feelings. But for most children, the ratio of anxiety experiences to assuring experiences is small enough for them to be able to cope with anxieties as they arise—or at least learn socially acceptable defenses against them. For lower-class children, particularly lower-class Negro children, the anxiety experiences occur so early in life, so pervasively, and are so overwhelming, and their training for coping with anxiety is so poor, that most of them do not learn to cope with it. At worst, they learn to evade the realities that produce it. That is, they learn to avoid experiencing it. This literally forces these children to "close out" or detach themselves from the external world around them—including school.

The process of genuine communication, learning, and change can all be seen for these children as anxiety producing. In a sense, the children's attempts to dissociate themselves from anxiety experiences are simultaneously desperate attempts to retain and to avoid altering their own sense of identity. It would further appear that one's own identity, or self-concept, is perceived as preferable to any loss or change in identity—especially when most of the changes experienced in the past have produced or threatened a worsening of one's identity. The hostility of the children may function as a means of cutting off anxiety and of deterring the learning process and self-change—an attempt to refrain from altering their sense of identity.

In a sense, when adults respond self-defensively to a child's hostility, they are responding as well to the child's demand to structure the situation so he can dissociate himself from the experience of anxiety, learning, and the altering of his identity. If adult responses fall into this pattern often enough (and I suspect they do), then not only is the child assured continued success at avoiding the anxiety experiences inherent in school and learning, but both child and adult remain hostile, and continually close themselves off from each other. Ultimately the child is denied the experience of learning. With further distance thus created between adult and child, the all-too-familiar and recurrent pattern appears, whereby children become tough, rebellious, sullen, defiant, or even worse, apathetic; and adults torment themselves at never being able to reach—or teach—these kids.

TRUST IN ADULT-STUDENT RELATIONSHIPS

What must occur between child and adult to lead more productively toward genuine communication and learning can be understood as what it takes for any two people to open themselves to each other. The essential quality, I believe, is trust. Trust, instead of hostility, can lead to more openness in adult-student relationships and consequently allow for a freer experiencing of the anxiety of learning and identity-change.

Trust (like love) is not enough. Productivity of school experience depends upon the adequacy and presentation of subject matter, as well as the child's ability to grasp it. But unless the child is open to the content, unless he is willing to attempt to grasp it, no progress can be made. The child's willingness to try to learn is, in my opinion, a necessary condition for learning to occur. In *The Culturally Deprived Child*, Riessman (1962, p. 94) quotes a teacher who was successful with these children: "Once you have established a basic relationship to them, you can teach them anything." Here, of course, I would specify the "basic" relationship must be a personal and trusting one. If trust in adult-student relationships in school can lead to willingness to learn, then we must explore the meaning and conditions of trusting.

Erikson (1958, pp. 55–56) distinguishes "basic trust"—"an attitude toward oneself and the world derived from the experiences of the first years of life"—from the more ordinary "trust"—"what is commonly implied in reasonable trustfulness as far as others are concerned." He says the general state of trust implies "not only that one has learned to rely on the sameness and continuity of the outer providers but also that one may trust oneself and the capacity of one's own organs to cope with urges; that one is able to consider oneself trustworthy" (p. 61).

An attitude toward oneself and an attitude toward the world cannot be separated (Fromm, 1947). A person who trusts, trusts himself, and is ready to trust the world. One who mistrusts, mistrusts himself, and the world as well. This can be traced to the mother-infant relationship in which, according to Erikson, basic trust is first established. An infant whose needs are cared for learns trust. The infant who does not have his needs cared for learns mistrust. The infant, so utterly helpless and dependent upon mother to attend to his needs, cannot separate his needs from mother.

If we equate the infant's needs with his sense of self or "being," then "mother," "needs," and "self" are all experienced by the infant as one. It is within, and possibly because of this state of oneness, that trust and mistrust develop.

Trust, then, is established in the open communication between mother and infant, whereby the infant freely acknowledges and expresses his needs (self), through the process of having these needs (self) adequately cared for by mother. His needs being cared for, and also his capacity to acknowledge them, enables the infant to develop a positive sense of identity, of self. Mistrust, on the other hand, is established by the infant's not having his needs (self) adequately cared for, because of the nature of communication (or lack of communication) between mother and infant; therefore the infant cannot acknowledge, much less express, his needs (self) freely, and consequently he develops a negative sense of identity.

The child who has learned trust perceives others and the world around him in a trusting manner. He is capable of "reasonable trustfulness as far as others are concerned." The child who has learned mistrust, perceives the world around him as a place where nothing and no one can be trusted. Further, the child who has learned trust has learned, from the care of his needs, a positive sense of being, or self, which then enables him to relate positively to the world around him. The child who learns mistrust, has learned, from lack of care for his needs (self), a negative image of himself, and then relates in negative fashion to the external world around him.

Here we can see some basis for the importance of human relationships in the development of trust and mistrust. The capacity to trust and the sad incapacity to trust, are not simply something we are born with. Trust and mistrust develop out of a multiplicity of interactions between human beings involving communication and the care of personal needs, as can be seen in the early development of trust or mistrust between mother and infant. Thus the nature of trust and mistrust cannot be viewed alone, but only as a quality of interpersonal interaction. Deutsch (1962) similarly discusses the nature of trust *within the context* of interpersonal relationships.

This developmental process raises a serious question. If certain children have never developed a sense of basic trust, how can they experience any form of trust, or trustworthiness in later years? How is it possible for any adult to establish a personal trusting relationship with such a child, once the child has reached school age?

Everyone experiences some degree of frustration, of deprivation in his early years. Such is the nature of human infancy. For all of us, deprivation is a matter of kind and a matter of degree. For example, infants from many middle-class homes not too long ago (today's adults) were fed according to the clock rather than when they were hungry. Undoubtedly such frustration leads to some mistrust.

Trust and mistrust are not qualities that either exist or do not exist in a person. Both exist in varying form and degree in each of us. This is significant for our work with these children. The fact that they have reached school age means that their needs have been cared for by someone, to some extent, and they have acquired some form of basic trust in their early years. What should concern us is how much or how little capacity for trust we have to work with in these children and in ourselves as well.

THE PROCESS OF MUTUAL REDEFINITION

The crucial factor that will determine whether personal trusting relationships develop between adults and children in slum schools is the adult's willingness to take the initial responsibility, in the course of his relationships with students, to enter a continuous and changing process of defining and redefining himself. This process begins with the demands made on adults by the children as expressions of their needs. This, in turn, leads the children to engage in an identical process of redefining themselves. As a result, both children and adults will communicate at more genuine levels, and alter their own sense of identity within the learning experiences shared between them. In other words, in a personal trusting relationship something must *happen* to both parties concerned, and the resulting change will have a mutual effect. In this paper I will call this process the process of mutual redefinition.

An example will illustrate how this process works. Not long ago I was working with a class of eighth-grade youngsters in a slum school. We had just completed a competitive class tournament. The teams had been closely matched, and I had had to arbitrate several close decisions. After the final round, two girls from the losing team walked over to me. "Boy, it's a good thing you're not a kid, Miss C. Y' dig?" said the spokesman.

Her tone of voice was half hostile, half joking. Clearly, she was angry. Her words and manner implied a direct challenging of me, and a flagrant violation of "appropriate school atmosphere" and my role as the guardian of that atmosphere. Fortunately, I knew the youngsters in the class; I knew the girl who spoke—and I knew myself. Though apparently she was threatening me, I did not feel threatened. Consequently, I did not have to defend myself by reprimanding her and reasserting the legitimate authority structure. Since I didn't have to concentrate on defending myself, I was able to intuit, however fuzzily at the instant, that her behavior represented an expression of her own needs, not, as it might have appeared, a threat to mine. My only response was a quiet, neutral, "Oh?"

As soon as I had a free hour, I called the girl into my office for a private discussion. (Common decency and respect for another human being, particularly one easily threatened, require a private, rather than public, discussion in such circumstances.) I began in a quiet tone, trying to communicate to her my genuine interest and desire to understand: "Arlene, do you have any idea why I asked to see you?" "No," answered Arlene, but not sullenly. "Oh . . . well . . . just think for a moment." Arlene did not reply. "Guess," I said. Arlene hesitated, then plunged, "Because of what I said to you after class this morning?" "Yes," I said. Another pause ensued. Arlene slumped in her seat and hung her head, looking sheepish but not defensive. I was also hesitating. What I had on my mind would not be easy to say. If my hunch was wrong, I would look pretty ridiculous. Even if I was right, but spoke in the wrong tone of voice, and Arlene got scared and denied it, we would be at a hostile impasse. Finally, I plunged, "Arlene, let me tell you what I think you were saying to me this morning. 'You're lucky you're not a kid, Miss C., 'cause if you were I'd beat your ass. Y' dig?" I paused only a moment. "Yes, Arlene, I think I dig. Do I?" I had begun this statement in a quiet, neutral, almost impassive tone of voice. But as I spoke, my feeling about myself, about Arlene, about our interaction, warmed. I was pleased with myself at being able to understand and use the "in" language. More important, I sensed as I spoke that I was right. I was pleased at my perceptiveness. I was pleased with Arlene for acknowledging, albeit at this point silently, almost imperceptibly, that I understood her. I was pleased with her spunkiness that morning, her daring to express to me her genuine feelings so openly, and her spunkiness in acknowledging them. Most important, genuine communication is intrinsically enjoyable. I am sure these feelings must have been reflected, at least to some extent, in my voice. and my face as I spoke. Arlene immediately slumped even further in her chair, hung her head, and with a shy tentative smile nodded her head yes. I smiled, now openly, and continued warmly, "O.K., I thought so . . . but wanted to be certain . . . Let's talk about it."

For the next hour Arlene and I discussed the tournament and Arlene's comment as well. I emphasized Arlene's right to feel, and express, whatever she might have felt about losing, and then spoke directly to what I thought Arlene felt to be the cause of her anger that morning. I pointed out that no one is perfect, and teachers are no exceptions; that though I did not feel any favoritism for either team, and had tried to call each decision exactly as I had seen it, there was always the possibility of human error. This was simply honesty on my part. It was also acknowledging my responsibility for Arlene's experience. After all *I* had initiated the tournament. Then gradually I turned the conversation toward what I considered the real cause of Arlene's anger that morning—the experience of losing. I pointed out directly and honestly that losing something that you want and are trying very hard to win is not pleasant, but that it is a reality of life for everyone. I was equally direct, but without a trace of punitiveness in my feelings or voice, in suggesting that maybe the anger Arlene had directed at me that morning had really been anger at her own fate, at being a member of the losing team. Was she justified in threatening me, or in feeling like beating me up just because she could not tolerate losing? In this discussion we both acknowledged the very real difficulty at accepting loss that had led Arlene to make the comment. I suspect that Arlene grew—and changed—a little in that hour. I know that I did.

Let us compare this, for a moment, with what might have happened if in recognizing Arlene's threat to me that morning, I had felt seriously threatened, and responded defensively. If I had automatically identified myself with a static teacher-authority role, I (my selfhood) would indeed have been threatened. My natural and spontaneous reaction then would be to defend my identity. I would lay down the law, and in no uncertain terms. Such an assertion would firmly establish the power (integrity, inviolability) and legitimacy (rightness) of my identity, myself. It would equally firmly establish the uselessness (impotence) and wrongness of Arlene's impulse (self). To carry this out I make a loud, public reprimand; guilt is assigned, punishment administered, and additional punishment threatened—all by tone of voice alone. It is clear to me, to Arlene, and to all of her classmates that Arlene is bad, guilty, and punished. If Arlene then defends herself by fighting back with overt hostility, or even a sullen pout, and if I have felt sufficiently threatened by the interchange, Arlene may be ordered out of the class, sent to the principal, etc., etc. And the fight is on!

To begin, adults *must* accept the idea that they must literally earn the children's respect. These children do not automatically respect us just because we have official authority roles. (This is so in spite of the frequent assertion that lower-class people have a kind of awe of school personnel. I suspect this kind of awe is mostly fear, tinged with bits of envy and admiration.) Therefore, one of the demands of these children is that we prove ourselves worthy of their respect. We must be willing to acknowledge and accept this challenge if we are ever to join these children in whatever it takes to get them to want to learn. Arlene's comment, for example, "You're lucky you're not a kid . . ." was a direct challenge to me to prove myself worthy of her respect.

Next, accepting this challenge means being flexible enough with the children to relinquish our authority-by-fiat, the authority conferred by our title and official role alone. It is precisely this official aspect of the teacher role that the children challenge. I am not suggesting that we renounce our authority as a person based upon professional competence, human sensitivity, or personal integrity. Far from it; at the moment of challenge this is what we must have and use. But we must be flexible enough to rely on our inner resources, and reinterpret not only for ourselves but for the children, the external symbols and their meanings. We must accept this challenge not *at* its face value but *for* its inner meaning to the children. In essence, we must be willing to alter our identity. This was done with Arlene by responding to her without reprisal . . . "Oh?" The discussion with Arlene and interpretation of her comment also required relinquishing this role. The fact that her language may have violated some form of "teacher code" was treated as irrelevant to the real situation—and fortunately so—for it enabled genuine communication to occur between us.

The next step involves being willing to engage in a series of testing-out processes with these children, and being able to recognize the underlying dynamics of these processes. As stated earlier, these children frequently appear hostile, particularly in our beginning contacts with them, and in a sense oppose or violate our standards and expectations of them. If we look beneath the appearances, however, we often find that this testing-out process does not represent only hostility or detachment. More important, it may also represent the child's attempt to find a place with adults, and school in general. It is as if the child were asking, "How much do I dare venture with you (the adult)?

Why (should 'I') venture at all? How do I know I can trust you? Dare I reveal my real needs (my real self)?"

As with Arlene, these children generally respond within the framework of the immediate discussion, or context of the lesson, but in a way that will allow them to become personally involved. That is, they will respond *to* the discussion, or class exercise, but *from* their own frame of reference or their own world. (Their "world" here includes language, ways of thinking and perceiving, all the realities of their culture and, most important, their concept of their own identity.) Though possibly startling to the adult (as I suspect Arlene's comment would have been to many adults who work in these schools), their comments generally have a direct meaning and relevance, not only *from* the children's orientation but *to* whatever is being presented. This testing-out process may best be described in their own jargon. They want to "get to the nitty gritty," or they want to "get where it's at." They want to see if the adult can grasp *their* meaning, not only of what they are verbalizing but of what they are saying in relation to what the adult is expressing. They want to see if they dare open up to the adult, trust him to care for their need of the moment, communicate with him. Also, they want to know what an adult will do when he is bluntly confronted with the realities of the children's own world. This tells them "who" the adult is—really is! On one level they are testing the adult to see how much he is with them; on another, *they are testing themselves to see how much they can get with him.*

It is in this testing-out process that these children open themselves, tentatively, to the adult, and school in general. The adult's response to the child at this time will determine the course of interaction between them, and the nature of the relationship that will be established between them. Whether the child will be able to face the anxiety of trying to learn the content being presented to him depends upon this relationship and this, at least partially, determines whether the child will or will not learn. In other words, at this time of testing out, the adult must be able to relinquish his authority-by-fiat role and also be flexible enough to enter the world of the child by responding in terms of what it is the child is demanding, and yet remain in the adult world of the immediate class or counseling discussion. Arlene's comment, for example, was prompted by the fact that she did not and could not accept loss or the anxiety (threat to identity) produced by losing. Her immediate reaction to losing, as revealed by her comment, was, in effect, a denial of losing, anxiety, identity-threat. Her substitution of externally directed anger for internally directed threat was an attempt to dissociate herself from the actual experiencing of the anxiety involved. Thus, the later discussion focused not directly on her comment, but the experience of losing. Arlene's comment was her genuine reaction to personal involvement with having to live with loss. (There are other possible reactions, as many of us who have worked in these schools know; she could have hauled off and slugged a member of the winning team.)

The standard counselor or teacher role does not measure up to the children's needs or demands in the testing-out situation. The child in effect presents a proposition that if verbalized would go something like, "I'll enter your world—if you'll but enter mine." This kind of mutual exchange is indeed a process of mutual redefinition.

SUMMARY

Hostility and apathy in children from slum areas are here interpreted as most probably manifestations of attempts to avoid anxiety. These children are made especially anxious by any threat of change in their self-concept. The learning process can be understood as requiring change, growth, development of the learner's identity. Learning, therefore, is particularly threatening to children such as these, for whom previous changes in self-concept have so frequently been negative.

Learning in school is an interpersonal process, the process of communication. Genuine communication, an art for any two people, is made particularly difficult by the large differences in manners, morals, attitudes, and habits that separate staff and children in slum schools. However, the children do "test out" the possibility of true communication. They do, often, reveal their real feelings about the material being presented, but often in an apparently hostile way, or via expressions uncongenial to the adult. If at the moment of testing out, the adult can trust himself, and trust the child, and respond to the child's real needs instead of self-defensively cutting off communication, the adult may succeed in winning the child's respect and saving the child's self-respect. The child may begin to trust the adult and trust himself. The process of developing mutual respect and mutual trust through genuine communication is called the process of mutual redefinition. By successfully entering the child's world, the adult redefines himself both to the child and to himself. The child who enters the adult world redefines himself to himself and to the adult. Because of the mutual openness and trust in the relationship, the anxiety of change is not overwhelming for either. In fact, it is only in the context of this process of mutual redefinition that learning for either child or adult can begin.

REFERENCES

Deutsch, Morton. 1962. "Cooperation and Trust: Some Theoretical Notes," *Nebraska Symposium on Motivation,* 275–316.

Erikson, Erik H. 1958. "Ego Development and Historical Change," *Psychological Issues,* 18–49.

Fromm, Erich. 1947. *Man For Himself.* New York: Rinehart and Co.

Karon, Bertram P. 1958. *The Negro Personality.* New York: Springer Publishing Co.

Kornberg, Leonard. 1963. "Meaningful Teachers for Alienated Children," in *Education in Depressed Areas,* ed. A. Harry Passow. New York: Teachers College, Columbia University.

Riessman, Frank. 1962. *The Culturally Deprived Child.* New York: Harper and Row.

The Influence of Emotional Disturbance and Social Class on Sensitivity to Vocal Emotion

Nelia Reynolds

INTRODUCTION

The purpose of this research was to compare normal and emotionally disturbed children with respect to their emotional sensitivity—experimentally defined as the ability to identify correctly, from vocal cues, the emotions of love, anger, sadness, and happiness.

In her intensive cross-sectional study of children from five to 12, Dimitrovsky (1964) found that the ability of a child to identify the emotional meanings of vocal expressions increased significantly with age. The study also showed that children of all age levels most frequently identified emotions of sadness, then of anger, happiness, and love, in that order. Children gave the responses "sad" and "angry" more frequently than the responses "happy" and "loving." Except with five year olds, the study found no significant relationship between verbal intelligence and the ability to recognize the emotions expressed.

Dimitrovsky's research examined the responses of normal children. A similar study by Turner (1964) used schizophrenic adults as subjects. Turner's results indicated that schizophrenics varied more than nonschizophrenics in the ability to identify vocal expressions of emotional meaning and, on the average, were inferior. Statistically, the higher average ability of normal persons was shown to be due to a more compact distribution which did not extend either as low as or appreciably higher than that of schizophrenics.

As one possible explanation of this finding, Turner suggests that schizophrenics are characterized, among other things, by disturbed interpersonal functioning and that such disturbances may interfere with the ability to identify spoken emotions. Following similar reasoning, Mattis (1965) hypothesized that since stress and anxiety tend to have a disruptive influence on interpersonal relations, people who are anxious would be more insensitive than people who are not. He compared a group of graduate students about to take a statistics exam with a control group of students, in terms of their sensitivity to vocal expressions of emotion. He found that the former, more anxious, group was less sensitive.

One question suggested by this past research is: how do emotionally disturbed children compare with normal children as judges of vocal expressions of emotions? Assuming that emotional sensitivity is a learned ability and that emotional disturbance is a learned reaction to environmental pressures, what is the most likely relationship between emotional disturbance and emotional sensitivity?

One possibility is that emotionally disturbed children are actually more sensitive than their normal contemporaries. It could be argued that a disturbed child has become disturbed precisely because he is especially sensitive to emotional expression. For example, consider two young children who overhear a parental argument without understanding the content of the argument. To the insensitive child, this experience will have little more significance than overhearing his parents discuss the possibility of rain. The sensitive child, however, may be deeply moved by the recognition of anger or unhappiness in his parents' voices. The argument may make him feel insecure or threatened. Similar experiences of this sort might cause such a child either to act out against or withdraw from the emotional pressures of his environment.

Although this reasoning is intuitively appealing, both Turner and Mattis' researches suggest the converse, that the normal child is more likely to have a great sensitivity to emotional expressions than the emotionally disturbed child. While schizophrenic adults are certainly not directly comparable to disturbed children, the two populations do have in common a disturbance in interpersonal functioning. Similarly, while there are many differences between an anxious statistics student and a disturbed child, the two do have intense anxiety in common. Thus, it could reasonably be expected that a disturbed child would be relatively less sensitive to vocal expressions of emotion than a normal child.

The present study originally intended to restrict itself to an examination of two groups of children paired by age and school grade, the independent variable being emotional health. However, after we had tested a group of normal children in Hartford, Connecticut, the Hartford Board of Education refused us permission to test any disturbed children in its school system. Therefore, two additional groups of children, one normal and one disturbed, were tested in Harlem public schools. As a result, quite by accident, the opportunity arose to consider the possibility of the influence of socioeconomic and racial variables on emotional sensitivity by comparing white, middle-class Hartford children and Negro, lower-class Harlem children. It was hypothesized that the children higher on the socioeconomic scale would be more emotionally sensitive.

METHODS

Subjects

There were three groups of subjects. The first consisted of 30 children
in the first through third grades in a Hartford public school. These children came from middle-class, white families. The second group consisted of 27 children in the second and third grades from a New York
City public school in Harlem, and the third group of 26 emotionally
disturbed children in the second and third grades from the same school.
This last group had been diagnosed by the school and was attending
special guidance classes for disturbed children. Both groups of Harlem
children were from lower-class Negro families. Throughout the remainder of this paper, the three groups of subjects will be referred to
as MCN (middle class, normal), LCN (lower class, normal), and LCD
(lower class, disturbed).

Instruments

To test emotional sensitivity, the present study used the tape developed
by Dimitrovsky. This tape consisted of 24 vocal expressions, 12 by male
speakers and 12 by female speakers. A short, emotionally "neutral"
paragraph was read by each speaker: "I'm going out now. I won't be
back all afternoon. If anyone calls, tell them I'll call back tomorrow."
The speaker repeated the paragraph in happy, angry, sad, or loving
tones. There were six randomly ordered expressions of each of the four
emotions. The tape was accompanied by four faces, next to each of
which was printed the emotion registered by the face (Figure 1). The
faces were drawn by the researcher as she imagined a child might
have done them. The second instrument was the vocabulary section of
the Stanford-Binet intelligence test for children.

Procedure

Each subject was tested individually. The researcher spent two or
three minutes talking to the child before starting, with the hope that
this would help the child to relax and feel less threatened by the situation. Then the Stanford-Binet vocabulary list was administered.

Next the child was shown the four pictures and given the following
instructions:

> I am going to play a record for you now. You will hear a lady saying
> the same sentence over and over, and I want you to tell me if you
> think [pointing to pictures] she is a happy, angry, sad, or loving lady.

Figure 1: Faces Used to Illustrate Four Emotions Being Studied

HAPPY   ANGRY

SAD   LOVING

You can tell me which kind of person she is or just point to the correct picture. Do you understand that? . . . Which picture would you point to if you thought she was a happy lady [etc., until it was clear that the child understood the instructions, as evidenced by correct identification of each picture]?

The child was praised during the instruction period. The record of the 12 female speakers was played and the child was told he was doing very well in identifying their emotions and that the rest of the record would be just the same except that the speakers would be men, so that he should point to the pictures of the happy, angry, sad, or loving man.

RESULTS

Table 1 presents the mean number of correct identifications made by each group. An analysis of variance shows that the difference between the means is significant beyond the .01 level.

TABLE 1

MEANS AND STANDARD DEVIATIONS OF
TOTAL NUMBER OF CORRECT
IDENTIFICATIONS FOR CHILDREN
IN EACH GROUP[a]

Group	Mean	Standard Deviation
MCN	12.5	2.84
LCN	9.3	1.97
LCD	9.7	2.96

[a]*Maximum possible score is 24.*

The means reveal that the MCN children are more sensitive to spoken expressions of emotion than either the LCN or LCD children, and that the latter two groups are very similar in sensitivity.

Because of the possibility that sensitivity to emotional expression might be correlated with verbal intelligence, each child was given the vocabulary section of the Stanford-Binet. The group means recorded on this test are shown in Table 2.

An analysis of covariance between the number of correct identifications and the number of correct vocabulary words was significant $(p > .01)$. This indicates that the differences in sensitivity between

TABLE 2

MEANS AND STANDARD DEVIATIONS OF
TOTAL NUMBER OF CORRECT
VOCABULARY WORDS FOR
CHILDREN IN EACH GROUP

Group	Mean	Standard Deviation
MCN	9.4	1.62
LCN	9.1	1.72
LCD	7.7	2.81

groups is a real difference, i.e., it is not just a difference in measured verbal intelligence.

Table 3, a breakdown of the information in Table 1, shows the group means of correct identifications for each of the four categories of emotional meaning. From these data we see that children in all three groups tend to identify sadness correctly most frequently, followed by anger, happiness, and love, respectively. The only exception to this order occurred among the MCN children, who tended to be correct in their identification of anger slightly more often than sadness. (The sad, angry, happy, loving order of recognition agrees with the findings of Dimitrovsky.) The data also reveal that while the three groups are very similar in their ability to recognize vocal expressions of happiness and

TABLE 3

MEANS AND STANDARD DEVIATIONS OF NUMBER OF
CORRECT IDENTIFICATIONS FOR CHILDREN
IN EACH GROUP FOR EACH CATEGORY
OF EMOTIONAL MEANING[a]

Emotion	Group	Mean	Standard Deviation
Happy	MCN	1.9	1.28
	LCN	1.7	1.08
	LCD	1.9	1.54
Angry	MCN	4.7	1.29
	LCN	2.7	1.22
	LCD	2.5	1.78
Sad	MCN	4.4	1.30
	LCN	3.5	1.42
	LCD	3.9	1.29
Loving	MCN	1.4	1.51
	LCN	1.5	1.00
	LCD	1.5	1.18

[a]*Maximum possible score is 6.*

love, the MCN children tend to identify anger and sadness correctly more often than either the LCN or LCD children.

In order to see if the differences in correct identifications are the chance result of different frequencies of emission, the percentage of responses was calculated for each emotional category. These data are shown in Table 4.

TABLE 4

PERCENTAGE OF EMITTED RESPONSES,
RIGHT AND WRONG

		Response		
Group	Happy	Angry	Sad	Loving
MCN	15.4	34.0	36.5	14.0
LCN	15.7	28.0	35.9	20.2
LCD	20.0	25.4	39.1	15.3

The results show that all children tend to use the angry and sad identifications more often than the happy and loving identifications. This factor could have contributed to the greater number of correct

TABLE 5

PERCENTAGE OF FREQUENCY OF ERRORS OF CHILDREN IN EACH GROUP
FOR EACH CATEGORY OF EMOTIONAL MEANING

		Correct Identification				
Identification Given		Happy	Angry	Sad	Loving	Totals
Happy	MCN		3.8	3.2	9.3	16.3
	LCN		5.9	3.5	7.4	16.8
	LCD		8.5	4.4	7.4	20.3
Angry	MCN	23.1		1.7	4.3	29.1
	LCN	15.6		4.6	5.6	25.8
	LCD	14.9		4.9	5.8	25.6
Sad	MCN	7.6	3.2		26.3	37.1
	LCN	8.2	7.7		17.9	33.8
	LCD	9.9	10.2		18.5	38.6
Loving	MCN	5.8	3.2	7.9		16.9
	LCN	8.4	7.1	7.4		22.9
	LCD	4.1	6.0	4.9		15.0
Totals	MCN	36.5	10.2	12.8	39.9	
	LCN	32.2	20.7	15.5	30.9	
	LCD	28.9	24.7	14.2	31.7	

identifications, for all groups, of sad and angry emotional expressions. (The data, of course, do not explain *why* the three groups of children heard anger or sadness more often than love or happiness. Further, while the data suggest that the MCN group's higher correct recognition rate of anger may have been partially the result of chance—due to the group's higher number of angry identifications—they do not explain why the MCN children were more sensitive to expressions of sadness than either the LCN or LCD children.) Finally, the data reveal that by chance alone, based on emitted responses, the LCD children should have correctly identified happiness most often and the LCN children, love. The three groups, however, had approximately equal success in identifying these emotions.

The kinds of errors made by the children in each group are shown in Table 5. The categories of emotional meaning on the left of the chart indicate the emotion identified by the children; those along the top of the chart indicate the correct emotion. The overall trend revealed by the table is that the LCN and LCD children tend to make similar errors, which in turn are different from the errors made by the MCN children. This tendency is particularly noticeable with respect to the greater tendency of both the LCN and LCD children to identify anger as happiness, sadness, or love, and their similarly less frequent tendency to confuse sadness with love.

The data also lend some support to Dimitrovsky's finding that children more often confuse either the active emotions (happiness and anger) or the passive emotions (sadness and love), and less often confuse one with the other. There are, however, exceptions to this.

DISCUSSION

The results of this research indicate that middle-class children are significantly more sensitive to vocal expressions of emotion than are lower-class children, regardless of I.Q. Also, the most consistent trend in the data appears to divide the children along socioeconomic and racial lines rather than according to degrees of emotional health.

It could be argued that the socioeconomic and racial divisions are also representative of divisions in emotional disturbance, that the average Harlem child, regardless of whether or not he has been diagnosed as disturbed, is more likely than the average Hartford child to be from a broken home, to know the meaning of poverty, to have difficulty in school, etc.—that, in short, the lower-class Negro child lives with more insecurity and stress than does the middle-class white child. It would follow, therefore, that the observed differences in sensitivity to vocal expressions of emotion do reflect differences between relative emotional health and relative emotional disturbance. Furthermore, if one accepts this argument, some support is given to the thesis of both Turner and Mattis, since the direction of the differences reveals that the presumably more emotionally healthy child is also the more sensitive child.

There is, however, an important artifact of the instrument used to measure emotional sensitivity that must be taken into account in interpreting the results, and that is that the basic record was made by middle-class, white speakers. Therefore, it is possible that the overall differences obtained do not reflect actual differences between the children but rather the inability of white speakers to communicate emotional meaning equally well to both Negro and white children. This interpretation assumes that there is a learning factor involved in the ability to recognize vocal expressions of emotion and that there are differences between Negro and white tonal articulation of the same emotions. These suppositions can be verified only through further research. Nonetheless, it is a distinct possibility that the use of white speakers in the present study may have increased the difficulty of the experimental task for the Negro children.

But, even if this were the case, it does not explain the qualitative differences revealed by the data in regard to specific emotions. We have seen that children of all three groups tended to identify anger and sadness correctly more often than happiness and love, and that this could be explained to some extent by the more frequent emissions of the negative emotions. The question remains, however, why children tend to hear anger and sadness more often than happiness and love. One possible explanation is that expressions of both anger and sadness, to a greater extent than happiness and love, often contain immediately identifiable cues, such as the characteristic loudness and blatancy of anger, or the shaking voice, crying, sobbing, and sighing sounds of sadness. Perhaps children tend to respond to these cues in the beginning of the speaker's paragraph, without waiting to consider that the loudness might be a boisterous expression of happiness, or the sigh a loving sigh, etc.

Although all children tended to say they heard sadness and anger more than happiness and love, the MCN group surpassed both the other groups in its ability to identify sadness and anger correctly. In fact, the greater failure on the part of the LCN and LCD groups to recognize these two spoken emotions seems to be the main cause both of their similar overall means and the fact that they were significantly lower than the means for the MCN children.

Unfortunately, the data presented here cannot tell us why the two groups of lower-class Negro children had more difficulty than the middle-class white children in recognizing vocal expressions of anger and sadness. The explanation for this difference, as well as for those previously described, will have to await further research. But if the results of this study are substantiated, then perhaps a new dimension to the effects of minority status is indicated, at least upon the lower-class Negro child. It may be that the need of such a child to adapt to a harsh environment induces in him a tendency to avoid the perception of painful and negative emotions.

REFERENCES

Dimitrovsky, L. 1964. "The Ability to Identify the Emotional Meaning of Vocal Expressions at Successive Age Levels," in *The Communication of Emotional Meaning*, ed. Joel R. Davitz. New York: McGraw-Hill Book Company.

Mattis, Steven. 1965. *Effect of Stress on Identification of Vocal Expression of Emotion*. Unpublished doctoral dissertation. Teachers College, Columbia University.

Turner, John le B. 1964. "Schizophrenics as Judges of Vocal Expressions of Emotional Meaning," in *The Communication of Emotional Meaning*, ed. Davitz.

Child-Rearing Practices in Lower Socioeconomic Ethnic Groups

Imogene D. Cahill

This study of child-rearing practices among lower-class mothers was undertaken in the hope that it might increase our understanding of lower-class culture. It is through its child-rearing practices that a culture transmits its customs and values, and its unique ways of thinking, feeling, and behaving.

Sixty mothers of the lower socioeconomic group were interviewed about the methods they had used to raise a five-year-old child from birth to the time of the interview. The questionnaire had been designed by Sears, Maccoby, and Levin (1957) and reported by them in *Patterns of Child Rearing*. The interviews were collected in the maternity ward of a hospital several days after the birth of a baby. In this environment, the mothers were relatively easy to approach; their attention was already focused upon child rearing, and they had plenty of time.

The interviews were supplemented by informal contacts with the mothers in the hospital setting, the outpatient clinic, or with their children in their own homes. Mothers and children other than those in the study, but coming from a similar background, were observed in the hospital setting, in nursery schools, playgrounds, school yards, and on public transportation facilities. Of the 60 interviewed, 20 each were Puerto Rican, Negro, and white. Their lower socioeconomic class was determined by their occupations and the length of their education, as well as by those of their husbands. The amount of income, if known, was considered. However, all were medically indigent. Hence, a low income was verified. Style of life, including type of housing, was also taken into consideration.

None of the mothers or their husbands had more than a high school education. The average number of years spent in school was 9.73 years for the mothers and 8.7 years for their husbands.

All but three of the women had been employed at different times for varying periods. For the most part, they were or had been factory workers or in service occupations. Their husbands also were in unskilled jobs, mostly as laborers, porters, or factory workers. Unemployment was common, however. Either no wages were coming in or the amount earned was barely enough for subsistence living. The average pay for the men who worked was reported to be about $55, regardless of family size. Several families, because of the number of their children, were having their incomes supplemented by payments from the department of welfare, even though the main earner had steady employment. At least 29 of the 60 families were receiving partial or full welfare payments.

The families lived either in slum areas or in public housing projects. The best-kept homes were in the latter, but even here the surroundings were drab and the buildings showed signs of approaching deterioration. The homes, in the slums of Harlem, Brooklyn, or the Lower East Side of New York, were unbelievably dilapidated. In most of the buildings in these areas, the hallways were dark and littered with garbage. Furniture was scarce and the little that was present was shabby. Heat was often inadequate or simply nonexistent. Vermin and rats were common. It was not unusual to see rat holes covered over with boards or strips of metal. Many of the women were poor housekeepers, understandable in such an environment, but some of the flats were kept quite clean. Misanthropy was evident everywhere. Doors were kept bolted and were opened cautiously. No one became intimate with neighbors. Social life was almost exclusively kept within the family. The exception was the men who sat or stood around in the streets and the doorways, idly talking and joking but often just staring into space or dozing. Some of the latter were under the influence of alcohol or narcotics.

This was a constant source of concern to the mothers. Women with teenage daughters were particularly concerned. "We live in a project so I can't let her out—too much goes on."

When one of the "caretakers" comes into the neighborhood, he is treated with distant politeness, but no one seems to know where anyone else lives. Doorbells often go unanswered. The person who is most unwelcome, yet often the most needed, is the welfare supervisor. He is the enemy.

There was a great deal of family disorganization within the population of the study. Nineteen of the marriages were consensual in type. However, some of these had been entered into seriously and were fairly stable unions. The reason for many of the consensual marriages was economic, but cultural influence was also important. It is a commonly accepted form of marriage among people of a low socioeconomic level in Puerto Rico and in the rural South. Seven of these unions, for example, were Puerto Rican and 11 were Negro, while only one was white. Seven other mothers in the study were divorced, seven were legally separated, and two were single. These mothers were living alone at the time of the study. However, this did not mean that their five year old had grown up fatherless. Some of the fathers visited often and took responsibility for their children. In other families, a father or a father surrogate had been present through most of the five-year period. Only four had reached that age with no father at all.

As a group, these mothers faced many other serious problems that rarely concern women on a higher socioeconomic level. Drug addiction, alcoholism, desertion, illegitimacy, imprisonment, beatings from husbands—all these were common.

There was no difficulty in obtaining a full sample of Negro and Puerto Rican respondents, since the hospital where most of the interviews were collected serves large numbers of both groups. Finding enough lower-class Caucasian mothers who had children of five, however, proved to be a time-consuming and frustrating task. The reasons for this are not clear. While there is a possibility that the most likely places were overlooked, it is likely that in the East Coast cities the bulk of the lower-class population is made up of Puerto Ricans and Negroes. Moreover, the criterion of having a five year old may have limited the selection away from the smaller Caucasian population on this socioeconomic level. In addition, it is reasonable to assume that the latter, being favored in eligibility for jobs and for membership in unions which provide such benefits as maternity care, are able to secure private or clinic care in private hospitals.

The ethnic background of the white mothers varied. Unexpectedly, the largest number came not from immigrant but from native American stock. There were eight of these. Five others were of Irish descent, another four were Italian, and one was Jewish. Two were foreign born but had lived in this country a number of years, one having come from Ireland and one from England. Combining these, for the purposes of the study, into one ethnic group might be dangerous in another time and place. Actually, this was logical considering these particular mothers. They did not live in ethnic neighborhoods, were mostly married to men of different ethnic backgrounds, and did not identify themselves as belonging to any particular group. The only mother who consistently varied from the others in her child rearing was Jewish. She had a more middle-class orientation than the others, probably an ethnic characteristic.

The Sears, Maccoby, and Levin (1957) questionnaire was chosen for several reasons. First of all, the study they had done was of the child-rearing practices of working-class and middle-class mothers, the results of which would be interesting to contrast with those of this study. Secondly, the questionnaire was designed for transcultural use. Landy (1959) had found it useful in a study he did in the cane fields of Puerto Rico. Minturn and Lambert (1964) had also employed it successfully in studying child rearing in six divergent and geographically separated cultures.

The questions, which were open-ended and worded so as to put the subject at ease and evoke a frank answer, were designed to elicit underlying characteristics as spontaneously as possible. Care was taken to enable the respondent to save face, to assume the existence of behavior valued negatively by the mother, and to make a wide range of answers seem acceptable. Responses can be grouped into traits or characteristics, such as showing warmth, permissiveness, dependency, and so on. Values can be contrasted against each other. Attributes or dimensions of behavior common to all mothers can be identified and compared, including such things as disciplinary techniques, degree of tolerance for negative behavior that is expected to change as the child grows older, the severity with which training is applied, and the mother's temperamental qualities.

The interview form, as modified, consisted of 72 major questions, many of which were broken up into several related parts, making a total of 189 separate items. The responses were transformed into 82 separate variables. These were rated against a scale of behavior patterns, usually graded in five categories, so that behavior could be measured quantitatively as well as qualitatively. For example, a statement such as, "What I like about her is her ways; she has nice ways," would help evaluate the mother as "warm." On the other hand, a father would be scored low because of the following comment (by the mother):

He don't have too much to say to them, except when I'm not feeling too good or if they are making too much noise—then he'll holler at them. But, other than that, he don't have too much to say to them.

The following is the scale used to evaluate dependency:

1. None. Wants little or no attention from mother. Takes care of self and others. Volunteers help. Does not mind mother's absence. Asks for little unnecessary help.
2. A little dependent. Does some of the above most of the time.
3. A moderate amount of dependency. Does not cling, but dependent if hurt or if mother is absent. Does most of the things under number one once in a while or one or two of them quite often.
4. Quite dependent. Often exhibits dependent behavior, such as shy-

ness or passivity. Does not want mother to go anywhere without him.

5. Very dependent. Wants much attention. Follows mother about. Constantly asks for help with things he knows how to do. Upset when mother leaves.

RESULTS AND ANALYSIS OF THE DATA

The First Hypothesis

The first hypothesis was: *There are differences in the child-rearing practices of Puerto Rican, Negro, and white families of the lower socio-economic group.* This hypothesis was rejected.

The chi-square test was applied and 22 variables were found to be at the .01 and .05 levels of significance. The overwhelming number of variables which showed no differences in the three groups made rejection of the hypothesis mandatory. Those which showed differences, however, were basic to the socialization process and are worthy of examination.

The Puerto Rican mothers were the most permissive about weaning. They started weaning later than the other mothers, ended it later, and were very permissive in the manner in which they went about it. All of the children were weaned gently or weaned themselves. At the age of five years two children had not been weaned! This is consistent with Landy's findings in his study in rural Puerto Rico, which reported some of the children carrying their bottles to school!

The Negro mothers showed a contrast to the Puerto Ricans in the manner in which they weaned their children. They began weaning earlier, ended it sooner, and were not as lenient. For example, at the end of 29 months, only two Negro children had not been weaned, while 15 Puerto Rican children had not.

The severity of the Negro mothers' manner of weaning bore even more of a contrast. While all of the Puerto Rican children had been weaned gradually or by their own choice, this can only be said of five of the Negro children. As an example of the degree of firmness of the Negroes, here is one mother's comment: "She do without . . . I let her go without it for days, and that was the end of it. I got the milk down her somehow."

The Caucasian mothers were not as lenient as the Puerto Ricans, but were more so than the Negroes.

Breast feeding was not popular with any of the groups. Thirty-nine did not breast feed at all and the majority of the remainder had discontinued by the end of one month. They spoke of it with distaste or embarrassment.

Bowel training practices varied in the same manner as weaning. The Puerto Rican mothers were later in starting it, in completing it, and were more permissive in the way in which they went about it. Again, the Negroes were the least permissive. All of their children were bowel trained by the end of 24 months while only 13 Puerto Rican children were. The white mothers were similar to the Puerto Ricans in this area. Although they began bowel training earlier, they did not complete it sooner. As could be expected, the later bowel training began, the more quickly it took place. Severity could not have been an intervening variable here, although the Puerto Ricans finished it the quickest, since the white mothers took as long as the Negroes but were no less permissive than the Puerto Rican mothers. Of the Puerto Ricans, 18 were rated as mild or moderate in their toilet practices, as were 16 white mothers. Only nine Negroes could be placed in that category while one was very severe. The following examples from Negro mothers show the variations in severity:

> *I used to make her sit on the pot, and when she got up and hadn't done anything, I'd make her get back on.*

> *I beats 'em. They're old enough to know better.*

There were no significant differences in the amount of bedwetting but there was a difference in the mothers' reactions to it. The Caucasian mothers were more permissive than those of the other two groups. The latter did not vary to any extent.

Negro mothers scored the highest in assigning regular chores to children, probably because a few had children with their families on farms in the South. Their chores consisted of difficult tasks, such as hauling wood or water. The Caucasian mothers were the least apt to give duties. The Puerto Rican mothers varied; some were lenient, but some were surprisingly strict. One of them described the following:

> *Johnnie I got picking up the house in the morning before they go to school. Henry got to do the dish washing. Earnie got to do the sweeping. And when they come home, they start mopping floors.*

Not only did they assign chores, but gave a lot of responsibility to their five-year-old girls. These were the least acculturated mothers:

> *She teaches the other girls manners. She changes their diapers. She washes them. She gets milk from the Frigidaire. She cleans the stove.*

The amount of dependency exhibited by children varied strikingly in the three ethnic groups. The Puerto Rican children were quite dependent; the white and, still more, the Negro children were very independent.

As a rule, Puerto Rican mothers were tolerant of dependency and rewarded it; Negro mothers punished it. Surprisingly enough, the white mothers were tolerant of it, yet in spite of this, the children were independent. We can only conclude from this that the process of developing independence in their children does not have the same value for white mothers as for Negroes. Some examples of variations in dependency attitudes among white mothers:

If he can dress himself, he will—but he prefers me to do it.

I stay out of it. "You fight your own battles," I say. I try to teach him not to hit little girls but it don't penetrate.

A few mothers, with many problems, were actually dependent upon their children: "They take care of me. When I'm sick they bring me food and nurse me. I don't know what I would do without them," said a Caucasian woman.

The Puerto Rican mothers were the least tolerant of aggression towards siblings, while the Negro mothers were the most permissive. The white mothers again fell in between the other two groups but tended to be more permissive in this respect than otherwise. None was permissive of aggressive behavior toward parents.

The Puerto Ricans were the least demanding of aggression and the Negroes put the most pressure on their children to be aggressive. This aggressiveness was for self-protection and was not valued for its own sake. The Puerto Rican children were comparatively quiet and passive, while the other two groups, particularly the Negro, were unquestionably rougher and more aggressive. The discrepancies between the actual behavior and the mothers' reports of the behavior could have been due to the value they put upon nonaggression, so that, consciously or unconsciously, they denied aggressiveness. The presence of a middle-class interrogator, whom they might have felt would disapprove of aggression, may have reinforced this tendency.

An interesting side note in this connection was provided by one Negro mother who had to work and leave her child with a Puerto Rican baby sitter. She considered this woman competent and kind. However, within several weeks' time, her 18 month old had changed from a lively youngster to a passive and rather dull child. She found that the Puerto Rican woman had been keeping him in a playpen the whole day. When she changed sitters, the boy became active again.

Another intelligent Negro mother said that she thought it was true that aggression was repressed at home, but that children "blew up" outside. She added, "We have to hold them down in the house. We haven't much room, and there are the neighbors to think about."

Some interesting responses were given to the question on how much demand is made of the child to be aggressive. These comments reflected the mothers' ambivalent feelings that, on the one hand, the child must learn early the value of staying out of trouble and that, on the other, he must learn to defend himself. The Puerto Rican mothers obviously hated aggression but were convinced that self-defense might be required because "we live in a bad neighborhood." For some it was a hypothetical question, since they were rearing their children "upstairs." This was literally true; the children were never allowed to go out alone and were even escorted to and from school.

The other two groups of mothers were also very restrictive of their children's mobility, feeling that it simply wasn't safe to permit them to be on the streets alone.

I don't like to teach fighting. I don't think it's very important for him to learn to fight. Once in a while my husband will box with him. (White)

I tell them they have to fight to take care of themselves. I say, "They will pick on you. You'll have to learn to take care of yourselves. I can't do it for you." They have to know when to hit and when not to, though, or the police will come with a warrant. I stay out of it . . . The neighbors say I'm evil, but I won't take up for them . . . I don't want no cowards in my family. (Negro)

I believe that he should be able—I wouldn't say to fight back—but I mean to stand his own ground and show he is willing and that he isn't afraid, because they take advantage of a child they know is afraid. But as for street brawling—no, I don't go for that. But he should be able to defend himself. Yes, definitely; you need to around here. (Puerto Rican)

There were differences in the comments about the extent to which the mothers threatened punishment without following through on it. Evidently the Puerto Ricans and Negroes were less prone to resort to threats than were the white mothers. The white mothers, however, used praise slightly more than the Puerto Ricans, but both groups used it more than the Negroes. White mothers seemed to feel that praise was a valuable way of encouraging their children in the socialization process. It also seems to be a way they express their affection. The Negro mothers, on the other hand, presented the point of view that their children were expected to behave in a certain way and that praise was not required. The Puerto Rican mothers, on the whole, tended to use praise moderately. It is of some interest that the four Puerto Rican women who scored high on the use of praise were long-time residents of New York and well acculturated. Not surprisingly, acculturation goes in the direction of the white rather than the Negro subculture.

Identifying the disciplinary parent was difficult because of some of the subtleties involved in the familial relationships. In the Puerto Rican group, it was the mother more often than the father who assumed the disciplinary function. However, she might discipline in the father's name, thereby implying that he was the final authority. The three Puerto Rican mothers who did not have a man in the home were the only ones who carried out discipline alone. On the other hand, the only Puerto Rican father who attempted to be the sole disciplinarian was a martinet (apparently emotionally disturbed) who beat both his wife and children. Several mothers sought to change their husband's attitude toward discipline. One used a subtle approach to sway a laissez-faire attitude: "Would you please tell him to mind?" Another used a quite mature approach to handle a very disciplinarian attitude: "He used to be too strict, but I had a conference with him, and now we talk it over first."

The Negro fathers scored higher than the Puerto Rican in disciplining the children. Five of the fathers were stronger disciplinarians than their wives, even though the responsibility was shared. An analysis of these five fathers reveals that three intimidated their children. According to one mother:

> *He is very strict on 'em, you know. He want—if he's home, then they—nobody messes up anything . . . They have to have some kind of freedom. You can't not forget about it. That's what I keep telling him . . . You can't raise nobody like he was raise' 'cause it ain't goin' to work. He got it from everybody. I guess he want to pay somebody back.*

One father assumed a stronger role than his wife for religious reasons. The family were Black Jews, and the roles of husband and wife were based upon Biblical tenets. Another family were Protestant Fundamentalists; both parents were disciplinarians, but the father was the stronger. Eleven Negro parents disciplined jointly, although in two of these families, the mother assumed a slightly stronger role. It is this group of 11 that seemed the most average and stable of the Negro families. The traditional matriarchal family pattern did not apply to this group, which was composed of nuclear families, pivoting around both father and mother. In six other families there was no father, so that the mother naturally assumed the disciplinary function—and sometimes with great effectiveness: "If I speak, they moves!" It is dangerous to speculate about small samples, but this group of 20 families raised in my mind the question: Is the Negro male ineffectual only when absent?

The frequency distribution of the white families forms an almost perfect curve, the greatest number falling into the category in which both parents shared discipline. There was only one fatherless family, so there was no skewing of one end of the curve. At the other end, however, were three fathers who were completely authoritarian. (The ethnic background of these men may have had something to do with their behavior. One was a native of Yugoslavia, one an American Indian who apparently was very alienated from society, and the third was a Southern white married to an Irish-American woman who reported: "He is so strict, I have to be lenient. He gives them discipline, and I give them love.")

In one family, the father's perennial failure to earn a living and even his absence while serving a prison term did not impair his authority. Orders to his family were delivered by mail! Only two white fathers refused to accept any disciplinarian role at all; both of these were ineffectual men with relatively strong wives, one of whom said plaintively, "He can't read or write hardly at all, so there are lots of things I have to do myself."

Puerto Rican and white women apparently put a higher value on their role as mothers than did Negro women. This is difficult to interpret, since the latter did not actually work outside the home any more than the other mothers. Only two really subordinated their role as mother to their jobs, and in both cases this seemed due more to rejection of the maternal role than to the attractiveness of a career: "Larry was a greedy baby. I didn't want any children. I was glad to get rid of him [when the child started to school]." It was more characteristic of the Negro mothers to prefer to be out of the home without wishing to relinquish responsibility. In many cases this was only wishful thinking.

> *I would rather go to work if I could afford a baby-sitter. I'd rather get out because I think it's very hectic, you know, staying in with that many children all day and half the night before they goes to bed . . . Sometimes you enjoy it and sometimes you get a little*

bored, a little tired. I find when I was working that the time I was
with them wasn't hard—because you're away for a certain time . . .
I think they learn to appreciate you a little more too if you work.

There was more sex-typing in my group than in either group of
Sears. Differences in sex roles were very important. The pride in relating how a boy behaved "like a little man" was common.

It is easy to understand why Puerto Rican women are so accepting
of the maternal role; traditionally, the Puerto Rican culture has placed
high value on this role. The difference between Negro and white
mothers in this respect might also be traced to tradition, since the
Negro woman has always—at least in the United States—been expected
to shoulder two jobs. During the period of slavery, it is probable
that a more homogeneous Negro society evolved than was possible
in the "melting pot" of the Caucasians at the lower socioeconomic
level. Among the whites, many traditions are represented, and various
traditions are blended even within the same family.

The Puerto Rican mothers had very little child-rearing anxiety.
Negroes had very little anxiety, but more than the former. The responses of the white mothers provided a striking contrast. While 17
Puerto Ricans and 11 Negroes showed no anxiety at all, only six white
mothers exhibited none. The Puerto Rican mothers, with their long
tradition of accepting child rearing as their expected function, probably felt only that degree of anxiety that was produced by acculturation
into a new society. This was not apt to be great as far as a child under
five was concerned. The Caucasian women, on the other hand, being
perhaps more familiar with white middle-class patterns, might have
been more self-conscious in talking to a middle-class interrogator and,
therefore, may have projected more anxiety.

Neither the Puerto Ricans nor the Negroes allowed their children
to dominate the family, the Puerto Rican mothers being the least permissive. Although the white group was most likely to permit child
dominance, these families were clearly not child centered.

Some of the responses were interesting, not because they showed
differences between the three groups but because the curves were
skewed so markedly, showing extremes in their attitudes. For example,
there were no feeding problems. All three groups were extremely nonpermissive when it came to nudity or sex play. All demanded immediate obedience, and the thought that a child would show aggression
toward his parents filled them with horror. All used threats and scolding to a marked extent. Expectations for achievement were similar.
Physical punishment was swift and harsh but the withdrawal of love
was never used. Physical immobility was extreme.

Sometimes, while attitudes were similar, cultural interpretations were different. For example, the requirement that Puerto Rican children be clothed at all times was satisfied, in the case of boys, by a shirt.

The 22 variables which showed significance when chi-square was applied were correlated by Pearson's r. The resulting matrix showed 15 relationships at the .01 level of significance and 24 at the .05 level of significance. The former were found to form clusters to indicate patterns of behavior. The largest of these grouped around the variable "mother's response to dependency." The kinds of behavior in this cluster were the earlier socialization processes such as weaning and toilet training; but they also included the amount of dependency, the use of praise, the extent of giving regular jobs, and the mother's attitude toward her role. From these correlations, one can see the intimate relationship between the timing of weaning and toilet training. It is not surprising to find the same attitude toward the one also operative in the other. There is a negative correlation between late starting and ending of bowel training and permissiveness of dependency. The later bowel training starts and ends, the more permissive the mother is about dependency.

The amount of dependency and the mother's reaction to it seems a logical relationship, but others are less obvious. It is interesting that "giving regular jobs" is linked to greater severity in weaning. Evidently both are the outgrowth of a disciplinary attitude, which in turn may make for a higher degree of dependency. The finding that more frequent use of praise goes hand in hand with rewards for dependency makes a nice argument for the interpretation that in both instances heteronomy instead of autonomy was intended. Finally, the significant correlation between response to dependency and the mother's attitude toward her maternal role suggests that the less comfortable the mother felt in her position, the more she encouraged independence.

In a second cluster, I discovered a relationship between the reaction of the mother to bedwetting and the severity of bowel training. This could hardly be otherwise, since the less permissive mother would be more likely to react strongly to bedwetting.

In the third cluster, the father's strictness is related to the variable concerned with which parent disciplines. The conclusion inferred from this would be that the father was, on the whole, stricter and tended to take over the task of disciplining. This impression was confirmed by direct observations.

Thus, we find that computation uncovers subtle relationships between important areas of child rearing. At no point were the findings incompatible with results by other statistical methods or conclusions based on observations.

Correlating was limited to those variables which showed significance when chi-square was applied, for the simple reason that it was decided to limit the size of the study. There is no reason to believe that many other interesting relationships would not be found if all of the 82 variables were correlated.

The Second Hypothesis

The second hypothesis was: *There are differences between the child-rearing practices of the families in the present study and those reported by Sears, Maccoby, and Levin.* This hypothesis was accepted.

While comparisons among the three ethnic groups in the present study can be made easily and with assurance, it is more difficult to compare our population with the Sears group. In the lapse of time since the Sears study was done, changes in child rearing have undoubtedly taken place. The present study was done by only one person, while the Sears study was carried out by a team. Furthermore, the sizes of the two populations (60 in contrast to 379) make a statistical comparison tenuous. It seems evident, however, that class differences, as well as disparities in time, location, and methodology are reflected in the data. Some of these differences are striking enough to give assurance that class differences surmount the disparities.

An important intervening variable in the current study is the fact that the presence of the father was not a constant factor. For example, 11 fathers had been absent for a year or more (although there might be a different man present) and four children had never known their fathers. (These statistics are not entirely reliable, since some of the women apparently interpreted the term "father" to mean the man who had been with the child for the longest period of time or who had taken responsibility for the child to the greatest extent.) The Sears group did not include any broken families.

My subjects began changing the mode of feeding later than the mothers in the Sears study. For example, at 15 months, six per cent of the mothers in the Sears group had not begun weaning, while in the current study 37 per cent of the mothers had not. I also found the duration of bottle-feeding much longer in my group, accompanied by a great deal more permissiveness. The permissiveness of the Puerto Ricans and the nonpermissiveness of the Negroes did not affect time of beginning, ending, or duration. However, the Negroes were more severe than the Sears group, if the two populations were contrasted separately. The Sears study showed no differences between their working-class and middle-class mothers so that, in this area, class continuity among the three groups was not evident.

Bowel training was begun later in my group, but both groups finished at approximately the same age. The duration was two and a half months less in my group, again supporting the principle that the later the training, the more quickly it comes about. My group was more severe than the Sears group. When the Sears group was broken down into working class and middle class, my population was most similar to the former, showing evidence of class continuity.

Class continuity was also evident in the amount of sex anxiety exhibited. My group was the most anxious, although the Sears working-class mothers were more so than the middle-class mothers. In my study, 71 per cent showed moderate to severe anxiety.

Behavior at meals did not differ greatly as far as attitudes were concerned, but did differ as far as the manner of eating was concerned. Sears found the working-class mothers stricter than those of the middle class in regard to behavior at meals. In my study, attitudes toward table manners and restriction of movement at meals were so divergent that comparison with the Sears study was not feasible. This is probably due to cultural factors. For example, Puerto Rican children eat together but usually perch at any convenient spot rather than at the table. Only the father and male adults in the family sit at the table, and the mother eats standing up after everyone has been served. This custom is changing, but it is still common. One woman told me, with some understandable pride, that the last time she visited the family in Puerto Rico, her father-in-law invited her to sit at the table with him. Negro women, too, if they come from the rural South, have a custom of not taking regular meals with the family present.[1] However, my families all reported having meals together.

It must be remembered that acceptable table manners are intracultural but that basic good manners are universal. One Negro father said pointedly, "I always make them pick up their biscuits with their forks and not handle it until it is on their plates. I makes any kids eating with us do the same."

My sample was more permissive than the Sears group about bedtime. Several women told me they thought children should go to bed early when they were attending school. It seemed that a mother would often let her children stay up so that she wouldn't be so lonely.

There was very little difference between the two populations in

---

[1] Several academic informants told me that every adult in the family prepares his meal and eats alone, although they might share with the children. It was suggested that this was a carryover from farming habits when the men worked late in the fields. An anthropologist thought it was more a symptom of poverty, stemming from the scarcity of food. He said that serving meals at the table to the whole family was a sign of upward mobility.

regard to neatness, orderliness, and noise control, but there was a wide disparity in restrictions on physical mobility. I found that 60 per cent of my families did not even let their children go to school alone, while only two per cent of the Sears children were so restricted. In the area of noise control, cultural patterns must again be considered. My Puerto Rican respondents asserted quite firmly that they didn't permit undue noise in the home, but to my ears the normal decibel level in their flats was painful.

Half of the mothers in my study wanted immediate obedience, while only a fourth of the Sears mothers expected this. The fathers in the Sears working-class group expected more immediate obedience than the middle-class fathers. The fathers in my group compared with the former. There were few behavior problems reported by my group, although some of the mothers acknowledged having trouble with older children. (One mother had a boy in prison.) Hylan Lewis (1961, p. 4) found similar difficulties in his study of child rearing among low-income families and speculated that Negro parents lose control of children as early as age six. He advances as one suggestion the possibility that the high demands made by parents are incompatible with the norms of peer groups in an urban society.

Although there was little effort on the part of the mothers in my group to teach the child before entering school, most expected him to do well. In contrast, Sears found that fewer middle-class than working-class parents had similar expectations. Only 45 per cent of my group had hopes that their children would be able to go to college, but apparently none fully expected their hopes to be realized. In the Sears middle-class group, 70 per cent expected college attendance of their children, but only 24 per cent of the working-class parents looked forward to it. Class continuity is evident here in an unexpected way, since a common stereotype is that lower-class parents do not value education.

Sears *et al.* found marked class differences in attitudes towards aggression. Neither of their groups condoned aggression towards parents but the middle-class group were much more tolerant of it. My group was even less permissive than their working class. They found class differences in permissiveness towards neighbor children, the middle class being slightly more permissive, but they found no differences in permission for aggression towards siblings or for aggression as a characteristic. My distribution was too widely spread to compare the attitudes of my mothers with the Sears population, probably because of the extreme differences between the Puerto Ricans and the other two groups in this area.

My group used deprivation of privileges more than Sears' middle class, but to the same extent as his working class.

There were no marked differences in the responses of the two populations on the use of physical punishment. This, however, was a very threatening area to discuss and differences were probably more qualitative than quantitative. In observing Negro and white mothers with their children, there never seemed to be any hesitancy in spanking. Some of those who acknowledged using physical punishment qualified their statements, as for example: "I never hits 'em on the head." "I don't use the buckle end of the belt." One mother lost custody of one child, a six-year-old girl, because of violent beating, and another court hearing was pending on a similar charge. With the Puerto Ricans, physical punishment may have had less occasion to arise, as their children were apparently well enough controlled. Yet I was told by informants that this was not the case, and some forms of punishment could be severe. Landy (1959) reported this, and Oscar Lewis (whose study on San Juan and New York Puerto Ricans, *La Vida,* was recently published) confirmed it in a personal communication.

The extent to which withdrawal of love was used as a technique for control was negligible in my group. As Sears put it, this is "the subtlest of all varieties of punishment." It is difficult to measure. From the child's point of view, love is withdrawn whenever he is being subjected to any kind of punishment. The Sears mothers used it moderately, but my group did so only negligibly.

According to the Sears study, reasoning was seldom used as a technique of control. My mothers did not use it at all. This is difficult to interpret, because of cultural differences in the meaning of reasoning. I finally added a new variable, "use of threats and scolding," because of the amount of information volunteered along this line. These forms of control were used to a considerable degree.

Sears found the middle-class mothers happier than the working-class mothers when they found out they were pregnant. My groups trailed the working class only slightly. This is perhaps surprising when one considers how often another child means more hardship. Reissman (1962, p. 37) suggests that lower-class mothers place a high value on children because of the emotional security the mothers receive when the children are young and the material security they get when the children are older. Class continuity is evident here.

Warmth is not an easy characteristic to measure unless it is conspicuous by its presence or absence. It is a pervasive thing. Sears *et al.* considered it a trait or dimension that encompassed many variables. They reported their middle-class mothers as being warmer than their working-class mothers. My mothers scored lower than either. Cultural differences may affect this, however. Only a few of my mothers were actually rejecting of their children. Respect and concern were not lacking, if warmth and demonstration of affection were. Many of the mothers felt that these things "spoiled" a baby or a child and that it was a mother's responsibility not to do so. Crying, for example, was beneficial for a baby, since it exercised its lungs. (It has not been too long since middle-class mothers thought the same. This may be an example of middle-class practices filtering down to the lower classes over a period of time and persisting long after middle-class practices have changed, as Bronfenbrenner suggests [1952].)

When the amount of dependency exhibited by the children was measured, there were no class differences in the Sears study. Many more of mine were dependent. However, when my Puerto Rican group was eliminated, there was very little difference. My group was less permissive of dependent behavior than Sears' middle-class group, but more permissive than the latter's working-class group. Again, if the Puerto Ricans were eliminated, my group was less permissive than Sears' working class.

The variables focused upon the father were, for the most part, unusual in that frequencies of the various behaviors were distributed in a bipolar fashion. This does not mean they necessarily exhibited extremes in behavior, but were reported so by the mothers. For example, the fathers rated high on warmth towards their children, but a third rated high on hostility or indifference towards them. A high esteem held by the mothers was reported for the most part, but a third held their mates in very low esteem. A strict division of labor by husband and wife was reported by some, but almost an equal number reported no division of labor. When the variables associated with the father were compared to the two groups of Sears, the odd distribution resulted in more similarity to the middle class at one end of the curve and similarity to the working class on the other. Many more of the fathers in my group were the family authority than in the Sears study. This shows no class continuity, since the latter's working-class fathers assumed familial authority even less often than the middle class. The figures in my study may be accounted for by the fact that several of my mothers were intimidated by their husbands.

He is a good worker but not a good husband. Nobody likes him. The children are glad when he leaves. He mistreated my son, so I didn't feel I had a right to have any more.

There was more disagreement in my study than in the Sears study on child-rearing policies. There was class continuity here, since the latter's working class disagreed more than the middle-class parents. The extreme disagreement in my group was probably due to the number of fathers who had left home, but still attempted to determine policies.

SUMMARY AND CONCLUSIONS

When the child-rearing practices of Puerto Rican, Negro, and Caucasian mothers were compared, more similarities than differences were found. This supports the assumption that there is such a thing as a culture or subculture of poverty. More important, it supports the assumption that social class exerts a stronger influence upon child-rearing practices as a whole than ethnogeny. On the other hand, though subtle differences in culture make the relative influences of each difficult to evaluate, the evidence for ethnogeny is overwhelming.

In spite of the fact that there are more similarities than differences in the child-rearing practices of the three ethnic groups, the practices that are different are important ones. Forty per cent of these were variables related to basic training procedures, such as weaning and toilet training. These variables were related to each other and to more than 60 per cent of the other chi-square significant variables. They seem to be much more sensitive to ethnic differences and assume more importance than the same variables in the Sears study, probably because the ethnic groups in my study are much less assimilated into the mainstream of American life than the ethnic groups included in the Sears study.

Other variables which proved to be affected more by ethnogeny than class are also important in the socialization and enculturation process, such as aggression, dependency, and anxiety about sex. The mothers' responses to dependency were the most significant of the variables which were positive when chi-square was applied. This suggests that this variable is a key to cultural differences, at least as far as these three ethnic groups are concerned.

Permissiveness in weaning and toilet training does not mean that permissiveness in other practices exists. For example, Puerto Rican mothers are extremely permissive in these areas but nonpermissive in almost all other practices. Negroes are the most nonpermissive of the three groups and the Puerto Ricans the least. However, all three are nonpermissive when compared to the working-class and middle-class mothers of the Sears study. There is no tolerance of nudity or sex behavior. Immediate obedience is expected, and aggression to parents is not tolerated. Physical punishment is swift and severe. Means of control are object-oriented. Withdrawal of love is never used. Physical immobility is striking. Aggression for self-protection and independence are valued, except among Puerto Ricans. Lower-class mothers are not child dominated and do not have anxiety about child rearing, at least not until their children are past the age of five. They are not likely to seek help from caretaking individuals or agencies about child rearing.

Many stereotypes of the lower-class family did not hold up. For example, one is that their life circumstances are too chaotic for norms in child rearing to exist. On the contrary, this population has unique, consistent, and identifiable beliefs about socializing children. Some of these, at least, are carried out and are observable. Lower-class women, in spite of not showing a great deal of warmth and of being nonpermissive, are very concerned with the well-being of their children. They do not have high aspirations for them, but they have high expectations of their educational performance. In spite of a great deal of family disintegration, most of the mothers attempt to provide as stable a home life as they can. There were only two cases of abuse or neglect. Another common stereotype that was not supported is the belief that lower-class men, particularly Negroes, are ineffectual in family life. On the contrary, when present, they assume an active role, take responsibility and assume authority.

When my data were compared to those of the Sears study, there was a great deal of evidence of class continuity from lower class to working class or from lower class to middle class. Social stratification was supported in almost all of the areas where the Sears study related it to child rearing. In addition, my study had many more variables where the influence of social stratification could be identified.

REFERENCES

Bronfenbrenner, Urie. 1952. "Socialization and Social Class through Time and Space," in *Readings in Social Psychology,* eds. Eleanor Maccoby, Theodore Newcomb, and Eugene Hartley. New York: Holt, Rinehart and Winston, Inc.

Landy, David. 1959. *Tropical Childhood*. Chapel Hill: University of North Carolina Press.

Lewis, Hylan. 1961. "Child Rearing among Low-Income Families." Address to the Washington Center for Metropolitan Studies. June 8.

Minturn, Leigh, and Lambert, William. 1964. *Mothers of Six Cultures.* New York: John Wiley and Sons, Inc.

Riessman, Frank. 1962. *The Culturally Deprived Child.* New York: Harper and Row.

Sears, Robert, Maccoby, Eleanor, and Levin, Harry. 1957. *Patterns of Child Rearing.* New York: Row, Peterson and Co.

A Report on the "600" Schools: Dilemmas, Problems, and Solutions*

Bernard Mackler

Consistent with the educational aim of a democratic society, that all children be given equal educational opportunities, new and expanding programs recently have emerged for exceptional children: the dull, retarded, blind, deaf, brain damaged, emotionally or mentally disturbed, and the gifted. These programs have sprung up quickly in a sincere effort to provide maximal educational opportunity for exceptional youngsters. A secondary consideration has been the need to alleviate the burden that the exceptional child places on the teacher and children in a regular classroom.

In smaller communities such programs consist of special classes or individual tutoring. In suburban and urban areas such classes have mushroomed into special schools. Indeed, exceptional children in urban areas demand ever greater specialization. Consequently special schools for specific handicaps—for the blind, the deaf, the physically handicapped, the disturbed—have sprung up. Chicago, Detroit, Kansas City, New York and, in fact, all major metropolitan areas now have special day classes, day schools, and residential schools for disturbed youngsters (Havighurst, 1964; Morse, Cutler, and Fink, 1964; Birch, 1956). (Detroit has had special classes for disturbed youngsters as early as 1883.)

The question is, to what extent are these special schools aiding their students? This paper is an analysis of the special schools for the emotionally disturbed in New York City, called the "600" schools.

SEGREGATION IN THE "600" SCHOOLS

Of all types of exceptional children, the emotionally disturbed is the hardest for the school to define, evaluate, treat, and educate. Often these children are categorized as such not because of their problems *per se*, but because of the school's need to isolate those who are disturbing classmates, teachers, administrators, and parents. In contrast,

* Portions of the empirical data assembled for this chapter were compiled by Elinor Bernstein and Nelia Reynolds. I gratefully acknowledge their assistance.

the matter of physical disability can be documented objectively. If a
child cannot see or hear, or has been crippled, diagnosis is both comparatively simple and unarguable. One would expect that treatment for
such a special group would be relatively uniform regardless of its
minority status, and one would expect that the racial composition of
these students would form a random distribution curve. Because the
disturbed are the most difficult group to diagnose, it is reasonable to
suppose that the greatest segregation and variation in treatment would
occur in special schools designed to aid it. White students are likely
to be defined as troubled, and placed in treatment schools, while
minority groups are likely to be defined as troublesome and placed in
custodial situations.

TABLE 1

ETHNIC POPULATIONS OF THE SCHOOL FOR THE DEAF AND SCHOOLS
FOR THE EMOTIONALLY DISTURBED IN MANHATTAN, 1963-64[a]

School	Number of Children	Percentage Ethnic Distribution		
		Puerto Rican	Negro	Other
Deaf				
P.S. 158 School for the Deaf (Day)	126	14.3	21.4	64.3
Disturbed				
P.S. 612 The John Barry School (Day)	200	38.0	58.0	4.0
P.S. 614 The Cyrus W. Field School (Day)	173	43.4	47.4	9.2
P.S. 615 Wiltwyck School for Boys (Residential)	101	14.9	72.3	12.9
P.S. 617 Villa Loretto (Residential)[b]	141	27.7	30.5	41.8
P.S. 618 Bellevue Psychiatric Hospital (Residential)	118	44.1	31.4	24.6
P.S. 619 St. Germaine's Home (Residential)[b]	207	25.1	7.7	67.1
P.S. 620 Pleasantville Cottage School (Residential)	160	0	0	100.0
P.S. 621 The Livingston School (Day)[b]	118	11.0	80.5	8.5
P.S. 622 The Manhattan School for Boys (Day)	182	22.0	58.8	19.2
P.S. 623 The Hillcrest School (Residential)	181	0.6	98.3	1.1
P.S. 624 Francis Parkman School (Day)	86	36.0	57.0	7.0

[a]*P.S. 615, 617, 619, 620, 623 are located in the suburbs but administratively are considered to be in Manhattan.*
[b]*Girls schools; except for P.S. 615 and P.S. 622, all other schools are co-ed.*

Let us look at Table 1 for a view of the ethnic differences that occur
in a school for the physically disabled (in this instance, deaf) and in a
group of special schools for the emotionally disturbed, all located in
Manhattan, in 1963–64.

The data substantiate my central point, for the school for the deaf
is integrated while *all* the schools (day and residential) for disturbed

youngsters are segregated. For emotionally disturbed youngsters, place-ment (hence treatment) seems determined not only by personal prob-lems but by minority status. Some of these schools service children from Manhattan; most service children from all five boroughs of New York City. If we trace the ethnic population of these schools back a few years, we note no differences from its composition in 1963–64. (The data for 1962–63 and 1961–62 are included in Table 2.) By the criteria of half or double of a community's ethnic population,[1] in this

TABLE 2

ETHNIC POPULATIONS OF THE SCHOOL FOR THE DEAF AND THE SCHOOLS FOR THE EMOTIONALLY DISTURBED IN MANHATTAN, 1962-63 and 1961-62

	1962-63 Percentage Ethnic Distribution				1961-62 Percentage Ethnic Distribution			
School	Number of Children	Puerto Rican	Negro	White	Number of Children	Puerto Rican	Negro	White
Deaf								
P.S. 158	95	12.6	13.7	73.7	81	12.3	11.1	76.5
Disturbed								
P.S. 612	195	32.8	58.5	8.7	201	34.3	56.7	9.0
P.S. 614	171	42.1	46.8	11.1	180	37.8	47.8	14.4
P.S. 615	91	14.3	68.1	17.6	99	11.1	63.6	25.3
P.S. 617	163	30.1	27.6	42.3	137	35.0	23.4	41.6
P.S. 618	100	27.0	39.0	34.0	159	35.2	36.5	28.3
P.S. 619	193	21.8	7.8	70.5	190	32.1	6.3	61.6
P.S. 620	144	0	0	100.0	144	0	0	100.0
P.S. 621	115	18.3	75.7	6.1	119	11.5	79.6	8.8
P.S. 622	181	21.0	63.0	16.0	166	22.3	60.8	16.9
P.S. 623	158	0.6	96.2	3.2	168	0.6	95.2	4.2
P.S. 624	(No data available)				(No data available)			

case Negro and Puerto Rican, we note that only one school in New York City (P.S. 619) approaches being integrated. Every other school for the disturbed either has an abundance of Negroes and/or Puerto

[1] A school would be segregated, in 1963, if it had less than six per cent or more than 30 per cent Negro students, and/or if it had less than five per cent or more than 17 per cent Puerto Rican students. See Mary Ellen Warshauer and Robert A. Dentler's discussion in this book, "A New Definition of School Segregation," for a detailed analysis of the criteria used here.

Ricans or else is mostly white. (In P.S. 620, the *entire* population is white.) What was true for 1963–64 was true for the years immediately preceding and is probably true today.

THE INADEQUACIES OF THE PROGRAM

I have no wish to damage the "600" program by indicting it. *The "600" school program represents a definite educational improvement over the programs and practices of the past.* (Previous practices included incarcerative truant schools, parental schools, probationary schools, youth houses, and other means of detainment, containment, or coercion.) The present "600" school program attempts to protect regular teachers and students from undue or damaging disruption, and to provide a therapeutic milieu for the disturbed child. But this program *is,* however worthwhile, ethnically segregated, inconveniently located, undersupported, organizationally unstable, and unable to meet the needs of its student body.

The "600" schools have been in existence for a decade and a half, during which they have grown from seven experimental units to 27 schools with 14 annexes, a pupil population of about 5,200, and a teaching staff of roughly 500, in addition to reading specialists, guidance counselors, medical and dental teams, clinicians, and social workers. Of the 27 schools, 14 are day schools serving about 2,000 pupils from ten to 18 years of age. The remaining schools are located in hospitals, treatment and remand centers, and residential institutions.

Only one day school serves girls. The other 13 serve boys, whose alleged common characteristics include repeated disruptive and aggressive behavior. Children who are withdrawn or disturbed in ways expressed other than through social misconduct are seldom assigned to the "600" day schools.

The most desirable screening and assignment procedure for the "600" day school students would involve a diagnostic evaluation by a clinical team. In practice, students are assigned on the basis, first, of referrals initiated by courts, social agencies, principals, and field assistant superintendents; then through a preliminary screening by guidance counselors; and finally, through a review of criteria including intellectual level, school performance, conduct record, and truancy.

The New York City Board of Education does not even determine which institutions will include "600" schools; moreover, it has not reviewed or in any other way concerned itself with the issue of the *educational* well-being of the children in these schools, most significantly those in the ethnically segregated residential institutions.

In addition to the problems posed by segregation, many "600" schools are beset by extremely severe problems of staff and pupil turnover, a shortage of trained staff, the inclusion of students unsuited to the present program, and an insufficient number of therapeutic and related treatment services.

Furthermore, many "600" students currently must travel long distances to attend day schools, even at the lower age levels. Thus, they are severed socially from their home localities. Similarly, as a result of the absence of community mental health clinics, outpatient services, and related facilities within the city, students in residential institutions are located many miles outside of New York City.

The placement of the schools leads to other problems. There are only two "600" high schools designated to serve the boys of New York City. At one of them, attended by boys who reside in all parts of four of the five boroughs, the average daily student attendance in 1964 was 68 per cent. Indeed, about 35 of these 185 students attend school only once a month.

In the elementary age "600" schools, location is complicated by the schools' lack of vacancies and by the residential mobility of the students' families or foster placements. Typically, a student waits about four months to be enrolled. Those who are arrested prior to enrollment wait in the Youth House until a court-ordered placement is arranged. Boys suspended by the regular school but not involved with the court wait at home.[2]

There is widespread agreement among staff in the "600" day schools that the schools are housed in buildings that are unsuitable castoffs of the regular school divisions; that the recommended teacher-pupil ratio of one teacher for every 12 students is seldom achieved; that staff morale is often low; and that ancillary services are gravely inadequate to needs. These are not my judgments but rather those of directly informed and experienced personnel.

In general, then, these are the problems that beset the special education program in New York in terms of its own goals, in the view of professional participants and according to the recorded data available to investigators.

A COMPARATIVE ANALYSIS OF SEGREGATION IN THE "600" SCHOOLS

The most striking examples of segregation in the "600" schools appear in those which are residential treatment settings. There are five such

[2] The period of waiting, incidentally, may include assignment and movement through several regular schools as well as the transfer of papers through two to three "600" schools to find a vacancy before placement is assured.

settings, all in suburban locations. (Four are in Westchester; one is in Ulster County.) All service New York City children.

Table 3 summarizes the data concerning the white, Negro, and Puerto Rican population of the five institutions. This table clearly indicates that of the five institutions, one is segregated white, two primarily Negro, and two Puerto Rican.

TABLE 3

ETHNIC POPULATION OF FIVE INSTITUTIONS FOR 1963

			Percentage		
School	Name of School	Number of Children	White	Negro	Puerto Rican
P.S. 615	Wiltwyck School for Boys	101	14.9	72.3	12.9
P.S. 617	Villa Loretto	141	41.8	30.5	27.7
P.S. 619	St. Germaine's Home	149	67.1	7.7	25.1
P.S. 620	Pleasantville Cottage School	160	100.0	0.0	0.0
P.S. 623	Hillcrest School	181	6.0	78.5	15.4

Table 4 traces back the composition of these schools. The data indicate that the 1963 situation represents a pattern of segregation that has been fairly consistent at least since 1958 (and probably longer).

The following survey focuses on three of these schools—the most segregated white, 620 (Pleasantville), the most segregated Negro, 623 (Hillcrest), and the school that is least segregated Negro, although segregated for Puerto Ricans, 617 (Villa Loretto). The survey was undertaken to evaluate the services at segregated schools and to verify my hypothesis that an extremely Negro-segregated school would have less adequate programs and facilities than a white-segregated school, or a moderately segregated school.

These schools function in the larger context of residential centers for emotionally disturbed children who are not able, for a variety of reasons, to remain in city homes. The Board of Education provides each school with the same kind of professional staff, which includes a principal, a secretary, and one teacher for every ten children. Assuming that the staffs are equally competent, it would follow that the three schools would be equally effective in educating and rehabilitating their students. However, this conclusion proves to be false, primarily because of differences among the schools in the types of children they service and in the amount of cooperation the children receive from their respective institutions. (The information was obtained through observa-

TABLE 4

ETHNIC POPULATION OF FIVE INSTITUTIONS
FOR 1958-1962 BY PERCENTAGE

School	Number of Children	Percentage		
		White	Negro	Puerto Rican
1962				
P.S. 615	91	17.6	68.1	14.3
P.S. 617	163	42.3	27.6	30.1
P.S. 619	193	70.5	7.8	21.8
P.S. 620	144	100.0	0.0	0.0
P.S. 623	158	3.2	96.2	0.6
1961				
P.S. 615	99	25.3	63.6	11.1
P.S. 617	137	41.6	23.4	35.0
P.S. 619	190	61.6	6.3	32.1
P.S. 620	144	100.0	0.0	0.0
P.S. 623	168	4.2	95.2	0.6
1960				
P.S. 615	99	18.2	47.8	35.3
P.S. 617	153	45.8	25.5	28.8
P.S. 619	178	65.7	6.7	27.5
P.S. 620	147	100.0	0.0	0.0
P.S. 623	157	4.5	95.5	0.0
1959				
P.S. 615	102	19.6	68.6	11.8
P.S. 617	135	45.9	28.1	25.9
P.S. 619	178	54.5	8.4	37.1
P.S. 620	155	100.0	0.0	0.0
P.S. 623		(No data available)		
1958				
P.S. 615	100	21.0	69.0	10.0
P.S. 617	127	48.0	21.3	30.7
P.S. 619	181	56.9	6.1	37.0
P.S. 620	153	100.0	0.0	0.0
P.S. 623		(No data available)		

tion, through discussions with principals, teachers, and social service staff members, and from an analysis of available records. All schools and institutions cooperated fully.)

The children at the white segregated P.S. 620 (Pleasantville Cottage School), mostly boys, range in age from eight to 15. The school's program is designed for this age range, and one of the aims of the institution is to discharge its children, if possible, before their sixteenth birthday. P.S. 617 (Villa Loretto), the least segregated Negro school, has teenagers, all girls, at ages ranging from 16 to 21. The 617 program is oriented toward helping the girls get high school diplomas; each girl is on an individual schedule depending on her previous education and vocational needs. Finally, P.S. 623 (Hillcrest Children's Center), which is segregated Negro, has mainly a male population, ranging in age from eight to 18. Children may enter the school when younger than eight if a sibling is already at Hillcrest. (Also, with new state legislation, some will be staying until they are 21.)

The children at 620 are all white and predominantly Jewish.[3] The family or other referral source has indicated a desire that the child be brought up with a Jewish education. These children come from lower-middle-income families, and all have had psychiatric or psychological treatment prior to admission. Many are considered severely neurotic. At 617, 60 per cent of the girls are Roman Catholic. All girls admitted to 617 must indicate that they do not object to its Roman Catholic orientation. Ethnically, the girls are approximately one-third white, one-third Negro, and one-third Puerto Rican. These youngsters are truant, delinquent, and disruptive, and come from financially poor families. The children at 623 are seriously disturbed, primarily acting out or withdrawn; their families are generally poor.

All three institutions receive the bulk of their referrals from the department of welfare, although 620 does receive referrals from clinics, schools, agencies, hospitals, and physicians.

Most of the children come from Brooklyn, Manhattan, the Bronx, and Queens, with a few from Staten Island, Westchester, and Long Island. Financial support is obtained through the New York City Department of Welfare, although the Greater New York Fund, the counties, and the courts also contribute to the schools' expenditures. (Sixteen children at 620 are paid for by their parents.)

The three institutions vary in the effectiveness with which they are able to deal with the children sent to them. In terms of appropriateness of treatment, 617 seems to be the most effective. The 617 girls are quite a homogeneous population within a narrow age-grade range. These girls, with their unhappy family lives and promiscuous and delinquent behavior, benefit noticeably from the loving and supportive atmosphere provided by the nuns and the competent social services

---

[3] While the 1963–64 statistics indicate a 100 per cent white population, on our visits in 1964–65, we did find one Negro boy, one of whose parents was believed to be Jewish.

staff of the institution, and from the academic and vocational high
school training provided by the school.

The 620 program is also excellent. However, since one of the major
problems of the 620 population is in the area of family difficulties,
and since the residential facility does not provide intensive care for
both families and children, it is not as effective as it could be. Because
620 has a large and experienced social service staff that emphasizes
milieu therapy, the 620 child receives and generally benefits from very
adequate treatment. In addition, although the age-grade range of the
school is large (from the fourth through the ninth), the school appears
to be very effective in academic terms as well. This success is largely
due to the presence of seven extra institution teachers helping the regular Board of Education staff and also the lack of seriously disruptive
behavior problems on the part of the students.

P.S. 623, in contrast, is not functioning very adequately. The Board
of Education provides an equal teacher-pupil ratio for all three schools.
However, the teachers at 623, in comparison with the other two
schools, are faced with the most seriously disturbed children who
present the greatest amount of acting out behavior and the lowest IQ's.
These facts alone suggest that 623 should have smaller classes than
the other schools. In addition, 623 has the largest age-grade range, and
the school receives no institutional teaching help. Lastly, of the three
institutions, the social services staff at 623 is both the smallest and the
least experienced and suffers from a high turnover. The 623 institution
is ill-suited for the job of reducing the acting out and withdrawal behavior problems of the children, especially when they occur in the
classroom.

As to the length of stay at the institutions—at 620, it is an average
of two years, four months; at 617, an average of 18 months; and at
623, an average of four years—and from institution estimates of success, the 617 program is most effective, with 620 second, and 623 well
behind the other two.

PREVIOUS REPORTS AND PROPOSALS

Unfortunately for New York City's emotionally disturbed children,
more is said about them than done for them. The "600" schools have
been studied by Hill (1956), MacIver (1957a; 1957b), the New York
State Education Department (1958), Kahn (1962), the Advisory Committee for the New York State Commissioner of Education—the "Allen

Report" (1964), the "600" Schools Supervision Association (1964), Mackler, Dentler, Bernstein, and Reynolds (1965), and most recently by Kahn (1965). These publicly available reports were completed by agencies and individuals independent of the Board of Education. Within the school system itself, there have been annual reports on the "600" schools. The most recent were *The "600" Schools, Yesterday, Today and Tomorrow* (King, 1965) and the report by the superintendent of schools, *Blueprint for Further Action Toward Quality Integrated Education* (1965).

It seems that every year sees a new report and a list of recommendations. Yet little, if any, meaningful implementation occurs. The major proposals presented by outside agencies are unheeded. Even the proposals that come from within the school system are either watered down, neglected, or forgotten. The reports fill files and perhaps soothe the conscience of some administrators, but the plight of the children remains unchanged.

Some "direct action" on the "600" schools has also been attempted. In the winter of 1964–65, there were protests, demonstrations, and a boycott against the schools, led by the Reverend Milton Galamison. The boycott was concerned with school segregation, per se, and one of its aims was to close all segregated junior high and "600" schools. Other objectives were: the upgrading of 200 Negro and Puerto Rican teachers to supervisory positions, a revision of the Board of Education construction program, a timetable for school desegregations, and improved "600" schools. The boycott, directed at first against P.S. 617 (The Nathanael Greene Day School in Brooklyn; this is a different school from Villa Loretto which is also P.S. 617), kept as much as 90 per cent of the students at home. The leader of the boycott, Milton Galamison, was criticized, by *The New York Times* among others, but the boycott continued, reaching out from Brooklyn, where it had begun, to "600" schools in both Manhattan and Queens, and to junior high schools in Manhattan. However, with the arrest of Galamison and another leader (Thelma Johnson) the demonstrations came to an end after approximately two weeks.

Nonetheless, the boycott is important, for it constitutes the first time that the problems of "600" schools were publicly exposed. Prior to the boycott, the schools had been rather tucked out of sight. For example, the Allen Committee was unsuccessful in obtaining data about their ethnic composition. The boycott pointed out the need to face the educational and ethnic problems of these schools.

Fuchs (1966), after a study of the boycott, concludes:

> *It would be missing the point entirely to blame the adult leaders of this boycott for stirring up trouble. The trouble is there and the shutdown was symptomatic of the problems. The young people's views of the schools and teachers give us some insights concerning their perceptions of what to them are intolerable conditions. Hopefully, school personnel, by studying those who feel strongly enough to walk out of school either by dropping out entirely or boycotting temporarily have much to learn about themselves and the children whom they would teach. The schools have failed with these youngsters. By their protest the young have given a "cry for help." We should listen.*

If we do listen, what can be done?

IMPROVING THE SERVICES

Many aspects of the "600" school program (or whatever might replace it) cannot be improved without an increased public awareness of the importance of special education for the disturbed or the disruptive child. It is easy enough, but irresponsible, to propose changes and improvements that would require resources not currently available to the New York City Board of Education and that will not be forthcoming until such public awareness exists. Therefore, in what follows, I have limited myself to listing improvements that could be accomplished within the existing resources of the school system. These improvements would not solve all of the problems facing special education, but they would produce some immediate progress in resolving several of the most serious failures, especially for the educators in the "600" schools.

1. Special educational programs currently located in psychiatric hospitals, remand centers, and residential institutions should continue their important work of educating nearly 2,000 children and youth. But the Board of Education should request these institutions to change their admission practices so that any child from New York City may be served, *regardless of ethnicity.*[4]

Inequities in the effectiveness of the programs of the three residential treatment centers analyzed above are due to differences in the types of children the centers service and the differing physical plants of the institutions, rather than to formal inequities in the educational provisions of the Board of Education. However, the data suggest several

[4] This proposal is directed toward private and sectarian institutions, and is inapplicable to prisons and most other public institutions.

possible measures by which the Board of Education could improve the implementation of its policies.

As noted earlier, in the analyses of the three residential centers, the Board of Education supplies each center with essentially the same goods and services. But excellent and equivalent school facilities are not enough. What the board ignores is the presence of segregation. Thus, though it satisfies the letter of the law, it yet does not fulfill the spirit. The board should ask all institutions to admit any child in the New York City area regardless of ethnicity. If the institutions refuse to alter their policies, the school system should then reconsider its position. It ought not to continue to service institutions that are segregated.

2. Most "600" day schools, both on the elementary and the secondary levels, should be *abandoned,* and their professional staffs deployed to elementary, middle, and senior high schools.

The present "600" day schools do not treat any of their youngsters. No special staff, psychological or psychiatric, is available for anything other than limited consultative duties. The tremendous turnover of teachers and students makes for an unstable situation. As stated earlier, a youngster assigned to a "600" school is assigned by a principal, field assistant superintendent, court, or social agency, and thus he is sent to a "600" school essentially to rid the regular school of a problem. At best, there is a sympathetic interest in his plight but no concerted effort to aid him. No diagnostic evaluation *with treatment considerations* is made and, as a result, the youngster bounces from one evaluation to another at different "600" schools.

The majority of the youngsters is neither withdrawn nor autistic. Their behavior problems range from disrupting a classroom to delinquency. Indeed, a number of youngsters are not behavior problems at all but suffer from severe academic retardation. The "600" schools staff, which provides no curriculum specifically designed for disturbed children, serves goals that are no different from those of a regular school staff as it tries to educate slow learners who are not behaviorally aggressive. The "600" day schools' major contribution in the youngster's behalf is smaller classes, and this can be achieved in the regular school, where additional personnel could also facilitate and support services and programs for the disturbed. Such special education teachers and pupil personnel staff could: (a) aid in the early identification and screening program within the school; (b) assist in assigning students to centers outside the district; (c) facilitate the return and education of children from residential treatment.

Within the regular schools, classes for disturbed and otherwise seriously disruptive children would serve about 2,000 students at the

eighth-grade level and below. Equitable assignment could insure that
the school would not have more than two classes. (Similar special
classes—exclusive of well-established programs for the deaf and the
blind—should be operated on the same decentralized basis for other
categories of students, such as the mentally retarded.)

3. At present, the board operates "600" schools in over ten treatment centers. A number of these centers operate as basic, clinical, and
educational research teams, in which teachers take direct part in
clinical conferences and in treatment itself. Administratively, most treatment centers select children pertinent to their research. Treatment centers currently serve as schools for no more than about 300 children.

I suggest that *one treatment center* in each borough be expanded
and developed, with the assistance of the appropriate bureaus of the
Board of Education and other municipal agencies, into a primary resource center for special educators in that area. Such centers could be
part of new building programs. Each of the five strengthened treatment
centers should be linked intimately with a nearby teacher training
college or university, a psychiatric hospital, and related treatment, training, and research resources.

Each treatment center should mediate (by liaison staff, if necessary)
between the special education program within its borough and the
Board of Education. It should offer diagnostic service, staff training
services, outpatient care that includes educational services, and in other
ways fill the gap that now obtains between isolated "600" day schools,
treatment centers, and residential institutions. My research, as well as
the report by Bloch and Behrens (1959), indicates the duplication of
diagnostic services that now exist for children from multiproblem
families. I also found much shuttling about of children within the
present system. Without a citywide or boroughwide policy there can
be no concerted effort by one clinic to remedy the situation.

Political change will have to foreshadow this new community approach if it is to be advanced, accepted, and implemented. I concur,
and unhappily so, with Bloch and Behrens' concluding statement: "The
most striking impression we have gained from this study is the hopeless
inadequacy of piecemeal attempts to treat the seriously deviant child"
(1959, p. 82). As more funds become available to community mental
health clinics and to centers for the treatment and education of retarded and otherwise handicapped children, the major treatment center
in each borough would become a model for the expansion of activities.

If these three recommendations were implemented, I believe that
the many problems that affect "600" schools—student transportation,
school location, assignment, reassignment, the constant movement of

special students, and the problems of staffing and housing "600"-type programs—would be resolved promptly. In addition, lines of authority would be clarified, while instructional programs would be kept flexible and close to home. Further, special school teachers and other staff could be supported by training and other services at the major treatment centers. Finally, implementation of these recommendations would stimulate the desegregation of schools within private and sectarian institutions.

REFERENCES

Birch, J. W. 1956. "Special Classes and Schools for Maladjusted Children," *Journal of Exceptional Children*, 22, pp. 332–337.

Bloch, D. A., and Behrens, Marjorie L. 1959. *A Study of Children Referred for Residential Treatment in New York State.* A report to the New York State Interdepartmental Health Resources Board. Albany: Department of Mental Hygiene, Community Mental Service.

Donovan, B. E. 1965. *Implementation of Board Policy on Excellence for the City's Schools.* New York: Board of Education, City of New York.

Emory, Helen T. 1965. "Manhattan to Get New '600' School," *New York World Telegram and Sun.* April 27.

Fuchs, Estelle. 1966. *Pickets at the Gates.* New York: Free Press.

Havighurst, R. J. 1964. *The Public Schools of Chicago.* Chicago: Board of Education.

Hill, J. W. 1956. *Report of the Committee to Survey the "600" Schools.* New York: Board of Education, City of New York.

Kahn, A. J. 1962. *New York City Schools and Children Who Need Help.* New York: Citizens' Committee for Children of New York.

———. 1965. *The "600" Schools: Sound Planning Still Needed.* New York: Citizens' Committee for Children of New York.

King, J. B. 1965. *"600" Schools Yesterday, Today and Tomorrow.* New York: Committee on the "600" Schools, Board of Education, City of New York.

Kirk, S. A. 1962. *Educating Exceptional Children.* Boston: Houghton Mifflin.

MacIver, R. M. 1957a. *The "600" Day Schools.* Interim Report No. III. New York: Juvenile Delinquency Evaluation Project, City of New York, The City College.

———. 1957b. *Students and Their Progress in "600" Day Schools.* Interim Report No. VI. New York: Juvenile Delinquency Evaluation Project, City of New York, The City College.

Mackler, B., Dentler, R. A., Bernstein, Elinor, and Reynolds, Nelia. 1965. *The "600" Schools and the Educational Complex.* New York: Institute of Urban Studies, Columbia University, Teachers College.

Morse, W. C., Cutler, R. I., and Fink, A. H. 1964. *Public School Classes for the Emotionally Handicapped: A Research Analysis.* Washington, D.C.: The Council for Exceptional Children.

New York State Education Commissioner's Advisory Committee on Human Relations and Community Tensions. 1964. *Desegregating the Public Schools of New York City.* (The Allen Report). Albany: The State Education Department, The University of the State of New York.

New York State Education Department. 1958. *A Survey of the "600" Day Schools in New York City.* Albany: The University of the State of New York.

The New York Times. 1965. January and February.

Saenger, G. 1960. *Factors Influencing the Institutionalization of Mentally Retarded Individuals in New York City.* A report to the New York State Interdepartmental Health Resources Board. Albany: Interdepartmental Health Resources Board.

Sheldon, Eleanor B., and Glazier, R. A. 1965. *Pupils and Schools in New York City: A Fact Book.* New York: Russell Sage Foundation.

"600" Schools Supervision Association New York City Schools. 1964. *The Improvement of the "600" Day Schools.* New York.

Superintendent of Schools, New York City Public Schools. 1965. *Blueprint for Further Action Toward Quality Integrated Education.* New York: Board of Education, City of New York.

The Contributors

IMOGENE CAHILL is an associate professor at the University of California School of Nursing (Los Angeles).

THELMA P. CATALANO, a former staff member of the Center for Urban Education, is an experienced teacher in the New York City public schools.

ROBERT A. DENTLER is director of the Center for Urban Education and professor of sociology and education at Teachers College, Columbia University.

CONSTANCE ELKINS has been a grade-school teacher and has done graduate study in the field of elementary school guidance.

MORSLEY G. GIDDINGS, a senior staff associate of the Center for Urban Education, has been a teacher in the public school system and for eight years taught science in a special service school in New York.

SOL GORDON, a professor of educational psychology at Yeshiva University, is director of Project Beacon, a graduate program of research and teacher training in the area of the disadvantaged child, at Yeshiva.

HAROLD GREENBERG is assistant professor of sociology at Long Island University in Brooklyn and the editor of Jewish Social Work Forum.

DOROTHY JESSUP is an advanced doctoral student in the sociology of education, in a joint program at Teachers College and Columbia University.

DAVID W. JOHNSON is an assistant professor of psychology at the University of Minnesota.

ROBERT LaFRANKIE is a high school principal in Rockland County, New York.

KURT LANG and GLADYS ENGEL LANG are the joint authors of Collective Behavior (*Crowell*). *Kurt Lang is professor of sociology at the State University of New York at Stony Brook, and* Gladys Engel Lang *is assistant director for social research and development at the Center for Urban Education.*

BERNARD MACKLER is assistant director of community research and development at the Center for Urban Education and associate professor of education at Teachers College, Columbia University.

ELIZABETH O'GRADY teaches emotionally disturbed children at the Essex Child Development Center—Garden School in Belleville, New Jersey.

JOE L. REMPSON, who currently is completing a study on school-parent relations in depressed areas of a large Northern city, is a staff associate at the Center for Urban Education.

NELIA REYNOLDS is an advanced doctoral student in clinical psychology at Teachers College, Columbia University.

DOROTHY SCHAEFER is director of special education in the Yonkers, New York, public school system.

DOROTHY SINGER is a psychologist and works with disturbed, retarded and brain damaged children at the Board of Cooperative Educational Services of lower Westchester, New York.

MARY ELLEN WARSHAUER, a staff associate at the Center for Urban Education, is the co-author (with Robert Dentler) of Big City Dropouts and Illiterates.